success

Intermediate
Students' Book

Unit	Page	Grammar	Vocabulary
1 Join the club	6–7	Present Simple and Present Continuous	Clubs, societies, organisations
	8–9		
	10–11 people		Phrasal verbs
	12–13	Reflexive pronouns; *each other*; Order of adjectives	Relationships; Clothes and accessories; Adjectives describing clothes
2 Keeping up-to-date	14–15	Present Perfect Simple and Present Perfect Continuous	
	16–17		Computers and mobile phones
	18–19		Phrasal verbs
	20–21		
	22–23	Think Back Revision 1 | Units 1–2	
3 An eye for an eye?	24–25	Past Simple, Past Continuous, Past Perfect	
	26–27		The courtroom; Law and punishment
	28–29	*used to/would*	Crimes and justice; Criminals; Anti-social behaviour
	30–31		
4 S(he)	32–33	Modals of possibility, ability, prohibition and obligation	Personality adjectives with negative prefixes
	34–35		
	36–37		Personality and behaviour; Synonyms
	38–39		
	40–41	Think Back Revision 2 | Units 3–4	
5 The world ahead	42–43	Future predictions; Adverbs of probabilty	
	44–45		
	46–47	Future: plans, intentions, arrangements, timetables, decisions	
	48–49		Natural disasters
6 Amazing animals	50–51	Zero, First and Second Conditionals; *If* and *When* clauses	Personality adjectives
	52–53		Animal similies; Synonyms; Animal categories
	54–55		
	56–57		
	58–59	Think Back Revision 3 | Units 5–6	
7 Success!	60–61	Third Conditional	
	62–63		
	64–65	*Wish, if only*	
	66–67		School, work; Success and failure

Reading	Listening	Speaking	Writing
	An interview with a person that belongs to a club	Why people belong to clubs	
	Radio discussion programme: Why young people join groups	**Speak Out:** Giving and justifying opinions	
Article: two gangs of young		Giving opinions: paintball games, conflicts	
Extracts from an article about young people		Relationships; Describing clothes	Description of a person
A personal website about a punk band		Interviewing a partner	
	The dangers of the Internet; Learning to use computers	**Speak Out:** Giving instructions	
Article: The first portable phones		Talking about mobile phones and communication	
Personal letters			A personal letter
Article: An unusual punishment		Interviewing each other about crimes	
Article: Laughter in court!		Deciding on appropriate punishments	
A newspaper report about a drink driving accident	Radio discussion programme: A famous person, who commited a crime	**Speak Out:** Agreeing and disagreeing; Expressing opinions	
A cartoon strip about how men and women are different		Talking about rules and obligations	
Article: male and female brains			
	How girls and boys are treated differently	**Speak Out:** Asking for and refusing permission	
A balanced for and against essay about single sex schools			A balanced for and against essay
Parts of a film script	Excerpts from a disaster movie	Making predictions	
Article: How the world might end		Discussing the future of mankind	
	A New Year's Eve party	Planning a party; Talking about New Year's resolutions	
	A student practicing giving a presentation	**Speak Out:** Giving presentations	
Article: Pets' views of humans		Talking about which animals make the best pets	
Article: The octopus			
	A lecture about African elephants; A dog show	**Speak Out:** Expressing probability	
An opinion essay about zoos			An opinion essay
Article: Comedian's success story			
A plot summary; An extract from a novel			
	Excerpts from a story; A popstar giving an interview	Talking about a successful person	Writing about being successful
	An excerpt talking about how to be a social success	**Speak Out:** Giving advice	An application form

Unit	Page	Grammar	Vocabulary
8 Taking a break	68–69	The Passive	
	70–71		Types of sports
	72–73		Travelling by plane; At the airport; Collocations
	74–75		Statistics; Describing places
	76–77	Think Back Revision 4 | Units 7–8	
9 To err is human	78–79	Reported speech: statements, time expressions	Reporting verbs
	80–81		Work; Education
	82–83	Reported speech: questions and imperatives	
	84–85		
10 Mysteries	86–87	Modals for speculation; Modal perfects	
	88–89		Verbs for descriptive storytelling
	90–91		Adjectives describing places and atmosphere
	92–93		
	94–95	Think Back Revision 5 | Units 9–10	
11 Beauty and health	96–97	Articles	
	98–99		Adjectives describing appearance
	100–101	*have something done*	Hair styles
	102–103		Adjectives for describing appearance
12 It's show time	104–105	Indirect questions	Types of cultural entertainment
	106–107		Art, theatre and music
	108–109		
	110–111		Base and strong adjectives; Describing films and TV programmes; Film reviews
	112–113	Think Back Revision 6 | Units 11–12	
13 Sports and games	114–115	Quantifiers: *both, neither, either, all, none, most*	
	116–117		Sports and venues; Linking words
	118–119	Possessive *s*	Football; Games and puzzles
	120–121		Sports; Collocations and phrasal verbs
14 Who cares?	122–123	Verb patterns	Describing food
	124–125		Advertising
	126–127		Shopping
	128–129		Collocations; Shopping
	130–131	Think Back Revision 7 | Units 13–14	

Culture Shocks p.132–139   Student Activities p.140   Irregular verbs p.144   Pronunciation table inside back cover

Reading	Listening	Speaking	Writing
Brochure: extraordinary hotels			
Website: extreme sports		Talking about extreme sports	
	Two girls arrive in UK	Checking in for a flight	
A school project about Edinburgh		**Speak Out:** Interpreting statistics	A description of a place
Three accident reports	Human errors		
Article: life after school		Giving a presentation	
	An interview with a careers guidance officer	Roleplaying a career guidance interview	A report of a careers guidance interview
	A speaking exam: discussing visual material	**Speak Out:** Discussing visual material	
	A TV programme trailer: The Piano Man		
Short story: The open window			
	Radio programme: a famous pilot	Speculating, giving evidence	A description of a place
A story about two rivals			Writing a story
Article: beauty through the ages		Talking about appearance	
Examples of different text types		Giving a presentation	
	A radio discussion programme		
A speaking exam: describing a person		**Speak Out:** Describing appearance	A description of a person
	A tourist visiting UK	Roleplay: a visit to London	
Article: New Orleans		Discussing visual material	
	People talking about modern art	Talking about modern art; **Speak Out:** Participating in conversations	
Film review: Curse of the Were-Rabbit		Talking about films	A film review
Computer games reviews			A computer game review
Article: Why we play games		Discussing sports and games	An opinion essay
	A radio programme about a football match	Giving a presentation about a game or pastime	
	Dialogues: making and responding to offers	Talking about sports and fitness **Speak Out:** Making and responding to offers	
	Radio adverts about food products		
Three letters to the editor		Discussing advertising	
	Buy Nothing Day	Presenting a topic **Speak Out:** Making and responding to complaints	
Two letters of complaint		Roleplaying negotiating compensation	A letter of complaint

CD 1.1 Texts recorded on Class CD   CD ROM Texts recorded on CD ROM

Join the club!

Read, listen and talk about clubs, societies, youth groups and lifestyles, clothes and accessories.
Practise the Present Simple and the Present Continuous, reflexive pronouns.
Focus on describing appearance, identifying speculation, giving and justifying opinions.
Write a simple description.

The Gentlemen's Clubs of London date from the 18th century. These are rather exclusive clubs which are like 'second homes' for many members.

GRAMMAR AND SPEAKING

1 Work in pairs. Tell your partner about any organisations you belong to or which groups you would like to join and why. Use these ideas to help you.

sports clubs/teams   sports team supporters club
a political party   school societies
the fan club of a group/singer   a charity
Internet groups/forums   a scouting organisation

2 **CD1.1** Listen and answer the questions.

• Who is Kay?
• What people belong to the club?

3 **CD1.1** Read and listen to the interview again. In pairs, discuss why you think the interviewer doesn't 'belong' in The Carshalton Club.

Kay So Lord Parkes, what kind of person joins The Carshalton Club?

Parkes Well, it helps if you have a moustache. I'm joking, of course. We are all top professional people – politicians, lawyers, even an ex-Prime Minister. Although more and more marketing people are joining these days.

Kay And what do you all do?

Parkes Well, people usually come here to play bridge or enjoy the food. Others come here to relax. Like Sir James over there. I usually only come here on Friday evenings.

Kay And … Tuesday lunchtimes?

Parkes Well, my wife is shopping at the moment so I decided to drop in. Anyway, The Carshalton also has a serious side. We do a lot of work for charity. For example, every day this week we're collecting money to renovate the bar in the Royal Opera House.

Kay I see. Finally, can I join your club? Lord Parkes … you seem terrified!

Parkes But, but, you don't understand, the thing is you're …

Kay A journalist? Even journalists join clubs, Lord Parkes. We're professionals, too …

Parkes No, that isn't such a big problem. It's just that you're … just not one of us. You're …

Work it out

4 Study the table. Then match sentences a–f with rules 1–6.

 a More and more marketing people are joining these days.
 b I usually only come here on Friday evenings.
 c My wife is shopping at the moment.
 d Every day this week we're collecting money.
 e You seem terrified.
 f Even journalists join clubs.

Present Simple and Present Continuous

We use the Present Simple:
1 to talk about habits and routines. ☐
2 to talk about facts and generalisations. ☐
3 with state verbs (*believe, belong, know, like, prefer, remember, see, seem, want, understand*) when we describe what is happening now. ☐
NOT ~~you are seeming terrified.~~

We use the Present Continuous:
4 to talk about actions happening now. ☐
5 to talk about temporary situations. ☐
6 to talk about changes. ☐

Mind the trap!

Adverbs of frequency normally come before the main verb with Simple tenses.

They **usually** have long hair.
I **occasionally** argue with my parents.

They come after the verb *to be* and other auxiliary verbs (*do, does, have* etc).

He is **often** late for school.
She doesn't **usually** phone during the day.

---

5 Complete the sentences with the correct forms of the verbs in brackets.

 1 The number of people who take part in Internet discussion forums _growing_ (grow) very quickly now.
 2 She's got a part-time job for the summer – she _works_ (work) as a waitress.
 3 My friend Mark is in the Scouts. He _often_ (often/go) camping at the weekend.
 4 I _I have ne_ (never/see) Hannah any more – she _studied_ (study) for her exams these days.
 5 Most of the kids in my class _listed_ (usually/listen) to soul and hip hop.
 6 _still belo_ (you/still/belong) to that Judo club?
 7 She's not here at the moment – she _visit/ing_ (visit) a friend. Can I take a message?

6 **CD1.2** Complete the text with the correct forms of the verbs in brackets. Then listen and check.

Every year, during the football season, I [1] _usually spend_ (usually/spend) Saturday afternoons at Dundee United games. There are also about twenty away games a year but luckily my friends and I all [2] _belong_ (belong) to the official supporters club so we [3] _travelled_ (travel) to the matches on the club's coach. It saves us a lot of money – train tickets [4] _are getting_ (get) so expensive nowadays! United are almost bottom of the league at the moment. These days we [5] _playing_ (play) quite well at home but our away games [6] _aren't going_ (not go) so well. But the atmosphere's always great and violence is a thing of the past. In fact, more and more families with young children [7] _are coming_ (come) to the games now. I [8] _always feel_ (always/feel) I'm part of a great big happy family!

7 Work in pairs. Choose a club from Exercise 1. Why do you think people join this club? Choose five of these ideas and compare your answers with another pair.

- find an alternative family
- have fun
- learn new skills
- have a strong identity
- help your career
- help other people
- feel special or different
- feel safe/stronger
- escape from everyday life
- make new friends
- find people similar to you
- be fashionable

8 Work in pairs. Think of a group of people your own age that you spend a lot of time with and answer the questions. Then tell your partner.

- How do you usually spend your time together?
- Is anything interesting happening or changing in your group at the moment?

New Romantics from the 1980s

Teddy Boys from the 1950s

Punks from the 1970s

THE ROYAL TOURNAMENT

EARLS COURT JULY

SPEAKING AND LISTENING

1 In pairs, look at the photos and answer the questions.

- Were/Are any of the fashions above popular in your country?
- Does the music you like influence the clothes you wear or your hairstyle? Why?/Why not?

2 Check you understand these words/phrases. Use a dictionary to help you.

(anti)commercial   role model   peer acceptance   fashion   youth (adj)

3 CD1.3 Listen and match speakers 1–3 with opinions a–c.

1 Jane Webb ☐
2 Mark Mondale ☐
3 Matt Hodges ☐

a Money and business is behind fashion and lifestyles.
b Gangs are a way to share music, have fun and find acceptance.
c Young people look for values and acceptance from people the same age.

4 CD1.3 Read the questions. Then listen again and circle the correct answers.

1 JaneWebb is an expert on
  a sociology.
  b psychology.
  c student unions.

2 According to Jane Webb, when young people reach their teens
  a they look for new role models in their lives.
  b they accept the values of the adult world.
  c their parents and older brothers and sisters are against them.

3 Mark Mondale believes that
  a teenagers are the same as sixty years ago.
  b business makes a lot of money from every new fashion.
  c teenagers look for answers from people their own age.

4 Matt Hodges thinks that
  a when young people become friends they start listening to the same kind of music.
  b music is the reason that many people become friends.
  c young people have fun with one group of people and look for help from another.

5 Both Dr Webb and Dr Mondale think that
  a Matt's answer proves their theories.
  b young people can't think for themselves.
  c psychology doesn't give easy answers for how teenagers behave.

6 The radio programme is
  a a phone-in.
  b a documentary.
  c a studio discussion.

Hippies from the 1960s

Hippies from the 1960s

5 CD1.4 Listen to the extracts. <u>Underline</u> the words/ phrases the speakers use to give their opinion. Circle the phrases when they start to explain or justify their opinion.

1 It seems to me that it's all part of becoming an adult. The thing is, when young people are in their teens, they start to question the values and lifestyles of the adult world they see around them.

2 As far as I'm concerned, becoming a Goth or a skater has absolutely nothing to do with looking for role models. Look at young people sixty years ago – they looked and behaved like younger versions of their parents.

3 Frankly, it's all about money. If you think about it, every new youth fashion makes millions of dollars.

4 Personally, I believe it's all about music. I'm into nu-metal, my favourite band is BioToxine.

6 Study Speak Out. Then complete the table with the phrases you chose in Exercise 5.

SPEAK OUT | Giving and justifying opinions

Giving opinions	Justifying opinions
In my opinion …	Everybody knows that …
If you ask me …	The reason why … is …
To be honest, …	I mean …
_____	_____
_____	_____
_____	_____
_____	

Mind the trap!

We only use **frankly (speaking)** to give an opinion which we think is controversial or unpopular.

Frankly, this lesson is a waste of time!

Personally, I love chocolate milkshakes!
NOT ~~Frankly~~

7 CD1.5 Complete the conversation with expressions from Speak Out. Then listen and check.

Kat Did you hear that discussion programme on Thames Radio last night? About why young people belong to different groups?

Jay Yes, I did. ¹_____ , I thought it was pretty awful. ²_____ , the presenter couldn't even control the guests!

Kat ³_____ , I found those two academics really irritating. ⁴_____ … making generalisations about young people is so unhelpful.

Jay I'm glad that young guy mentioned music though. ⁵_____ , that's the most important thing.

8 Work in pairs. Give your opinions on the topics below and justify them. Use Speak Out to help you.

1 Are friends more important than family for most young people?
2 Is it a waste of time and money to be fashionable?
3 Do people's tastes in music have the most influence on how they look and behave?
4 Is it useful to make generalisations about young people?

Off the streets

It's a typical Saturday afternoon on Cathedral Square in Peterborough, in the east of England. Two noisy gangs of young people are sitting in the centre of the square. One group are wearing tracksuits and baseball caps and brand-new white trainers. A lot of them are wearing jewellery like gold chains and earrings. They're the 'Chavs'. Opposite them are the 'Goths'. They're wearing black Doctor Marten boots, long black coats and black T-shirts with the names of their favourite bands on them. Some of them are wearing lipstick and eyeliner and a few of them have piercings. Nervous shoppers hurry past them, trying not to make eye contact. It seems to be quiet but you feel that at any moment a fight could start. The police say these young people are probably harmless – perhaps they just hang around the square because there's nothing better to do. But older people say they are tired of putting up with the noise and litter. These kinds of problems certainly aren't unique to Peterborough. But after trying several different methods, Peterborough City Council has a radical plan to change things.

The council's controversial plan to bring peace to the city starts on a Tuesday morning during the half-term holiday. A group of fourteen Chavs and Goths of both sexes are travelling by bus to a secret location in the countryside, ten miles out of town. There are more Chavs than Goths – maybe it's hard for some Goths to get up in the mornings! When they finally arrive, supervisors ask them to put on camouflage clothing. And then the two gangs spend the rest of the morning pretending to shoot at each other.

Don't worry – the guns are not real (they fire plastic balls filled with paint) and it's all for fun. But isn't it dangerous to fight aggression with aggression? Is a game of paintball really the best way to bring young people together? Steve Mayes, the organiser of the event, feels that it is. He thinks these controversial games give the two groups something to do and can start them talking. 'It gets rid of a lot of energy too – it's much better than playing games on Playstations and Xboxes,' he says. Meanwhile, the Chavs and Goths are fooling around: there's a lot of shouting and laughter and everyone appears to be having fun.

At the end of the day Steve Mayes believes the event was a success – the two groups are already talking to each other. 'It's like football,' says Denise, another organiser. 'You choose which team you belong to. But at the end of the day, Chavs and Goths are the same sort of people.'

Dan: 'I almost didn't come this morning but my friends persuaded me. There was a lot of aggression to begin with but everyone calmed down in the end. I bumped into an old friend from primary school who I hadn't spoken to for years but he seems just the same as ever – in fact I got on with him really well. The atmosphere in town is probably a lot better now.'

READING AND VOCABULARY

1 **CD ROM** In pairs, look at the pictures and the title of the article. What do you think it is about? Then quickly read the text and check your predictions.

2 Read the text again. Are the statements true (T) or false (F)?

1 The scenes that are described in the first paragraph don't happen very often. ☐ F
2 The shoppers in Peterborough are afraid to look at the young people in the square. ☐ T
3 The police don't think the young people are dangerous. ☐ NOT
4 Peterborough isn't the only place where you can find such problems. ☐ T
5 Only boys are taking part in the council's events. ☐ F
6 At the end of the day Chavs and Goths start playing football together. ☐ F

3 Look at this sentence from the text and answer the questions.

It seems to be quiet but you feel that at any moment a fight could start.

1 Which sentence best describes the statement above?
   a A definite fact – it is certain that the situation will end in violence.
   b Speculation – it is only the writer's guess/ impression that there will be violence.

2 Which words or phrases in the sentence helped you decide your answer to Question 1?

4 Find and underline the words which suggest that these sentences are speculation.

1 These young people are probably harmless.
2 Maybe it's hard for some Goths to get up in the mornings!
3 Everyone appears to be having fun.
4 Steve Mayes believes the event was a success.

5 Study Train Your Brain and check your answers to Exercise 4.

TRAIN YOUR BRAIN | Reading skills

Identifying speculation

Writers often use speculation when they don't know all the facts. To identify speculation:
1 Read the statement carefully and try to decide if it is a definite fact or an impression/guess.
2 Look out for typical words or phrases which suggest a statement is an impression/guess.

Words often used for speculation
Modal verbs – *could, might*
Other verbs – *seem, appear, look, think, feel, believe*
Adverbs – *possibly, probably, maybe, perhaps*

6 Read Dan's impressions of the day again. Underline the statements which are speculation. Use Train Your Brain to help you.

7 **Vocabulary** Find phrasal verbs 1–6 in the text and match them with meanings a–f.

1 hang around ☐ e
2 put up with ☐ c
3 fool around ☐ b
4 calm down ☐ a
5 bump into ☐ f
6 get on with ☐ d

a be quiet and relaxed after you have been nervous or excited
b behave in a silly or irresponsible way
c tolerate, accept
d have a good relationship with
e wait or spend time somewhere and do nothing
f meet somebody when you don't expect to

8 Complete the sentences with the correct form of a phrasal verb from Exercise 7.

1 I only started to go on with ~~bump into~~ my sister after she left home!
2 Your boyfriend never helps you. I don't know why you put up with his laziness.
3 The kids always hang around when the teacher isn't in the room.
4 Guess what! I got on with Matt in the supermarket yesterday. He's married now!
5 Try not to worry … just have a cup of tea and try to calm down.
6 The gang used to fool around in the park until the neighbours started complaining.

9 Work in pairs and answer the questions.

1 Do you think that the paintball games are a good idea or not?
2 Could they work where you live? Give your opinions, using Speak Out on page 9.
3 Which things lead to conflicts between young people where you live? Give your own opinions or use the ideas below to help you.

- supporting a different football team
- listening to different types of music
- living in a different district of town
- looking different
- attending a different school

11

ONE OF THE GANG?

A I met my friends at college so they all live in different parts of town but we have one thing in common – we're all crazy about nu-metal. In fact, we're teaching ourselves to play the guitar. We always really enjoy <u>ourselves</u> when we meet up at weekends.

B I think gangs are pathetic. People in gangs think they're better than anyone who's different to them – they take <u>themselves</u> so seriously. I prefer to decide what music I buy and what I wear <u>myself</u>. I don't want to be just one of the crowd.

C I think it's really important to belong to a gang. I hang around with other people from the estate. We're all into different clothes and music but we all grew up together and that's really important. We spend a lot of time on the phone to <u>each other</u> and help <u>each other</u> with our problems.

GRAMMAR AND READING

1 **Quickly read texts A–C and answer the questions.**

Which person …
1 doesn't belong to a gang? ☐
2 has known the people in his/her gang since childhood? ☐
3 has similar interests to other people in his/her gang? ☐

Work it out

2 **Look at texts A and B and complete the table.**

Reflexive Pronouns			
	1st person	2nd person	3rd person
Singular	_____	yourself	himself herself
Plural	_____	yourselves	_____

3 **Look at the sentences and answer the questions.**

1 We always enjoy ourselves when we meet.
2 I decide what clothes I wear myself.

- In which sentence does the reflexive pronoun mean without any help/independently?
- Where does the reflexive pronoun go in the sentence when it has this meaning?

4 **Look at the sentence and decide what the context is.**

We make fun of each other a lot.

a I laugh at myself and my friend laughs at herself.
b I laugh at my friend and she laughs at me.

> ### Mind the trap!
>
> We don't normally use reflexive pronouns with these verbs: *wash*, *dress*, *shave*, *brush*.
>
> I **shave** before I have a shower. NOT ~~I shave myself~~.

5 **Complete the sentences with the correct reflexive pronoun. Tick the sentences in which the pronoun means *independently*.**

1 You shouldn't blame _____ for not passing the exam. It was very hard. ☐
2 Mike's working part-time. He has to pay for his studies _____ . ☐
3 Be careful with that knife – you don't want to cut _____ ! ☐
4 I grew these tomatoes _____ . ☐
5 Nobody helped us so we had to do it _____ . ☐
6 Please behave _____ . You're both being very naughty. ☐

6 **Complete the sentences with the correct reflexive pronoun or *each other*.**

1 Richard and Kate are the perfect couple. They really love _____ .
2 Tom's vain. He's really in love with _____ .
3 Although they both live in Spain, they speak to _____ in French.
4 She's weird – she's always talking to _____ .
5 Everyone in our gang really gets on with _____ .

7 **Write sentences about your relationships with your friends. Use reflexive pronouns or *each other* and the verbs below. Use the texts in Exercise 1 to help you.**

argue with   get on with   understand   text
believe in   help   make fun of   enjoy   phone

My friends and I spend a lot of time together and text each other in the evenings. We often meet on Saturday afternoons and we always enjoy ourselves …

VOCABULARY AND WRITING

1 Think Back! Work in pairs. Put each word into the correct group. Then add as many other words as you can think of in three minutes.

(gold) chain boots eyeliner sweater trainers coat
earrings lipstick tracksuits T-shirt

clothes	make-up	footwear	jewellery

2 Look at the texts below and complete the table for the nouns in pink/bold.

Describing clothes – order of adjectives

opinion	size/length	colour/shade	style/cut	material	(compound) noun	preposition + noun phrase
trendy	–	–	baggy	–	top	with a hood
–	long	–	baggy	–	combat trousers	–

3 Put the adjectives in the correct order. Use the table in Exercise 2 to help you.

1 striped/a(n)/old-fashioned/cotton   **shirt**
2 silk/large/a/blue   **blouse**
3 black/leather/tight   **trousers**
4 nylon/cheap/white/a   **tracksuit**
5 cotton/beige/baggy   **shorts**
6 red/bright   **lipstick**
7 horrible/grey/woollen   **socks**
8 long/with a band logo on it/a   **T-shirt**
9 ripped/with a patch/denim   **jeans**

4 Work in pairs and follow the instructions.

- Look at the photos of the Chavs and Goths on page 10 and choose one person.
- Describe what he/she is wearing.
- Try and guess who your partner is describing.

5 Choose a fashion or style that is popular with a group of people in your country. Write a description of about 200–250 words.

- Paragraph 1
  Mention the clothes, accessories and make-up they usually wear.
- Paragraph 2
  Mention the kind of music they listen to.
- Paragraph 3
  Mention how they typically spend their free time.

WHAT'S NEW ON THE HIGH STREET

FASHION TRENDS

Callum is wearing a trendy baggy top with a hood, a brown cap, long baggy combat trousers, a chain and trainers. He's also wearing a charity bracelet.

Hannah is wearing a stylish cotton T-shirt with a design, a short denim jacket, blue cropped jeans, a studded belt and long leather boots. She's wearing eyeliner and mascara.

02 Keeping up-to-date

Read, listen and talk about modern communications and technology.
Practise the Present Perfect Simple and the Present Perfect Continuous.
Focus on giving instructions.
Write a personal letter.

 Getablog.com Want your own personal website? A place where you can post your thoughts and images, interact with others and more? Get a blog! Click on the link, and you can get your own blog in only five minutes. And it's all for FREE!

ABOUT DAVID LEAD GUITARIST

ABOUT STEPHEN DRUMMER

ABOUT TRACY RHYTHM GUITARIST

ABOUT CRITICAL AGE

We've been together for ten months.
We've already played more than thirty gigs.
We haven't signed a deal with any record companies ... yet! But we've made a demo CD!

Email Critical Age: Criticalage@zmail.com

ABOUT COLIN LEAD SINGER/BASS GUITARIST

I write the songs and I write this blog.
I've been playing the guitar since I was four.
I've been the bass guitarist for three months – since Brian left the band.

21 Oct @ 02:24

Have you been listening to Southgate FM recently? Nick Rhodes has been playing our CD all week! I'm amazed! He loves us. He hasn't been talking about anyone else. He's played _So Happy_ three times tonight! We've been rehearsing a lot lately. We're playing a gig at _The Rock Garden_ on Nov 5 @ 9p.m. Come along. It'll be explosive! I've been writing songs all day – I'm exhausted. I've written four new songs.

POST REPLY   READ ALL REPLIES

SO FAR 9 8 7 PEOPLE HAVE VISITED THIS BLOG

GRAMMAR AND READING

1 Read the Getablog.com advert. Tick the sentences that are true.

1 A blog is an easy-to-use personal website. ☐
2 On a blog, you can write your opinions and post photos. ☐
3 You can't communicate with other people. ☐
4 It takes a long time to set up a blog. ☐
5 It doesn't cost anything to set up a blog. ☐

2 In pairs, read the blog and answer the questions.

1 How many people have visited this blog?
2 What does it tell you about the band?
3 Do you think they are a successful band? Why?/Why not?

Work it out

3 Think Back! Look at the sentences. What tense is used? Why?

1 *We have played more than thirty gigs.*
2 *We have made a demo CD.*

4 Think Back! Complete these sentences from the blog. When do we use these two time expressions?

We've been together _____ ten months.
I've been the bass guitarist _____ Brian left the band.

5 Match sentences 1–3 with the uses of the Present Perfect Simple and Present Perfect Continuous (a–c).

1 I've been writing songs all day. I'm exhausted. ☐
2 I've written four new songs. ☐
3 I've been writing songs since I was sixteen. ☐

a An action that started in the past but is still continuing.
b A past activity that may be continuing. It has a result in the present.
c A finished action.

Check it out

Present Perfect Simple and Continuous

We use the Present Perfect Simple to talk about:
• news and recent actions.
  We **have made** a demo CD!
• a finished action if we don't say exactly when it happened. We may say how many times it happened.
  We **have** already **played** more than thirty gigs.

We use the Present Perfect Continuous to talk about:
• an action that started in the past but is still continuing.
  I **have been writing** songs since I was sixteen.
• a past activity with a result in the present. It may be continuing.
  I **have been writing** songs all day – I'm exhausted.

We use *since* to say when the situation started.
We use *for* to say how long this situation has been true.

6 For each example write one sentence in the Present Perfect Simple and one in the Present Perfect Continuous.

Colin has been writing songs since 2001.
He has written hundreds of songs.

1 Colin/write — songs since 2001 / hundreds of songs
2 Colin/go out — with Tracy for about a year / for a drink with Tracy
3 Tracy/play — in public many times / the piano since she was six
4 Stephen/act — in three music videos / in a music video all day
5 David/save up — his money / almost €3,000

7 Use the Present Perfect Continuous and the words in brackets to explain these situations.

Colin needs a drink. He's been rehearsing since 6.30.

1 Colin needs a drink. (rehearse/6.30)
2 David's very tired. (play games/ages)
3 Stephen's arms are sore. (lift weights/gym/two hours)
4 Tracy feels stressed out. (teach Colin drive/two o'clock)
5 Colin's looking thin. (not/eat much/recently)
6 I know all the lyrics to *So Happy*. (listen/song/all day)

8 Complete the text with the correct forms of the verbs in brackets. Use the Past Simple, the Present Perfect and the Present Perfect Continuous.

8 Nov @ 12.30

My ear is sore! I ¹_____ (talk) to a guy from a record company all morning. He ²_____ (call) me six times since the Rock Garden gig! He ³_____ (offer) us all sorts of things if we sign with his company. Last night he ⁴_____ (offer) to take us all on tour in America! We ⁵_____ (try) to decide if we should accept his offer, but we ⁶_____ (not/make) a decision yet. ⁷_____ (you/ever/be) on a plane? Well, right now, I feel the way you do when the plane is taking off – I ⁸_____ (never/feel) so excited. I ⁹_____ (think) about the future – and it's looking good.

9 Work in pairs. Use the prompts below to roleplay the interview. Then Student A, look at page 141 and Student B, look at page 142.

Interviewer	David
How long/know/Colin?	years
Where/meet?	primary school
How long/play/guitar?	five years old
Ever/meet/anyone famous?	yes/Ewan McGregor
What/listen/recently?	punk from the 70s

15

VOCABULARY

1 Match the verbs with pictures 1–6.

attach ☐   click ☐   delete ☐   download 1
install ☐   press ☐

2 Work in pairs. Use a dictionary to check the meanings of the <u>underlined</u> words. Then complete sentences 1–6 with the verbs from Exercise 1.

1 Put the <u>plug</u> in the <u>socket</u>, and then _____ the power button to switch on the computer.
2 To send a message move the <u>cursor</u> onto the <u>toolbar</u> and _____ on the envelope.
3 Use a <u>search engine</u> like Google to find some <u>freeware</u> to _____ .
4 It's a good idea to read the <u>manual</u> before you _____ the <u>program</u>.
5 If you think an email has a virus, you should _____ it immediately.
6 First, open the <u>folder</u> 'My docs', then use the <u>icon</u> of the <u>paper clip</u> to _____ the document to the email.

3 [CD1.6] Listen to the conversation and number these words and phrases in the order that you hear them.

battery ☐   phonebook ☐   ring tone ☐
signal strength ☐   vibrating alert ☐
voicemail ☐

4 Match the beginnings of sentences 1–6 with endings a–f.

1 If the signal strength is too low, ☐
2 If the battery is low ☐
3 The phonebook ☐
4 The ring tone ☐
5 With a vibrating alert ☐
6 Voicemail ☐

a is a service which answers your calls for you.
b is what you hear when someone calls your mobile.
c is where you store your friend's numbers.
d you can receive calls without disturbing other people.
e you can't make or receive calls.
f you need to charge it.

LISTENING

1 [CD1.7] Listen to Daria, Neil and Hanif talking about the Internet. Tick true and cross false.

1 Daria doesn't think the Internet is as dangerous as some people say. ☒
2 Hanif thinks it's a wonderful invention. ☑
3 Neil thinks that you can do lots of cool things online, but you should be careful. ☑

THE FIVE DEADLY DANGERS OF THE
Internet

1 You can get arrested if you download copyrighted material.
2 You don't know who you're really talking to on chat sites.
3 People can <u>manipulate</u> photos that you send on the Internet.
4 Spyware programmes can steal your personal information.
5 You can get a computer virus.

What do I look like? I'm a cute fluffy bunny.

2 Work in pairs. Read the text. Then look at the cartoon and decide which of the dangers it suggests.

3 [CD1.7] Listen again, and complete the advice the people give. Then match advice a–e with dangers 1–5 in the leaflet.

a Don't _send_ any _photo_ that you don't want the whole world to see. ☐
b You should be careful about what kind of _____ you _____ . ☐
c You can't always _____ what people tell you on _chatsite_ . ☐
d You should only register with _____ that you can trust. ☐
e Don't _open_ any _email_ from strangers. ☐

4 Work in pairs. Which of the opinions from Exercise 1 do you agree with the most? Why?

SPEAKING AND LISTENING

1 Work in pairs. Describe the photo then answer the questions.

- Is it more difficult for older people to use computers? Why?/Why not?
- Have you ever used a computer with your parents or grandparents? If so, what for?

2 **CD1.8** Listen to the people in the computer class. Tick the reasons they give for learning to use computers.

1 to save money ☐
2 to keep in touch with young people ☐
3 to buy presents on the Internet ☐
4 to help with a hobby ☐
5 to find a job ☐

3 **CD1.9** Listen to the students in the computer class. Then match students 1–5 with things they want to do a–e.

a attach something to an email ☐
b join a chat group ☐
c print a document ☐
d send an email ☐
e switch on the computer ☐

4 **CD1.10** Complete extracts 1–3 below with phrases a–g. Then listen and check.

a the one with
b the thing that looks like
c do you see
d that's right!
e make sure you
f don't forget to
g the next thing you need to do is

1 **Teacher**	So press the big blue button, ¹___ power written on it.
Woman 2	This one?
Teacher	Yes, ²___
2 **Teacher**	First click on the attachment icon ... ³___ a paper clip ... ⁴___ ?
3 **Teacher**	and now ⁵___ to click on the icon that says new message ... . Now, type in the address ... ⁶___ get it right ...
Man 2	Bill Hickey at easymail.com
Teacher	That's it ... and ⁷___ put the subject of your email.

5 Complete the Speak Out box with the words and phrases from Exercise 4.

SPEAK OUT | Giving instructions

Saying what to do	**Identifying objects**
The first thing you've got to do is ... ¹_____	It's a bit like ... ⁵_____
First .../Then .../Next ... ²_____	The big thing with ... ⁶_____
You don't need to ... ³_____	It's made of ... It's used for ...

Checking	**Saying someone has understood**
Alright?/OK? (Have) you got that? ⁴_____ Have you done that?	⁷_____ That's it!

6 Work in pairs. Make a list of six things that you associate with computers. Then use Speak Out to describe things from your list.

A It's a large object. It's made of plastic and metal and glass. It's a bit like a television.
B A monitor?

7 **CD1.11** Complete with one word in each gap. Use Speak Out to help you. Then listen and check.

The ¹_____ thing you've got to do is to find a phone box. It isn't easy nowadays. Don't ²_____ to check that it accepts money. A lot of them only take phonecards now. ³_____ , you lift the receiver, and put the money in. Make ⁴_____ you put enough money in the slot or you won't get connected, ⁵_____ ? ⁶_____ , you dial the number and hope you don't get an answering machine, because if you do, you won't get your money back. OK. Have you ⁷_____ that?

8 Work in pairs. Use the language in Speak Out to explain how to use a mobile phone. Student A, look at page 141. Student B, look at page 143.

Portable Phones —
Walk and **Talk!**

Have you ever called up a friend and heard this: 'Sorry, he's not in. Can you call back later?' Have you ever been in a dirty phone box on a cold night and found the phone out of order? Have you ever thought how wonderful it would be if you could talk to your friends any time you wanted to? If so, then read on …

A

Ever since Bell patented the telephone in 1876, we've been living in the age of instant communication. But there has always been a restriction – you need to find a phone. And that isn't always easy. OK, we've had car phones since the 1950s. But the first car phones were enormous. The machinery filled the boot of the car! More than a portable phone, it was a mobile phone box! One of the first users was a doctor in Sweden. Unfortunately, the phone needed so much power that he could only make two calls before the battery went dead. The first to his patient, and the second to the garage to get someone to come and fix his flat battery.
By the mid-1960s phones were small enough to fit into the front of a car, but unfortunately, they were still too heavy for people to carry around. They were also extremely expensive. So, it was no surprise that they didn't become popular.

B

And then Mr Cooper made a call. On 3 April 1973, while walking along a street in New York, Motorola employee Martin Cooper took out his portable phone, dialled a number and made a call to a rival phone company. I don't know what he said – perhaps, 'Nobody has ever done this before!' – but I bet he felt pretty happy when he hung up. He knew that his company was ahead of the competition.

C

Now – just over ten years later – the DynaTAC 8000X portable cellular phone has arrived in the shops, and this week I've been testing it. I must say I'm impressed. The first thing you notice is how small and light it is. It weighs a little less than a bag of sugar and is about the same size as a brick – about twenty centimetres long. It looks really smart, too. And you can talk for almost half an hour without recharging the battery! You can also turn down the volume in case the phone goes off when you're in a meeting. The disadvantage? The price. It costs almost £3,000!

But don't worry. The price will come down and soon everyone will have one.

D

And while I have my crystal ball out, here are some more predictions about how we will communicate in the future … . Firstly, I think people will forget how to write because all communications will be oral. And one day before too long we will have phones with 3D video screens which allow you to see your friends and watch TV! More good news: phone calls will be free – they'll be paid for by advertising! And finally, I believe that eventually humans in the future will have phones in our brains! With a speaker in an ear, and a microphone in a tooth, we will be able to dial numbers just by saying them.

But until then, you could do worse than buy yourself a Motorola DynaTAC. Become mobile and say goodbye to those cold calls in dirty phone boxes.

Science Times

April 1 1984

Personal computers – will every home have one?

Disposable cameras – snap and throw.

Windows or Apple? Which is better?

Male baldness – the cure is near.

Cover story
Portable Phones
Walk and Talk!

… plus lots more fascinating articles!

READING

1 Look at the front cover of the magazine and answer the questions.

1 What kind of magazine is this?
2 When was it published?
3 What is the main story of this issue?
4 Do you ever read any magazines like this?

2 **CD ROM** Read the magazine article. What is it about?

a The history of communications.
b A new mobile phone.
c Technology in the future.

3 Match headings 1–4 with paragraphs A–D in the text.

1 The future
2 The first call
3 Testing the product
4 The historical background

4 Read the text again and choose the best answers.

1 Which of these problems with traditional phones in 1984 does the writer not mention?
  a The person you want to talk to is often not at home.
  b Public phones don't always work.
  c Not all your friends have a phone.

2 The main disadvantage with the first car phones was that ...
  a you could only use them in Sweden.
  b they only worked inside phone boxes.
  c they used too much power.

3 Why were car phones still not popular in the 1960s?
  a They were too small.
  b They weighed a lot and they cost too much.
  c They used up batteries too quickly.

4 Why is Martin Cooper important in the history of mobile phones?
  a He made the first mobile phone call.
  b He worked for the mobile phone company, Motorola.
  c He invented the first portable phone.

5 What does the writer not like about the DynaTAC portable phone?
  a the price
  b the size
  c how long the battery lasts

6 What does the writer think of the future of mobile phones?
  a He's sure they will be successful.
  b He's not sure they will be successful.
  c He's sure they won't be successful.

5 **Vocabulary** Complete with these words and phrases from the text.

out of order dead fix dial
turn down go off come down

1 Excuse me, could you send someone to _____ my phone. It's not working.
2 First, pick up the receiver. Then, _____ the number you want to call.
3 Has your mobile phone ever _____ during an exam?
4 It's always the same with new technology. At first, it's really expensive and then the price _____ .
5 Do you know how to _____ the volume of your mobile phone?
6 Suddenly, the line went _____ . Lesley felt scared.
7 This phone is _____ . Have you got a mobile?

6 Work in groups. Discuss these questions.

1 How have mobile phones changed since 1984?
2 Which of the predictions the writer makes in his article have/have not come true?
3 Which ones do you think will/won't come true?
4 How do you think communications will change in the future?

7 Work in groups. Use the prompts and your own ideas to discuss the statement below. Use Speak Out on page 9 to help you.

The more people use technology, the less they communicate.

- Too much information, no time to think.
- Technology helps you to keep up-to-date.
- Talking with technology is impersonal.
- You can always keep in touch with your friends.
- Technology lets you use language in new ways.
- Emoticons and texting are killing language.

"I'VE HAD A HIGH-SPEED INTERNET CONNECTION WITH WIRELESS TECHNOLOGY FOR MORE THAN A YEAR. I'VE LEARNT TO TEXT FASTER THAN I CAN SPEAK. MY NEW MOBILE IS THE BEST ONE I'VE EVER HAD. SO, WHY HAVE I BEEN FEELING SO LONELY?"

7 November

Dear Hanif,

Where have you been recently? Have the aliens finally come and taken you away to their planet? Or have you been playing so many computer games that you haven't had enough time to answer your friends' emails?!

It's too late to send me an email, anyway, 'cause I'm staying with my uncle and aunt in the country. I've been here since Friday, and I'm going to stay until the end of the month. It's wonderful here! So quiet and peaceful! Why don't you and Neil come down for a weekend? The only thing is there are no computers here! And I can't even use my mobile! The signal strength is too low. That's why I'm writing you this letter – I think it's the first time I've written a letter for more than a year!

What was the Critical Age concert like? Did you enjoy it? What a pity I missed it! I've been listening to the radio all morning, but they haven't played So Happy yet.

Anyway, I've got to stop now. My uncle's going into town and he's going to post this for me. Write me a letter if you still remember how to use a pen! OK?
I want to hear all your news.

Best wishes,

Daria

WRITING

1 Work in groups. Ask and answer questions to find the most popular way of communicating personal news in writing. Use the ideas below to help you.

- a letter
- a postcard
- a text message
- an email
- a message on an instant messenger site

How many times have you written a letter to a friend in the last month?

2 Look at the letter that Daria sent to Hanif, and tick the true statements.

1 She tells Hanif her news. ☐
2 She starts each new topic with a new paragraph. ☐
3 She uses questions and imperatives to communicate more directly with her reader. ☐
4 She doesn't say anything about Hanif's life. ☐
5 She gives a reason why she can't write anymore. ☐
6 She uses a formal written style. ☐

Nov 11

1 _____ ,

It's alright. You can stop worrying. I haven't lost my memory and forgotten all my friends. Only you! :-) Seriously, I'm really sorry I haven't written for so long.

I'm pretty tired at the moment because 2 _____ . No, it isn't because of too many computer games! I've been working really hard … and partying even harder! <u>The big news is</u> 3 _____ ! We went backstage after the Rock Garden gig and we spoke to him for about half an hour. He's really excited about the group. <u>Apparently</u> they're going to be on national TV next week.

4 _____ . It sounds great. Just what I need – a bit of rest and relaxation. I'm not sure what time we'll be there, so 5 _____ on Saturday morning! OK? <u>Anyway</u>, got to go. 6 _____ . Oh, <u>by the way</u>, 7 _____ ? I haven't heard from him for ages.

8 _____ ,

Hanif

6 Work in pairs. Complete the letter with suitable words and phrases. Then go to page 140 and compare your answers with the original.

Dec 22

Hi Daria,

Sorry I haven't written sooner, but I've been 1 _____ . I'm exhausted! I've been 2 _____ . I've got a big Maths test tomorrow. What else? Well, I've been taking driving lessons, too! My grandma is 3 _____ . I can drive quite well already. I want to pass my test so that I can 4 _____ .

The big news is that 5 _____ a present! The new Critical Age CD signed by Colin! We've been 6 _____ quite a lot recently. He's really 7 _____ . You'd love him.

Anyway, that's enough about me. What about you? Have you decided to 8 _____ yet?

Oh, before I forget, Chris called me up. Apparently, there's a really good 9 _____ course on at the youth centre next week. Do you want to go? Come on! It'll be fun. I've got to go. My 10 _____ is calling me!

Write back soon.

Love, Neil.

3 Complete Hanif's reply to Daria with extracts a–h.

a All the best
b don't go out
c have you had any news from Chris
d Hi Daria
e I haven't been getting enough sleep
f I'm meeting Neil at the café
g Neil and I met Colin from Critical Age
h Thanks for the invitation to the country

4 Match the <u>underlined</u> words and phrases in Hanif's letter with their synonyms below.

before I forget guess what? it seems that so

5 Circle the best words and phrases.

1 *Have you heard / Before I forget* the latest news.
2 *Anyway / Apparently* they've expelled Chris from school! I don't know why. Give him a call and ask him.
3 *By the way / Guess what*, have you seen Vicky? Could you give her my address?
4 *Anyway / By the way*, I imagine Chris is feeling pretty bad. Maybe you could go and see him. What do you think? I've got to go now.
5 *Cheers / Yours sincerely,* Daria

TRAIN YOUR BRAIN | Writing skills

Personal letters

1 Start with expressions like *Hi/Hello/Dear … .* and finish with expressions like *Cheers/All the best/Best wishes.*
2 Tell your reader your news.
3 Comment on and ask about your reader's life.
4 Start a new paragraph for each new topic.
5 Use imperatives and direct questions to engage your readers.
6 Give a reason to end the letter.
7 Use an informal conversational style.

7 Study Train Your Brain and write a letter to a friend with some personal news.

- Note down a) the most important things that have happened in your life recently, and b) what you want to find out about your friend's life.
- Organise your notes into paragraphs.
- Use vocabulary from Exercise 6.
- Write a first draft of the letter and then give it to a classmate to check it for errors.
- Write the finished version of your letter.

VOCABULARY AND GRAMMAR

1 Complete the sentences. Make new words from the words in capital letters.

1 A lot of people like to be _____ because it makes them feel better. **FASHION**

2 Wearing _____ and other types of jewellery can be a sign that you belong to a group, for example Goths. **EAR**

3 UNICEF is an _____ which looks after children in underdeveloped countries. **ORGANISE**

4 People usually join political parties because they _____ with their views on politics, economics and social issues. **IDENTITY**

5 Some young people join gangs because they're looking for _____ . **ACCEPT**

6 The battery in my mobile is flat – I need to _____ it. **CHARGE**

2 Complete the sentences with the correct verbs from the box.

bump calm fool get go hang put

1 In hot weather, the kids usually _____ around the village square.

2 When you live in a big city, you have to _____ up with noise, traffic and pollution.

3 You can _____ into an old friend from school anywhere – even on holiday.

4 The doctor tried to _____ the patients down.

5 He is often punished by his teacher because he likes to _____ around.

6 Teenagers often do not _____ on with their younger brothers and sisters.

7 Which is the most embarrassing place where your mobile can _____ off?

3 Complete the text with one word in each gap.

Dear Sir,

I get very annoyed by old people complaining about mobile phones all the time. They always talk about loud ring ¹_____ but forget what life was like before. Trying to find a phone which was usually ²_____ of order. To ³_____ honest, I can't imagine life without my mobile. I've had mine ⁴_____ 2004 and, if you ⁵_____ me, its my most important possession. I've ⁶_____ ten texts already today. My advice to anyone reading this, don't be miserable, get a mobile phone and enjoy ⁷_____ !

Jane Silver

4 Complete the sentences so that they mean the same as the original sentences.

1 My sister started studying Maths at 4 o'clock. She is still studying it.
My sister _____ Maths since 4 o'clock.

2 Jane is really selfish – she doesn't like anyone else.
Jane is really selfish – she only _____ .

3 My mum started cleaning the windows after lunch. Four windows are clean already.
My mum _____ four windows since lunch.

4 It is a long time since Kate emailed me.
Kate hasn't _____ a long time.

5 Tom can take care of himself. Bill can take care of himself, too.
Tom and Bill can both _____ .

6 Nobody helped us – we did it on our own.
Nobody helped us – we did it _____ .

5 Complete the email. For each gap circle the correct answer.

_____
Latest news
Reply Reply All Forward ⊟ 🖨 ✂ ✖ ⬆ ⬇ Follow Up A ▾

From: kate@abc.co.uk
To: jessica@yes.com
Subject: Latest news

Hi, Jessica,

Thank you for your last email. I ¹_____ very busy this week, so please don't be angry with me for writing back so late. I ²_____ four tests already and the week is not over yet! I ³_____ this project on famous British monarchs for nearly two weeks now and I still haven't finished. I know it's a long time but I ⁴_____ it to be really good. What else? I usually ⁵_____ to school with my dad but this week he is on a business trip so I ⁶_____ the bus to school. You know that I ⁷_____ to a horse-riding club? Well, I ⁸_____ my friends from the club this Saturday at ten o'clock. I can't wait to see them. Got to go now. I'll write more on Sunday, I promise.

Take care,
Kate
_____

1 a am
  b have been
  c was
  d am going to be

2 a have
  b had
  c have had
  d have been having

3 a wrote
  b have written
  c am writing
  d have been writing

4 a will want
  b want
  c have wanted
  d wanted

5 a am going
  b am going to go
  c have gone
  d go

6 a take
  b am taking
  c have taken
  d am going to take

7 a belong
  b have belonged
  c belonged
  d am going to belong

8 a am seeing
  b see
  c am going to see
  d have seen

PRONUNCIATION

1 **CD1.12** Listen to the words in the table. Now listen to the words in the box and write them in the correct column. Then listen and check.

uncle tracksuit toolbar apple cup
card fun fan fashion radical bump
mascara mark club park recharge

æ	ʌ	ɑ:
cat	cut	bath

LISTENING SKILLS

1 **CD1.13** Listen to a radio programme in which different people give their opinion about fashion and appearance. Match speakers 1–5 with statements a–f. There is one extra statement.

1 Katie ☐
2 Tom ☐
3 Brian ☐
4 Lisa ☐
5 Veronica ☐

a Some clothes in fashion shows are not designed to be worn by ordinary people.
b If you buy clothes from the same shops as everyone else, you don't show your own style.
c You may become a fashion victim if you pay attention to new fashions in magazines and on TV.
d The clothes people wear can tell us something about their character.
e Fashion is really important and we should obey it.
f There is a link between what you wear and what kind of music you listen to.

SPEAKING SKILLS

1 Describe the photo and answer the questions.

1 Why do you think the people have decided to go shopping together?
2 Do you agree that shopping has become a popular leisure activity for families nowadays? Is this right or wrong? Justify your opinion.

2 Roleplay this conversation.

Student A
You are on a language course in England. You have found out that the school is next to a theatre. You would like to join the theatre. Ask one of your teachers for information. In the conversation:
• ask the teacher for their opinion of the activities at the theatre.
• explain that you are not sure whether your knowledge of English is enough for you to be able to take part in shows put on by the theatre.
• show your interest in the theatre and ask how to join it.

Student B
You are a teacher on a summer language course in England. One of your students wants to find out details of the local theatre. In the conversation with the student:
• say that, in your opinion, participation in the theatre is a way of studying English.
• tell the student that all students from the school can participate in the activities at the theatre.
• explain how to go about becoming a member of the theatre.

An eye for an eye?

Read, listen and talk about crime and punishment.
Practise the Past Simple, the Past Continuous and the Past Perfect, *used to* and *would*.
Focus on agreeing and disagreeing.

GRAMMAR AND READING

1 **Work in pairs. Describe the photo then answer the questions.**

• Where are the two young people and what are they doing?
• This is their punishment for a crime. What do you think they did?

a destroyed a statue
b insulted some police officers
c stole a car

2 **Read the article and check your answers to the questions in Exercise 1.**

Work it out

3 **Identify the tenses of the verbs in bold: Past Simple/ Past Continuous/Past Perfect. Then circle the correct words in the explanations.**

1 When I reached the front, the police **had stopped** the traffic.
The police stopped the traffic *before / at the same time as / after* I reached the front.
2 When I reached the front, two teenagers **were walking** along the street.
The teenagers were walking *before / at the same time as / after* I reached the front.
3 When I reached the front, I **asked** one of the cops a question.
I asked a question *before / at the same time as / after* I reached the front.

Newsletter from America

Liz Connery on what's happening across the Atlantic.

Rough ■Justice

Last weekend I was staying with some friends in Ohio. I needed a break from New York and someone had told me it was a nice, quiet place.

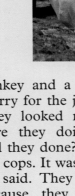

It was Sunday at 10 o'clock and I was jogging in a park. I was running near the street when I saw a crowd of people, a police car and a donkey! I ran forward and pushed through the crowd. When I reached the front, the police had stopped the traffic and two teenagers were walking along the street with the donkey and a sign that said, 'Sorry for the jackass offence.' They looked miserable. Why were they doing this? What had they done? I asked one of the cops. It was a punishment, he said. They were doing it because they had stolen a statue from a church and destroyed it. A judge, Michael Ciccnetti, had sentenced them to 45 days in jail, ordered them to pay for a new statue, and given them this unusual punishment. This was not the first time that this judge had thought of an original way to punish continued p7

4 Look at sentences 1–3 in the Past Continuous. Match them with descriptions a–c.

1 I was staying with some friends in Ohio. ☐
2 It was 10 o'clock. I was jogging in the park. ☐
3 I was running near the road when I saw some people. ☐

a a description of an action or situation in progress at a specific time
b a description of a temporary situation
c a longer action interrupted by a shorter one

Check it out

Past Simple, Past Continuous and Past Perfect

We use the Past Simple:
• to describe finished actions.
• to tell the main events in a story in order.
I ran forward and pushed through the crowd.

We use the Past Continuous:
• to describe things which were in progress at a specific time in the past.
It was 10 o'clock. I was jogging.
• for temporary situations/ habits.
I was staying in Ohio.
• for longer actions interrupted by shorter ones.
I was running when I saw some people.

We use the Past Perfect:
to talk about an action that happened before another action in the past.
They were doing it because they had stolen a statue.

Mind the trap!

We generally use the Past Simple, not the Past Continuous, to talk about finished actions, even if they lasted for a long time or were repeated.

They spent 45 days in jail. NOT were spending

He planned the robbery for several years. NOT was planning

5 **CD1.14** Work in pairs. Match questions 1–4 with answers a–d. Listen and check.

1 Where were you? ☐
2 What were you doing? ☐
3 What happened? ☐
4 What did you do? ☐

a My neighbours started shouting at each other.
b I got up and put on the TV really loud.
c I was trying to get to sleep.
d I was at home.

6 Work in pairs. Roleplay the situation. Student A, look at page 142. Student B, look at page 143.

jackass *American English* **1** a male donkey **2** stupid or annoying

7 In pairs, read these unusual punishments. Guess the crimes the people committed. Use the Past Perfect.

Perhaps Andy had parked his car in the wrong place.

1 Andy had to work as a school crossing guard.
2 Bill had to visit nine fire stations and apologise to the fire fighters.
3 Carl had to wear a dress, a wig and make-up in a busy shopping street.
4 Dan invited a family to his house and asked them to take anything they wanted.
5 Ed had to run a five-mile race.

8 Complete sentences a–e with the Past Perfect. Then match the crimes with punishments 1–5 in Exercise 7.

a He _____ (make) a false call to the fire station. ☐
b He _____ (drive) too fast near a school. ☐
c He _____ (break) into their house and he _____ (steal) their property. ☐
d He _____ (run) away from the police after they _____ (see) him drinking beer while driving . ☐
e He _____ (insult) a woman and he _____ (throw) beer cans at her car. ☐

9 Complete the sentences. Use the Past Simple, the Past Continuous and the Past Perfect.

1 When he crashed the car,
   a he _____ (drive) at 160 kph.
   b he _____ (drink) six bottles of beer.
   c an ambulance _____ (arrive) and _____ (take) him to hospital.

2 When the judge returned to the courtroom,
   a everyone immediately _____ (stand) up.
   b she _____ (make) her decision.
   c the journalists _____ (still/write) their reports.

3 When she came out of the prison gate,
   a she _____ (learn) her lesson.
   b her husband _____ (wait) for her.
   c she _____ (kiss) her husband and then they _____ (go) home.

READING AND VOCABULARY

1 Look at the picture of a courtroom. Match people a–e with the words below. Use a dictionary to help you.

accused ☐   judge ☐   jury ☐
lawyer ☐   witness ☐

2 **CD ROM** Read newspaper headlines a–f. Check the meanings of the <u>underlined</u> words. Then read texts 1–6 opposite and match them with the headlines.

a # Toilet <u>injuries</u>

b Criminal <u>takes</u> victim <u>to</u> <u>court</u>

c From cookies to <u>court</u> <u>case</u>

d *I'm <u>guilty</u>! Arrest me!*

e Teacher <u>sues</u> pupil for <u>lost</u> <u>earnings</u>

f Six chairs, a table and some <u>compensation</u>

3 Read the texts again and answer the questions. Tick true and cross false.

1 Kathleen Robertson sued her own son. ☐
2 Daniel Allen didn't mean to hurt Ms Blau. ☐
3 The teenage girls from Colorado wanted to frighten their neighbours. ☐
4 Terrence Dickson is a burglar. ☐
5 Kara Walton couldn't open the door of the toilet. ☐
6 Helmut Bleibtreu had felt guilty for 80 years. ☐

4 Complete the sentences with the highlighted words in the text.

1 'A _____ consists of twelve persons chosen to decide who has the best lawyer.' – *Robert Frost*
2 After the witness had given his evidence, the _____ confessed to the crime.
3 Was this the first time that a teacher had _____ a student?
4 The _____ shouted out, 'Order in court!'
5 A football player took an opponent to court to ask for _____ for a broken leg.
6 The police are looking for _____ to the robbery which took place at Murphy's Jewellery late last night.

5 Work in groups. Imagine you are the jury and decide if these people should win or lose their cases. Then look at page 140 and check.

• Kathleen Robertson
• Wanita Young
• Terrence Dickson
• Kara Walton

Laughter in Court!

1 ☐ Kathleen Robertson of Austin, Texas took a furniture store to court for medical costs and physical and mental suffering. She had broken her ankle after falling over a little boy who was running wild inside the store. The store owner was rather surprised to be the accused in a court case. The little boy was Ms Robertson's son!

2 ☐ Eleven-year-old New Jersey boy Daniel Allen was running to catch a bus when he accidentally knocked over school teacher Eileen Blau. Daniel cried when he found out he had hurt the teacher. But two years later, she took him to court because of the injuries she had suffered. Apparently, the Allens' insurance company had still not paid compensation for her medical care and lost earnings. During the court case Daniel told the judge, 'I'm sorry I ran into her. It was an accident!'

3 ☐ A Colorado woman has sued two teenagers for giving her some cookies! Instead of going to a dance, Taylor Ostergaard, 17, and Lindsey Jo Zellitti, 18 decided to stay home and bake cookies for their neighbours. After they had finished baking, they added a heart shaped card to every packet of cookies. The card read, 'Have a great night. Love, The T and L Club!' Then, the girls went from house to house, and left a dozen cookies at every home where the lights were on. When the teens knocked on Wanita Young's door, the 49-year-old woman called the police. She was afraid because there were suspicious people at her door. They hadn't answered when she had asked them who they were. Later, Taylor explained that they hadn't answered because they had wanted the gift to be a surprise. There were no witnesses, and the police decided that the girls had not committed a crime. However, the next day, Young went to hospital suffering from anxiety. A year later, she sued the girls for the cost of her medical bills.

4 ☐ Terrence Dickson had just robbed a house in Pennsylvania. However, he discovered that he couldn't get out of the garage because the automatic door wasn't working correctly. And he couldn't get back in the house either because the door was locked. The family was on holiday, so Mr Dickson was stuck in the garage for eight days. He survived on a case of Pepsi and a large bag of dried dog food. When he finally got out, Mr Dickson sued the homeowner's insurance company. He claimed the situation had caused him mental anguish. It seems that even a burglar can ask a jury for money.

5 ☐ Kara Walton of Delaware went to court to get damages for something that was her own fault. She sued the owner of a night club because she had fallen from a bathroom window and lost her two front teeth. Why was she climbing through the window in the club? Was the door blocked? No, it was because she didn't want to pay the $3.50 for using the toilet!

6 ☐ Some people just can't accept responsibility for their own problems, but that's not the case of Helmut Bleibtreu. In 2006, this 84-year-old German pensioner went to the police and confessed to a crime. He had placed a firecracker on a railway track in 1926, and had run away when railway police saw him. For 80 years he had lived with his guilt, but finally he felt he had to admit to the only bad thing he had ever done. The police told him not to do it again and set him free.

GRAMMAR AND VOCABULARY

1 Read text A. Why did the little girl run and hide from the police?

a I was really naive. I believed everything my sister told me. One time she said, 'It's illegal to play a board game if you're not old enough.' I played games with my family anyway, but anytime I heard a police siren, I didn't hesitate. I ran and hid in case they arrested me.

b I <u>used to be</u> really naive. I used to believe everything my sister told me. One time she said, 'It's illegal to play a board game if you're not old enough.' I used to play games with my family anyway, but anytime I heard a police siren, I didn't use to hesitate. I used to run and hide in case they arrested me.

c I used to be really naive. I used to believe everything my sister told me. One time she said, 'It's illegal to play a board game if you're not old enough.' I <u>would play</u> games with my family anyway, but anytime I heard a police siren, I wouldn't hesitate. I would run and hide in case they arrested me.

Work it out

2 Compare text A with text B and <u>underline</u> all the differences between them. Then compare texts C and B in the same way.

3 Study the words you <u>underlined</u> in texts B and C. Then decide when we use *used to* and *would*. Tick the correct boxes.

	used to	*would*
habitual/repeated actions in the past		
past states with verbs like *have, be, believe …*		

Mind the trap!

We use the Past Simple, and not *used to* and *would*, to talk about something which was not frequent or habitual.

One time she **said**, (NOT ~~used to say~~ or ~~would say~~) 'you're not old enough.'

4 **CD1.15** Rewrite the <u>underlined</u> verbs in the text with *used to*. There is one verb you can't change. Then listen and check.

I <u>was</u> really silly. I <u>thought</u> that the expression 'Don't drink and drive' meant that it was illegal to drink anything in the car. So when I was drinking Pepsi in the car, I <u>hid</u> every time I saw a police car. I <u>didn't get up</u> until the police had gone. On one trip to Florida this <u>happened</u> six times!

5 **CD1.16** Decide which of the verbs you changed in Exercise 4 can be replaced with *would*. Then listen and check.

6 Work in pairs. Complete the sentences with *used to*. Then write similar sentences that are true for you.

1 Now I know the world is round, but … .

Now I know the world is round, but I used to think it was flat.

2 I get on really well with my little brother now, but … .
3 I can come home any time I want now, but … .
4 My mum goes to the gym every day, but … .
5 My dad doesn't smoke any more, but … .
6 I know you live in London now, but where … ?
7 Now I want to be a doctor, but … .

7 Complete sentences 1–6 with the words in the box.

blackmailers burglars kidnappers muggers serial killers shoplifters

When I was a little kid, I used to believe that …

1 _____ were very strong people who picked up shops.

2 _____ were people who stole burgers.

3 _____ were people who hit you on the head with a mug.

4 _____ were people who sent black envelopes to people.

5 _____ were murderers who put poison in breakfast cereals.

6 _____ were people who would catch kids and force them to take a nap.

8 Correct the definitions in sentences 1–6 in Exercise 7. Follow the example. Use a dictionary to help you.

Shoplifters aren't people who pick up shops, they're people who steal from shops.

Shoplifting is a serious crime

VOCABULARY

1 Think Back! Complete the table with words from the box.

blackmail burglary courtroom kidnapping judge jury lawyer mugging robbery sentence shoplifting trial

Crimes	Justice
blackmail,	

2 Work in pairs. Check the meaning of these acts of anti-social behaviour. Then, Student A, look at page 142. Student B, look at page 143. Listen to your partner and say what the people did.

noise nuisance vandalism graffiti dropping litter racial abuse speeding swearing in public bullying

3 Work in pairs. Check the meaning of these punishments. Then decide on the best punishments for the anti-social behaviour in Exercise 2.

electronic tagging a rehabilitation programme community service a fine a prison sentence

4 CD1.17 Complete the text. Write one word in each gap. Then listen and check.

When he was only 15, Norman Fletcher committed a
[1] _____ . He got away with £8.25 and six packets of chewing gum. Unfortunately for him, he had robbed his local shop, so the police arrested him and he had to pay a [2] _____ of £82.50. Later on, he became a [3] _____ , but he was caught after he had taken a tin of beans from a supermarket. He went to court, and during the [4] _____ his [5] _____ argued that Norman needed to go on a [6] _____ programme. She also said that her client was prepared to do some [7] _____ service. However, the [8] _____ sent him to prison for eight weeks.
Brilliantly, Norman broke out of prison the day before his [9] _____ ended. He stole a car to get away, but he was stopped for [10] _____ – he was going at over ninety miles per hour – and was sent back to prison. When he was released, Norman decided to become a [11] _____ . He tried to steal a handbag from an old woman, but she hit him so hard with her umbrella that he started screaming for help and he was arrested for noise [12] _____ !

3 [CD1.18] Listen again to both conversations and complete the arguments for and against this statement: *Farrah Keating's punishment is fair.*

FOR
- £50,000 is a large fine.
- She was _____ and she panicked.
- She cannot drive a car for _____ years.

AGAINST
- She was driving at _____ miles per hour in a thirty miles per hour zone.
- She didn't stop to _____ the victim.
- She was _____.
- She didn't have a _____ _____.
- She _____ when she was arrested – she said her _____ was driving.

SPEAKING AND LISTENING

1 Read the newspaper article. Check you understand the underlined words.

2 [CD1.18] Listen to two conversations about the Farrah Keating story and match them with photos A and B. Which conversation is more formal?

Guilty!

Celebrity dancer Farrah Keating has been found guilty of drink-driving and of failing to report an accident. The judge has given her a £50,000 fine and an eight-month suspended sentence. She has also been banned from driving. Last September, the dancer, who recently got divorced from actor Leonardo Boom, knocked down eight-year-old London girl, Maira Abbasi, with her car. She didn't stop to help the girl, who suffered severe injuries to her back and legs. The victim's father complained that the punishment was too lenient, and would not act as a deterrent to other irresponsible drivers.

4 [CD1.18] Decide which of the phrases in bold are formal (F) and which are informal (I). Then listen again and check.

- **I'm afraid I can't agree with** you. Of course it's not fair! ☐
- Oh, **come off it!** I don't believe this! ☐
- **I agree with you up to a point**, but I'm not sure a prison sentence is the best punishment. ☐
- **Well, maybe,** but think about it for a second. ☐
- **I couldn't agree more.** Her greatest punishment is the guilt she must be feeling. ☐
- **You're dead right!** She lied when the police arrested her. ☐

5 Complete the Speak Out box with the phrases in bold in Exercise 4.

SPEAK OUT | Agreeing and disagreeing

Informal	Neutral/Formal
Agreeing	
1 _____ That's so true. No doubt about it.	Absolutely! That's a good point! 2 _____
Partial agreement	
3 _____ You've got a point, but …	That may be true but … 4 _____
Disagreeing	
5 _____ No way!	I totally disagree with you. 6 _____

6 Read the conversations. Decide if they are formal or informal. Then complete them with expressions from Speak Out.

Amy	I think the death penalty is justified in some cases.
Ben	What are you saying? 1_____ I think it's totally barbaric!
Carl	2_____ Amy, but the problem is that the police aren't perfect. They make mistakes.
Judge	Will the lawyers come up to the bench, please? … Look, this case has gone on long enough. We need to reach a conclusion soon.
Lawyer 1	3_____ . I'm ready to make my closing speech right now.
Lawyer 2	4_____ . I still have several witnesses to call.
Dave	There is no justice for the poor. The rich can buy the decisions they want.
Emily	5_____ . I saw this case the other day. This rich guy had killed his wife, but he got away with it because his lawyer was really good.
Fay	6_____ you guys! That's not true at all!
Politician 1	And to conclude, let me say that the government is too soft on crime. We need a harder approach.
Politician 2	7_____ , but we have to be hard on the causes of crime, too.
Politician 1	8_____ ! Hard on crime and hard on the causes of crime!

7 Work in pairs. Use Speak Out and the arguments from Exercise 3 to roleplay the situation.

Student A
You are Farrah Keating's sister. You meet the father of the child who was knocked down. Explain how the accident happened and say how sorry you are for what happened. Say how you feel now. Explain why Farrah Keating's punishment is fair.

Student B
You are Maira Abbasi's father. You meet Farrah Keating's sister. Ask how the accident happened and why the driver didn't stop to help your daughter. Explain how it has affected your family. Explain why you think Farrah Keating's punishment is not fair.

8 Work in groups. Discuss the punishments in situations 1–4 below. Express your opinions and agree/disagree with each other.

1 A 15-year-old boy bullied other children and stole their money and valuables. He insulted teachers and tried to burn down the school. He was suspended for three weeks.

2 An 18-year-old student created a virus which infected millions of computers around the world. He received a ten-year prison sentence.

3 A US citizen blew up a government building and killed 168 people. He received the death penalty.

4 A man drove the get-away car in a bank robbery in which a security guard was killed. His sentence was life imprisonment.

(S)he

Read, listen and talk about gender differences, family life, personality.
Practise modal verbs.
Focus on asking for and refusing permission, synonyms.
Write a for and against essay.

Why Men Are Impossible

They have no opinions about clothes ...   **... but they can buy a pair of trainers in thirty seconds.**

I'm not sure about this skirt. Perhaps I **should** look for another one?

It looks fine.

Don't you think you **ought to** try them on first?

They'll be fine.

They have no interest in details ...   **... unless it's a car that they'll never own.**

It's Carol's birthday on the 14th ... We **must** buy a card.

Mmm ...

It **can** go from 0 to 100 in 5.28 seconds!

Mmm ...

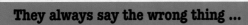

They always say the wrong thing ...   **... or don't want to talk at all.**

It looks awful.

You can still take it back.

So it does look awful?

You **mustn't** take it personally.

Can we talk about where our relationship is going?

What now? But I **have to** go to football practice.

They're boring to argue with ...   **... but it can be nice to have them around.**

... sentences for you?

I suppose so.

If you must.

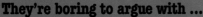

Why do you always have to finish my ...

Can we join you?

GRAMMAR AND LISTENING

1 In pairs, look at the cartoons and choose two words to describe the men and two words to describe the women. Use a dictionary to help you.

(un)complicated   (in)decisive
(im)practical   romantic   (in)sensitive
(un)sympathetic   (un)predictable
diplomatic   talkative

The cartoon suggests that men are insensitive because they always say the wrong thing.

Work it out

2 Look at the cartoons. Then, for each phrase 1–7 below find a phrase with a verb in bold which has the same meaning.

1 I feel it's important for us to buy …
   a *… we must buy …*
2 It's necessary for me to go …
   b …………..
3 Stop taking it personally.
   c …………..
4 It's a good idea to look for another one.
   d …………..
5 Isn't it sensible to try them on?
   e …………..
6 It has the ability to go from 0 to 100.
   f …………..
7 Are we allowed to join you?
   g …………..

Check it out

Modals and related verbs

- We use *must* and *have to* to talk about necessity.
  I **must** get up early tomorrow. (personal preference)
  I **have to** go to football practice. (external obligation)

- We use *mustn't* to talk about prohibition.
  You **mustn't** take it personally.

- We use *should* and *ought to* to talk about duty or give advice.
  You **ought to** try on those shoes first.
  Perhaps I **should** try another skirt?

- We use *can* and *could* to talk about ability in the present/past.
  It **can** go from 0 to 100 in 5.28 seconds!
  I **couldn't** understand men, but now I can.

- We use *can* to talk about possibility.
  You **can** still take it back to the shop.

- We use *can* to ask for permission or make requests.
  Can we talk about our relationship?
  Can we join you?

3 For each sentence, circle the best option.

1 You *don't have to / mustn't* tell anyone – it's a secret!
2 I *must / have to* stay late at school today – we've got a rehearsal for the play.
3 Since the accident he *hasn't been able to / couldn't* speak.
4 In your country *must men / do men have to* do military service?
5 I *ought to / mustn't* send her an email – she must be very worried.
6 I *can't / couldn't* swim when I was younger.
7 I *must / have to* go to the dentist's – I've got really bad toothache.
8 Don't worry about losing your library card – you *can / should* get a new one.

4 **CD1.19** Listen to the dialogue. Why does Jerry finally decide to go to the kitchen?

5 **CD1.19** Complete the sentences with the correct verbs. Use the clues in brackets. Then listen again and check.

1 Hey girls, _____ *(request)* you make us some sandwiches?
2 Even men _____ *(ability)* put some cheese between two bits of bread.
3 No Lisa, you _____ *(prohibition)* listen to them. Dave! You _____ *(advice)* be so lazy!
4 Remember when you _____ *(ability)* understand why your printer wasn't working and I _____ *(necessity)* fix it for you?
5 Men _____ *(duty)* help women with technical problems.
6 You love _____ *(possibility)* to show how much you know about computers.
7 I _____ *(ability)* eat this rubbish!

6 Work in pairs. Answer the questions. Use the verbs in bold.

1 Are there any rules that you **have to** follow at home?
2 What things **could** you do when you were younger but you can't now?
3 Does your school have any rules about things you **mustn't** do?

Like Father, Like Son? Perhaps Not …

A new report suggests that our brain chemistry at birth is as important as our upbringing

Go into a busy newsagent's and have a look at what kind of things people are reading. The chances are that the women are reading about fashion, beauty, romance or relationships and the men are reading about cars, photography, equipment or sport. This ought not to be a surprise. After all, these choices are also seen in typical male and female hobbies – men generally enjoy things such as looking after their cars, buying new parts for their stereos, bird-watching or playing computer games while women seem to prefer keeping in touch with friends and entertaining.

For a long time, experts thought that these differences between male and female interests depended on how parents brought up their children and indeed society in general. However, when we look at young babies, we see that boys and girls have interests which we can call typically 'male' or 'female' from a very early age. A baby girl, as young as 12 months old, is sympathetic when she sees a sad or worried face – she also looks sad and makes comforting sounds. Baby girls also make more eye contact and look longer at other people. Boys of the same age look longer at mechanical objects – toys that spin, light up or move. Later, when they become toddlers, boys usually enjoy putting things together and building towns or bridges or vehicles. Boys are often more selfish and aggressive when they play with other children while girls are better at joining in with others. Just like the adults.

So where do these differences between male and female behaviour come from? Although it is true that culture and upbringing play an important role, many scientists now believe that the answer also lies in the amount of male and female hormones in the mother's body before a child's birth. Research has shown that this balance of hormones leads to three different types of brain: type E, type S and type B. People who are born with a type S or male brain are generally interested in systems: constructing and organising things and working out how things work. They tend to be good at working out where they are, from maps, making things from plans or collecting things. Others have a type E or female brain which means they are good at understanding other people's emotions and treating people with care because they are sensitive themselves. Others are born with characteristics of both these male and female brains – this is called the type B or balanced brain.

Perhaps the most crucial thing that the researchers found out was that the type of brain you have does not have to depend on your sex. Not all men have the male brain, and not all women have the female brain. But on average, more males than females have a type S brain, and more females than males have a type E brain.

So does this mean that one sort of brain is superior? No, not at all. Some people find some things easier to do than others but both sexes have their strengths and their weaknesses. Researchers hope that understanding how people are born with different types of brain can help make all of us more tolerant of difference.

READING AND VOCABULARY

1 Work in pairs. Describe the photo then answer the questions.

- Do boys of this age behave differently to girls? In what ways?
- In which ways do men and women differ in their hobbies and interests?

2 **CD ROM** Quickly read the article and answer the questions.

1 How many types of brain are there?
2 Does the type of brain you have depend on your gender?
3 Is there a type of brain which is better than the others?

3 Read the article again. Tick true and cross false.

1 Generally speaking, women and men both prefer reading about people than reading about gadgets or equipment. ☐
2 Experts used to believe that parents had a lot of influence on what hobbies their children liked. ☐
3 Even when they are babies, girls seem more interested in people than boys. ☐
4 It seems to be easier for little girls to get on with people than for boys. ☐
5 People with a type S brain get lost easily. ☐
6 It is extremely unusual for women to have a type B brain. ☐

4 Match these adjectives from the article with definitions 1–6.

sympathetic (para. 2) ☐
comforting (para. 2) ☑ 5
selfish (para. 2) ☑ 6
aggressive (para. 2) ☑ 3
balanced (para. 3) ☑ 4
tolerant (para. 5) ☐

1 allowing people to do what they want especially when you do not agree with it
2 showing that you understand and care about someone's problems
3 behaving in a violent and angry way towards people
4 having not too much of any one thing
5 making someone feel better when they are anxious
6 caring only about yourself and not other people

5 Try the personality test. Then look at page 140 to find out what your answers suggest. Do you agree?

How balanced is your brain?

Tick six sentences which you can identify with the most.

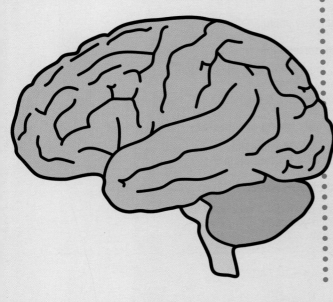

1 I dislike listening to gossip. ☐
2 I enjoy collecting things (eg CDs, magazines, aircraft numbers). ☑
3 I enjoy getting to know other people. ☑
4 I like finding out how something works or fixing things. ☑
5 I love reading about any of these things – military history, science, the universe, instruction manuals, computers. ☑
6 I sometimes make a faux pas when I'm with people. ☐
7 I think I often know what other people are thinking. ☐
8 I usually trust my intuition or first impressions when I meet people. ☐
9 I worry when one of my friends is having problems. ☐
10 I'm hopeless at doing several things at once. ☑
11 I enjoy being a host/hostess – for example organising a party. ☐
12 It's easy for me to read maps. ☐
13 It's important for me to have close friends. ☐
14 It's quite easy for me to 'fit in' in a new situation or with new people. ☐
15 Literature is one of my strongest subjects. ☐
16 Maths is one of my strongest subjects. ☐

SPEAKING AND LISTENING

1 **CD1.20** In pairs, look at the photo. What do you think the situation is? Then listen to the conversation between Anna, Damon and their dad and check.

2 **CD1.20** Listen again and tick the statements that are true.

1 Damon thinks that Philip wore a skirt for fun. `F`
2 The boys in Damon's school are allowed to wear shorts in hot weather. `F`
3 None of the teachers appreciated what Philip was doing. `F`
4 Damon believes that Philip's protest was a good thing to do. `T`
5 Damon thinks that the pupils are too old for rules about what to wear. `T`
6 Damon's dad doesn't think that what pupils wear has any influence on a school's reputation. `F`

3 Work in pairs and answer the questions.

• Do you sympathise with Philip's protest?
• Whose point of view do you agree with most – Damon's or his dad's?
• Do you think that boys are treated differently at school?

4 **CD1.21** Listen to the last part of the conversation. Then, in pairs, answer the questions.

• Who seems to find it harder to get permission – Damon or Anna?
• Do you think parents are stricter with girls than with boys?

5 **CD1.21** Study Speak Out. Listen to the last part of the conversation again and tick the phrases you hear.

SPEAK OUT | Permission

Asking for permission

Direct/informal

▲ Please let me + infinitive ☑ *May I*
   Can I … ? ☐
   Could I (possibly) … ? ☐
   Is it OK if I … ? ☑
   Do you mind if I + Present Simple? ☑
▼ I was wondering if I could … . ☑

Indirect/very polite

Giving permission

That's fine by me./No problem./Sure. ☐
Yes, of course./Please, do. ☐
(Do you mind …?) No, I don't. ☐

Unwillingly giving permission

I suppose so./If you must. ☐
As long as + Present Simple ☐

Refusing permission

Actually, that's not a very good idea. ☐
I'm afraid you can't. ☐
Sorry, but … . ☐

VOCABULARY

1 Think Back! **Add prefixes** *-in/-im/-un* **to make the opposites of the adjectives below. Use a dictionary to help you.**

predictable   sensitive   tolerant
decisive   practical   sympathetic

2 **Decide if the adjectives below have a positive (+) or a negative (–) meaning. Use a dictionary to help you.**

big-headed   cruel   greedy   sociable
cheeky   forgetful   laid-back   stubborn
considerate   gloomy   quick-tempered   vain

3 CD1.23 **Listen and write down an adjective from Exercise 2 that describes the four people best.**

1 stubborn   3 forgetfull
2 sociable   4 considerate

TRAIN YOUR BRAIN | Dictionary skills

Synonyms

Dictionaries are a good way to find synonyms (words which have a similar meaning). These often come after a definition of a word.

absent-minded /æbsənt-maɪndɪd/ *adj 1* likely to forget things (= forgetful)

Sometimes a dictionary may also have a study box for very common words – a list of words with similar meanings.

WORD FOCUS: UNKIND
similar words: nasty, cruel, mean, thoughtless, insensitive, unsympathetic

4 **Use a dictionary to try to find synonyms of the words below.**

1 funny _____   4 kind _____
2 timid _____   5 nice _____
3 intelligent _____   6 rude _____

5 **Write a short description of your partner. Use the words in Exercises 1–4 to help you. Then read out your answer. Does he/she agree?**

Mind the trap!

You should always give a reason when you refuse somebody permission in order not to sound rude.

'Can I sit here?'
'Sorry, but the seat's already taken.'

6 CD1.22 **Listen to the three conversations. Which one is the most formal/informal? Which phrases from** Speak Out **suggest this?**

7 **Work in pairs. Act out the conversation. Replace the** underlined **phrases with another phrase from** Speak Out **which has a similar meaning.**

Anna Sandra has got us tickets for the Jason Trembelin concert tonight. <u>Do you mind if I go?</u>
Dad Well, as long as it doesn't finish too late.
Anna No, I'm sure it won't. Err … actually, <u>I was wondering if I could spend the night at</u> Sandra's afterwards. I mean it is Friday night after all.
Dad <u>Actually, that's not a very good idea is it?</u> I mean you've got the dentist's early in the morning.
Anna But Dad. You let Damon stay out with his friends, why can't I?
Dad Damon's a year older than you, Anna.
Anna What you really meant was Damon's a boy.
Dad Nonsense … you know that we treat you both the same.
Anna Go on, <u>please let me</u> stay over.
Dad Oh, <u>I suppose so</u> – as long as you phone us after the concert.
Anna Thanks! Err … just one more thing. <u>Could I possibly borrow £15?</u> There are these gorgeous T-shirts … .

8 **Work in pairs and act out the situations. Student A, look at the situations below. Student B, look at page 143. Use** Speak Out **to help you.**

Student A
1 You want to visit your friend this evening.
2 You are a young male student travelling on a train. A pretty woman gets on the train with a heavy suitcase. You offer to help her.
3 A stranger at a party asks you about your weight. You refuse to answer – you think it isn't his/her business!

9 **Work in pairs. Use** Speak Out **to roleplay a conversation. Student A, look at page 142. Student B, look at page 143.**

WRITING

1 **In pairs, look at the photos and answer the questions.**

- What kind of schools do you think these are?
- What sort of school is more popular in your country?
- Do you think that girls and boys should go to separate schools? Why?/Why not?

2 **Read the essay. In pairs, answer the questions.**

1 Does the writer mention any of your opinions from Exercise 1?
2 What is the writer's personal opinion?
3 What is the tone of the essay? Tick the best answer.
- formal and controlled ☐
- emotional and moralistic ☐
- informal and personal ☐

English Worksheet 1

'Girls and boys should be taught in separate schools.'

Write an essay giving arguments for and against this statement and also state your own opinion.

1 Everyone agrees that education is a very important matter but not everyone agrees about the best way to teach children. One controversial question that people disagree on is whether girls and boys should be educated separately.

2 There are several advantages to single-sex schools. <u>Firstly</u>, schools can concentrate on teaching subjects that interest students most. <u>For example</u>, girls are often more interested in languages and an all-girl school can find more time for such subjects in the timetable. <u>Secondly</u>, many people think that girls and boys learn better in classes of the same sex. They say that there is more competition between students and that generally results are better. <u>Finally, supporters of single-sex schools also believe</u> that students are calmer and behave better, too.

3 However, there are many arguments against single-sex schools. Firstly, <u>critics of such schools say</u> that they encourage young people to make stereotypical choices about their futures. <u>This is because</u> students often don't have the chance to try things which are less typical for their gender. But perhaps <u>the biggest disadvantage is</u> that they do not give boys and girls a chance to socialise with each other. This can make it hard for people to adapt to the 'normal' world after they finish school.

4 <u>In conclusion</u>, although single-sex schools can be a good thing, especially academically, they also have a negative side. <u>In my opinion</u>, the biggest argument against these schools is that they do not give young men and women the chance to understand each other better.

(249 words)

Essay Plan

Paragraph 1: Introduction _____ _____
Paragraph 2: Arguments for
Paragraph 3: Arguments against
Paragraph 4: Conclusion _____ _____

3 Look at the essay again and put sentences a–d into the correct paragraphs in the essay plan above.

a A very short summary of the debate.
b Some general points about the subject that everyone can agree with.
c The fact that the question is controversial and causes a lot of debate.
d The writer's personal opinion.

4 Look at paragraphs 2 and 3 of the essay. How many arguments does the writer give in each paragraph?

5 Look at the <u>underlined</u> words/phrases in the essay and put them into the correct place below.

- Introducing each new argument: *First of all; To begin with; Next; _____ ; _____ ; _____*
- Giving examples/reasons to support an argument: *For instance; _____*
- Introducing your own opinion: *Personally, I believe … ; _____*
- Introducing a conclusion: *To sum up; _____*

6 Complete the missing information in Train Your Brain. Use Exercises 3–5 to help you.

TRAIN YOUR BRAIN | Writing skills

For and against essay

Paragraph 1 – Introduction
- Make some general points that [1] _____ can agree with.
- Perhaps give a definition of a difficult concept or say that the issue is controversial.

Paragraph 2 – Arguments for
- Give two or three arguments for an issue.
- If necessary, give examples or reasons to [2] _____ an argument.

Paragraph 3 – Arguments against
- Write a paragraph similar to paragraph 2 for arguments against.

Paragraph 4 – Conclusion
- Give a short [3] _____ of the debate.
- You can add your own [4] _____ at the very end.

The tone of such essays should be rather formal – not emotional, moralistic or personal.

---

7 Work in pairs and follow the instructions.

- Read the essay question below and check you understand it.
- Think of some arguments for and against the statement to put in the table. Do you need to add any examples or reasons to explain your arguments?
- Tell each other what your personal opinion is.

'Adolescence is the unhappiest time in most people's lives.'

Write an essay giving arguments for and against this statement and also state your own opinion.

Arguments for the statement	Arguments against the statement

8 Compare your ideas for the essay with other pairs. Who has the most convincing arguments? The most original?

9 Which of the statements below could you include in an introduction to the essay in Exercise 7? Choose three. Use Train Your Brain to help you.

1 According to the dictionary, adolescence means the period of time in someone's life between being a child and an adult.
2 Four years ago, on my thirteenth birthday my big brother said to me, 'You're a teenager now. Welcome to the club.' I glanced at his long, serious face – he looked really, really sad.
3 It is a disgusting lie to say that adolescence is the unhappiest time in your life. And I should know!
4 Everyone knows that this is a challenging time when young people have to make sense of the world … and themselves.
5 For some people the challenge makes it an enjoyable time, for others it can be the opposite.

10 Write the essay in Exercise 7. Write 200–250 words. Use your answers to Exercises 5, 7, 8, 9 and Train Your Brain to help you.

VOCABULARY AND GRAMMAR

1 **Complete the sentences. The first letter of each word is given.**

1 There should be a stricter punishment for **d**_____ litter.
2 If someone shouts at you in public, you can **t**_____ them to court.
3 Do you know Sting's song 'If you love somebody, **s**_____ them free'?
4 It always takes me hours to choose what I want to buy – I'm very **i**_____ .
5 I have to buy special cosmetics because I have **s**_____ skin.
6 Most Hollywood films are quite **p**_____ – you always know what's going to happen.

2 **Write the following words and phrases under the right headings.**

community service   rob   vandal
blackmailer   steal   insult   shoplifting
robbery   fine (n)   judge (n)   sue
mugger   serial killer   vandalism
prison sentence   drunk-driving
life imprisonment   accuse   burglar
kidnap   robber   suspended sentence

Crime and punishment			
crimes	punishment	people	verbs

3 **Complete the second sentence so that it has a similar meaning to the first sentence using the word given. You must use between two and five words including the word given.**

1 I read the newspaper before I ate dinner.
   ALREADY
   By the time I ate dinner _____ the newspaper.
2 I often went swimming when I was a child.
   TO
   I often _____ swimming when I was a child.
3 It is necessary for me to wear a tie at work.
   TO
   I _____ a tie at work.
4 I can stay at home today. The school is closed.
   GO
   I _____ school today.
5 Is it OK if I come round this afternoon?
   IF
   Do _____ come round this afternoon?
6 I can't sing now and I couldn't sing when I was young.
   ABLE
   I have _____ sing
7 When he was young he would never argue or fight.
   TO
   He _____ argue or fight.

4 **Circle the correct answer.**

1 My dentist says I *have to / can* stop eating sweets.
2 *Could / Should* you turn down the music? I have a headache.
3 You *mustn't / don't have to* smoke here – it's bad for the baby.
4 I *should / can* do some shopping today – I don't have any soap or shampoo.
5 Although she is only five, she *can / ought to* swim without any help.
6 When I was younger, my grandma *would / must* tell us a bedtime story every night.
7 Tom *used to / would* be crazy about hip hop when he was younger.
8 I *have to / must* go to the hairdresser's – I look terrible.

5 **Complete the text with the correct forms of the verbs in brackets.**

Last week I was alone at home. I
[1]_____ (do) my English homework so I was really concentrating. Everything was very quiet. I [2]_____ (switch) off the telly and the radio before I started. I [3]_____ (write) an essay about ghosts when suddenly I [4]_____ (hear) a loud noise from the kitchen. I [5]_____ (go) to check – the window was open! I thought someone [6]_____ (lock) the windows when I sat down to do my homework. I [7]_____ (feel) scared. We [8]_____ (live) on the ground floor so anybody could get in through the window. I had just got up to investigate when my mobile [9]_____ (start) ringing. It was my parents. They were phoning me to say that they [10]_____ (forget) to close the windows before leaving for the cinema and wanted me to close everything because a storm [11]_____ (come)!

PRONUNCIATION

1 CD1.24 **Read the words. In each group circle the word that has a different vowel sound. Then listen and check.**

1 law / low / court / report
2 lot / cope / tolerant / from
3 blow / knock / know / host
4 order / property / soft / gossip
5 opponent / phone / storm / open
6 got / floor / rob / hot

READING SKILLS

1 Read the article. Are the statements true (T) or false (F)?

1 Boys have always scored better in exams than girls.   F
2 Boys don't do well at school because of what happens in class.   F
3 Some boys are not sure of themselves because of their family situations.   T
4 Boys prefer to work on large projects.   F
5 Boys pay too much attention to girls to learn well at school.   T
6 In all the countries in the study girls were better at reading than boys.   T
7 A lot of British girls read more than two hours a day.   F

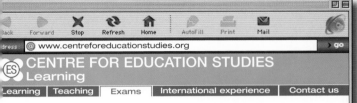

www.centreforeducationstudies.org

CENTRE FOR EDUCATION STUDIES
Learning

Learning | Teaching | Exams | International experience | Contact us

CLOSING THE GENDER GAP IN OUR SCHOOLS

Education is an issue which concerns many people in the UK as well as round the world. In England, Wales and Northern Ireland pupils sit GCSE (General Certificate in Secondary Education) exams followed two years later by A (Advanced) levels. Pupils in Scotland follow a different system, finishing their time at school with the Higher Leaving Certificate. One particular worry – why are boys doing so badly? Vote and tell us what you think.

Some twenty years ago, the performance of girls and boys in class was compared. Boys scored better in exams, so various measures were introduced to improve the performance of girls, including having single sex girl-only classes. Now, the situation is reversed, with girls consistently out-performing boys.

So, what has gone wrong with boys, and what can be done about it? John Dunsford, leader of the association of head teachers of secondary schools in Britain, says that that the academic failure of boys is a problem which has its roots in society rather than the classroom. Girls, more than boys, see education as a passport to a good job. On the other hand, according to Penny Lewis, a head teacher, young men lack confidence, which they hide with a show of bravado. They're uncertain about their place in society. This could be due to the fact that some boys grow up in families where there is no male role model to follow.

Moreover, boys may learn in a different way to girls, preferring small amounts of work with immediate deadlines rather than large projects stretching into the distance. And education is not seen as 'cool'. As one secondary school teacher said, 'Girls achieve more at school because the are watching the future while the boys are watching the girls.'

This is not just a problem in Britain. In a study by the Organisation for Economic Cooperation and Development and UNESCO, girls out-performed boys at reading at the age of 15 in all 45 countries, where the study was made. The UK ranks ninth out of the 45 countries for reading despite the fact that pupils in the UK spend less time reading than in most other countries. Only 3.5% of girls in the UK survey said they read for two hours a day or more and only 2.5% of boys said the same.

Now have your say:
Are single-sex classes best?

SPEAKING SKILLS

1 Describe the photo and answer the questions.

1 Are the girls doing something unusual, do you think? Why?/Why not?
2 Do you think that all games and sports are suitable for both young girls and boys? Why?/Why not?

2 Roleplay this conversation.

Student A
You are on a language camp in Ireland. Your school is organising a disco. You would like to go to it and stay until the end.
• Ask the family you are living with if you can go to the disco and return at midnight.
• Convince the family that you will return with a friend from the school and that someone will definitely walk home with you.
• Promise that you definitely won't be late.

Student B
You live in Ireland and rent rooms to students who are spending time on language courses. One of the students staying in your care is planning to go to a disco.
• Say that you agree that they can go to the disco but you don't agree with the time he/she is planning to return home. Explain why you don't agree with such a late return.
• Agree with the suggested solution.
• Ask for the name of the friend who will walk home him/her.

The world ahead

Read, listen and talk about the future, natural disasters.
Practise future forms.
Focus on reading effectively, giving presentations.
Write a leaflet.

GRAMMAR AND LISTENING

1 Work in pairs. Look at the photo and read the extracts from the film script. Then answer the questions.

 1 What kind of film is the photo from?
 2 Have you ever seen any films like this one? If so, tell your partner what you liked/didn't like about it.

2 **CD1.25** Read sentences 1–5. Then listen to the film script. Tick true and cross false.

 1 The President is the first person to see the meteor. ☐
 2 There isn't much time to prepare for the impact. ☐
 3 The meteor will kill millions of people immediately. ☐
 4 The consequences of the meteor will not last a long time. ☐
 5 The plan is to destroy the meteor with a nuclear bomb. ☐

SCENE 2   INTERIOR/DAY – The White House

Scientist 1:   Look at that meteor, Mr President …
        It's going to hit the Earth!
President: How long have we got?
Scientist 1:   Just 72 hours!
President: Where is it going to hit?
Scientist 1:   New York City!
President: Oh my God! There will be millions of
        deaths … How bad will it be?

SCENE 4   INTERIOR/DAY – The White House

President: Will anyone survive?
Scientist 2:   Some will, but not many.
President: Is there nothing we can do?
Scientist 2:   I have a plan … We place a nuclear
        bomb on the meteor and …
President: Will it work?
Scientist 2:   I'm not sure, but it might work!
President: But who's going to do it? It's suicide!
NASA pilot: I'll do it!

SCENE 5   INTERIOR/DAY – Cape Canaveral

NASA pilot: It probably won't work, baby, but
        I've got to try.
Girlfriend: I'll miss you, Troy! Be careful!

Work it out

3 Look at the script in Exercise 1 again. Who says these sentences?

1 It's going to hit the Earth! _____
2 There will be millions of deaths. _____
3 It might work! _____
4 It probably won't work. _____

4 Match sentences 1–4 in Exercise 3 with functions a–c.

A prediction based on something someone:

a can see now. ☐
b is not so sure about. ☐ ☐
c is sure about. ☐

Check it out

Future – predictions

We use *will*, *won't* and *might* to talk about predictions based on opinions: something that we believe or calculate.
There will be millions of deaths.

We use adverbs such as *certainly*, *definitely* and *probably* to say how sure our prediction is.
It probably won't work.

We use *might* when we're not sure about something.
It might work.

We use *going to* to talk about predictions based on evidence that we can see, hear or feel: something that is sure to happen.
Look at that meteor! It's going to hit the Earth.

Mind the trap!

In affirmative sentences we put adverbs between *will* and the main verb.

It will probably work. NOT It probably will work.

In negative sentences we put adverbs before *won't*.

It probably won't work. NOT It won't probably work.

5 Work in pairs. Decide if predictions 1–6 are based on opinions (O) or evidence (E). Then complete them with the forms in the box.

am going to   are going to   is going to
might   probably won't   will definitely

1 I think computers _____ become more intelligent than humans. I'm sure of it. ☐
2 Oh my God! He _____ die! – No, he isn't. He's the hero! ☐
3 Nobody really knows but one day people _____ colonise another planet. ☐
4 Maybe that will happen, but I _____ live to see it. ☐
5 I feel awful. I _____ be sick! ☐
6 Listen to those engines! They _____ explode! ☐

6 **CD1.26** Order the words in the predictions below. Then listen and check.

1 a/crater/definitely/huge/It/make/will
2 A/cloud/dust/into/of/rise/sky/the/will
3 able/be/see/sun/the/to/We/won't
4 and/be/cold/dark/for/It/many/will/years
5 be/food/much/probably/There/won't

7 Work in pairs. Look at the scenes from the film and predict what is going to happen. Use the verbs below.

fight   land   give

8 Work in pairs. Make predictions about the things below. Use the time expressions in the box and the examples to help you.

very soon   in the next twenty years   never
fifty years from now   in my lifetime
by the end of the century   in 1,000 years

- discover intelligent life on another planet
- aliens come to Earth
- people live to be more than 150 years old
- robots take over the planet
- a nuclear war
- a world parliament
- humans become extinct
- humans live on the Moon
- solar power replaces petrol

A Do you think we will discover intelligent life on another planet some day?
B Yes, I think we will discover intelligent life somewhere else in the universe in my lifetime.

'This is the way the world ends.
Not with a bang but a whimper.'

(T.S. Eliot)

Some say the human race will go out with a bang; others predict a long slow death; while the optimists think we will live for ever. What are the dangers we face and how probable is it that they will occur in the next seventy years?

1 During this century the quantity of greenhouse gases will probably double and the average global temperature will rise by at least 2°C. That's a bigger increase than any in the last 1.5 million years. This could completely alter the climate in many regions and lead to disasters such as world food shortages, mass migration, wars for water and other resources. **Probability: High**

2 In the last century we have had four major flu epidemics as well as HIV and SARS. There will certainly be another one in the near future. A virus probably won't wipe out the whole human race. However, in 1918 influenza killed twenty million. A similar epidemic could be even worse today. **Probability: Very high**

3 It hasn't happened yet, but one day it is almost certain that a terrorist group will get the necessary materials and technology to use weapons of mass destruction. A nuclear, chemical or biological terrorist attack will almost certainly happen in the next thirty years. **Probability: Very high**

READING

1 Match dangers a–f with pictures 1–6. Use a dictionary to help you.

a Meteorite impact ☐ **d** Super volcanoes ☐
b Robots taking over ☐ **e** Climate change ☐
c Terrorist attack ☐ **f** Viral pandemic ☐

2 Study Train Your Brain. Check you understand the meaning of the words in bold. Use a dictionary if you need to.

TRAIN YOUR BRAIN | Reading skills

Reading effectively

You need to use different strategies depending on what you are looking for in a text:

Strategy	What do you do?
Skimming to understand the general idea of a text.	Look at the title, the photos, the introduction and the final paragraph.
Finding the **main idea** of a paragraph.	Read the first sentence which often summarises the main point. Look for the key words.
Scanning to find **specific** information.	Underline the key words in the questions, find synonyms and similar expressions in the text, and read carefully around the key words.

3 Quickly look at Exercises 4–6 and decide which strategies from Train Your Brain you should use to do them.

4 [CD ROM] Read the text and tick the best summary.

1 A study of the worst disasters that have ever affected people on Earth. ☐
2 A description of the threats facing humanity and how probable they are. ☐
3 An essay about how humanity will change in the future. ☐

5 Match paragraphs 1–6 in the text with dangers a–f in Exercise 1.

6 Read the introduction and paragraphs 1–3 and answer the questions.

1 By how much will the Earth's temperature have increased by 2100 AD?
2 How many consequences of climate change can you find? What are they?
3 How many people died in 1918 as a result of an epidemic?
4 What kind of terrorist attacks will probably happen one day?

4 ☐ Over a long period, the risk of dying as a result of a meteor hitting the Earth is about the same as the risk of dying in a plane crash. A huge meteor hits the Earth about once every million years. It will happen again, and when it happens, an enormous cloud of dust will rise into the atmosphere. This will block out sunlight and kill plants. However, the most adaptable species (cockroaches and humans, for example) will probably survive.   **Probability: Medium**

5 ☐ By 2050 robots will probably be able to think like humans. They will look after us at home like mechanical servants. But they will also carry out more complex tasks. For example, they will be able to work as doctors or teachers. Some people think that the fantasies of science-fiction films will come true. Humans won't become extinct, but we will join together with advanced robots and make a new species that will live for ever.   **Probability: High**

6 ☐ Approximately every 50,000 years a super-volcano erupts. The consequences are terrible and can last for years. It covers the land with ash, and a huge cloud of sulphuric acid circles the Earth. Daytime is like a moonlit night. Ice forms in the tropics. A super-volcano is twelve times more likely than a large meteorite impact.   **Probability: Very high**

So, there you are. The future is full of dangers and the world will end one day. However, I really don't feel too worried. It may be irrational, but I actually feel optimistic. I think it's going to be very hard to kill off the human race. And I'm quite looking forward to having my robot servant.

7 Read paragraphs 4–6 and the final paragraph. Use the appropriate strategy from Train Your Brain to answer the questions.

1 Which happens more often?
  a a very large meteor hits the Earth, or
  b a super-volcano erupts?
2 What will happen after both a meteorite impact and a super-volcano eruption?
3 Which species will probably not die out completely after a large meteorite impact?
4 When will robots' minds be similar to ours?
5 Why does the writer feel optimistic about the future of humanity?

8 Find these verbs in the text and match them with words 1–7. You can use some of them with more than one noun.

alter   become   double   face
lead to   rise   wipe out

1 _____ a danger
2 _____ extinct
3 quantities _____
4 temperatures ~~rise~~ _____
5 ~~rise~~ _____ the climate
6 _____ disaster
7 _____ a species

9 Work in groups. Use the language from Exercise 8 and the prompts below to discuss this statement.

I feel optimistic about the future. There is, of course, the risk that humanity will disappear in some disaster, but I believe that we will evolve into a more intelligent species.

• Say what you think the future will be like.
• Mention the dangers in the text. Say how probable you think they are.

A I believe the biggest danger we face is climate change.
B I don't agree. The climate will definitely change, but we will probably survive.
C I think people will be happier in the future.
D I agree. In my opinion, the world will be a fairer place than it is today.

THE END IS NEAR MERCHANDISE STORE

GRAMMAR AND LISTENING

1 Work in pairs. Look at the picture and answer the questions.

   1 What are these people celebrating? How do you know?
   2 What do you like/dislike about parties?

2 **CD1.27** Complete gaps a–d with sentences 1–4. Then listen and check.

   1 My flight leaves at 10a.m.
   2 I'm going to go on a diet!
   3 I'm meeting my mother for lunch.
   4 I'll have some more cheesecake, please.

Work it out

3 Match sentences 1–4 in Exercise 2 with descriptions a–d, below. Then complete the table below with the words in bold.

   a She's just made a **decision**. ☐
   b He's made an **arrangement**. ☐
   c It's written on a **timetable**. ☐
   d She's got a **plan/intention**. ☐

Present Continuous	arrangement
going to + infinitive	_____
Present Simple	_____
will	_____

Check it out

Future plans, arrangements, timetables, decisions
We use *going to* to talk about plans, intentions and ambitions. I'm going to go on a diet. I'm going to work for NASA when I'm older.
We use the Present Continuous to talk about arrangements such as appointments, meetings or events. These tend to be in the near future, often with a definite time or place, and suggest that the future is as certain as the present. I'm meeting my mother for lunch.
We use the Present Simple to talk about information on a timetable (because it happens habitually). The flight leaves at 10a.m.
We use *will* when we make a spontaneous decision. I'll have the cheesecake, please.

4 Work in groups. Make decisions with *will* for these situations.

   1 You're buying a new jacket. – get the *blue/black one* …
   2 You're at the restaurant. – have the *pizza/meat* …
   3 You're feeling stressed out. – *have a bath/go to bed* …
   4 The party's almost finished. – *go home/go clubbing* …
   5 It's late on Sunday and you haven't done your homework yet. – *do it now/forget about it* …

I think I'll get the blue one. Which one will you get?

5 Work in pairs. Write your plans and intentions for the prompts below. Then take three guesses to find out what your partner is going to do.

- after this class
- this weekend
- the next time you're alone at home
- next summer
- on your next birthday
- on your last day of school
- the next time you go shopping

A *Are you going to go for a run in the park after the class?*
B *No, I'm not going to go for a run in the park.*
A *Are you going to go shopping?*

6 Work in groups. Study the train timetable for one minute. Then take turns to cover it up and to test your memory.

ONERAIL

TRAIN TIMETABLE

Depart: Edinburgh

| 12:00 | 12:30 | 13:05 | 14:00 | 14:45 | 16:00 |

Arrive: London

| 16:58 | 17:31 | 18:05 | 18:47 | 19:53 | 20:53 |

A *Your train leaves Edinburgh at 12 o'clock tomorrow. What time do you get in to London?*
B *I get in at just before five o'clock.*

7 `CD1.28` Circle the correct answers. Then listen and check.

1 Kelly Have you published any books?
Sean No, but I'm writing a novel and *I'm going to / I'll* send it to a publisher.

2 Tony The phone's ringing!
Monica *I'm going to / I'll* get it!

3 Lee Brilliant! Wow, you're really good! When's your next gig?
Kirsty *We're playing / We'll play* at the Zenith next Friday at nine.

4 Amy Have you made any resolutions for the New Year?
Jimmy Yeah, *I'm going to / I* give up smoking.

5 Sarah Do you mind if I go with you? The first bus *isn't going to / doesn't* leave until 10a.m.

8 `CD1.29` Complete the conversation with the correct forms of the verbs in brackets. Then listen and check.

Brenda I [1]_____ (go) to Madrid on Friday. I got a ticket on the Internet.
Amy What [2]_____ (you/do) in Madrid?
Brenda Remember that Spanish guy at Monica's New Year Party? Well, I [3]_____ (visit) him.
Amy Really? What time [4]_____ (your flight/leave)?
Brenda In the morning some time … Let's see … Yeah, it [5]_____ (leave) at 11.30.
Amy Here, just a minute – where's my diary? … Um … Listen, [6]_____ (not/do) anything on Friday morning. I [7]_____ (drive) you to the airport if you like.
Brenda Cool! Thanks. I [8]_____ (bring) you back something nice from Spain.
Amy Thanks … What [9]_____ (you/wear) for the trip on Friday?
Brenda I don't know … Oh! I know! I [10]_____ (wear) my denim skirt and my pink top.

9 `CD1.30` Look at Monica's diary and describe the arrangements for the party. Then listen and check.

Monday 5

Sort out music - Kirsty
Get drinks - Nick and Amy
Pick up pizzas - Juanma and Sandra
Get DVDs - me   Party - 9p.m.

Kirsty is sorting out the music.

10 Work in groups. Use the checklist to organise a party. Decide who is doing what.

When?	Drink?	Games?
Where?	Music?	Transport?
Food?	Films?	

A *Let's have a party next Saturday!*
B *Great idea. I'll sort out the music.*
C *And I'll … . Who will … ?*

11 Find a partner from another group and tell him/her about your party. Mention the arrangements you have made and your intentions.

We're having a party next Saturday at 10. Gaby is sorting out the music. I'm going to wear my new blue top.

12 Work in groups and follow the instructions.

- Write a different New Year resolution on four identical pieces of paper.
- Put all the resolutions face down on the desk.
- Take turns to read out the resolution and to guess who wrote them.

A *I'm going to stop annoying my little brother.*
B *Is it Anna?*
C *No, it's not me … Is it you Arthur?*

SPEAKING AND LISTENING

1   Work in pairs. Look at the picture and answer the questions.

    1 What are the students doing?
    2 What is the subject of the presentation?
    3 Have you ever made a presentation?

2   Work in pairs. Look at the presentation plan below. Decide which aspects of life from the ideas wheel would be relevant/appropriate to discuss the topic.

3   CD1.31 Listen to Simon and Meg discussing the presentation. Which aspects of life is Simon going to talk about?

IDEAS WHEEL

religion · technology · leisure · personal life · politics · sport · history · society · work · the environment · transport · morality · art · education · health

---

Presentation plan

'How will technology change our lives in the next 20 years?'

Introduction
Say what you think the question means
Explain your plan for the presentation

Aspects of life
_____
_____
_____

Conclusion
Summarise the arguments
Give your opinion

Homework

Prepare a 3-minute presentation on this question:

How will technology change our lives in the next 20 years?

4 **CD1.32** Listen to Simon's presentation and tick the advice that Meg and Rhona give him.

During the presentation

1 Don't read your presentation. Use notes. ☐
2 Don't speak too fast. ☐
3 Try to sound interested. ☐
4 Pause to give your listeners time to think. ☐
5 Look at your listeners to check they understand you. ☐
6 If you make a mistake, start your sentence again. ☐
7 If you can't remember a word, use another one. ☐
8 Don't get into personal details. ☐
9 Observe the time limit. ☐

5 **CD1.33** Listen to the extracts from Simon's presentation and complete the Speak Out box with the expressions he uses.

SPEAK OUT | Giving presentations

- Begin your presentation with:
  I'd like to begin by …ing/[1] I'm ____ ____ ____ about/ I've chosen this topic because …

- Introduce new points with:
  Firstly/ Secondly/ Moving on to/[2] ____ to

- Give yourself time to think with fillers:
  Well/ Right/ So/ Where was I?/[3] ____ ____ [4] ____ I ____ is/ The thing is/ You see

- Summarise your points at the end:
  Finally/[5] To ____ ____ / Last but not least

6 Prepare a presentation on the topic below. Use the presentation plan and the ideas wheel to help you.

How will global warming change the way we live in the future?

7 In the next class, give your presentation. Follow the advice in Exercise 4 and use the language in Speak Out.

VOCABULARY

1 Complete the leaflet with the correct form of the words in capitals.

ACTION ecology

The real weapons of mass [1] ___ (DESTROY) What is the biggest danger facing [2] ___ (HUMAN)? Is it a [3] ___ (TERROR) attack or is it a flu epidemic? Could it be a [4] ___ (NATURE) disaster? A meteor or a volcanic [5] ___ (ERUPT)? Well, actually there is something much more [6] ___ (DANGER).

The way we live!
Our [7] ___ (WASTE) lifestyles produce vast amounts of greenhouse gases. And this is causing climate change. If we don't change the way we live, cities will disappear under the sea. There will be food [8] ___ (SHORT) and mass [9] ___ (MIGRATE) from the south to the north.

So if you want to save the planet, take action now!

Find out more about Action Ecology at www.actieco.com

2 Check the meaning of disasters a–g and of the underlined words below. Use a dictionary to help you. Then match disasters a–g with quotes 1–7.

a drought   e hurricane
b earthquake f tsunami
c flood   g volcanic eruption
d forest fire

1 'It was 6.3 on the Richter scale.' ☐
2 'The city is covered in ash and mud. There is a stream of molten lava.' ☐
3 'Tanya is heading for Florida with winds of up to 170 miles per hour.' ☐
4 'The Thames has broken its banks.' ☐
5 'After years without rain there is no food or water.' ☐
6 'The high winds are making it very difficult for the emergency services to put it out.' ☐
7 'A massive undersea earthquake caused a ten-metre-high wave.' ☐

3 Work in groups. Imagine you want to raise money to help people after a natural disaster. Use the ideas on page 140 to help you.

A I think organising a concert is a good idea because everybody likes music. We could raise a lot of money from ticket sales.
B I disagree. A photo exhibition is a better idea …

49

Amazing animals

Read, listen and talk about the animal world.
Practise Zero, First and Second Conditionals; phrases used instead of *if*.
Focus on talking about probability; taking notes when listening.
Write an opinion essay; clauses of addition and contrast.

Lifestyle

Those crazy humans!

What would our pets say about us if they knew how to talk? *Lifestyle* asked two pet-owners to imagine how their pets might describe living with them.

Wally, a six-year-old golden retriever, describes life with Lucy, an architect.

I absolutely adore Lucy – my human. There's nobody like her. As soon as she goes out, I start missing her terribly. A few minutes can seem like weeks. I'm always pleased to see her again.

I've trained my human well. She even does little tricks for me – when I look at the front door and whine she immediately jumps up and starts putting on her shoes. It works every time! I've even taught her to share some of her food with me. I hope that if I keep training her, she'll eventually give me all of it!

Often when we're out she does silly things like throw sticks. I think she expects me to bring them back. If she knew how pointless it is, perhaps she'd stop doing it. But as long as it makes her happy, I'll do it – it's a very small sacrifice, isn't it?

Humans are loveable creatures – so easy to please and easy to train!

Kika, a nine-year-old tabby cat, describes life with Gavin, a graphic designer.

I don't know when my human started living in my home. He's been here for a very long time. Luckily mine goes out quite often. I've no idea what he does but it can't be for pleasure. Maybe he goes hunting but if he does, he's not very good at it – he's always hungry and irritable when he gets back. If I were him, I'd practise at home first – he could start by hunting flies and spiders and then try the bigger things later.

Humans are lazy animals. If Gavin's at home, he spends about eighty percent of his time asleep or resting. They're not very clean, either. Mine only washes twice a day … unless he's in love.

There's a theory that humans are solitary creatures but I'm not sure. For several months mine smelled of another human! But eventually it stopped. Then he started going out less in the evenings and spent hours staring hypnotised at that noisy glass box. So my conclusion is that humans do have partners but just for short periods each year.

I'm afraid that Gavin is going to be here for ever. But provided he fills up the big white thing in the kitchen with food, I'll let him stay.

GRAMMAR AND READING

1 Work in pairs and follow the instructions.

- Check you understand the meanings of the words below. Use a dictionary to help you.
- Do you prefer dogs or cats? Why? Tell your partner using the words below.

> (be) good company   intriguing   arrogant
> cruel   lazy   obedient   independent
> playful   loyal

> *I prefer cats – I think they're very independent, they always do what they want.*

2 Read the text. Which pet seems to like its owner more?

Work it out

3 Match sentences 1–3 with situations a–c.

1 **If** she **knew** how pointless it is, perhaps she**'d** stop doing it. [b]
2 If Gavin**'s** at home, he **spends** eighty percent of his time asleep. [c]
3 **If** I **keep** training her, she**'ll** eventually give me all of it. [a]

a a situation that has a realistic chance of happening in the future
b a situation which is very unlikely to or cannot happen now or in the future
c a situation that is always true; a fact

4 Match sentences 1–3 in Exercise 3 with the type of conditional. Which tenses do we use to form them?

Zero Conditional [2]
First Conditional [3]
Second Conditional [1]

Zero   *if* +___ , Present Simple
First   *if* + Present Simple, ___ + infinitive
Second *if* + ___ , *would* + infinitive

5 Look at the sentences and the definitions. How would you say the <u>underlined</u> words in your language?

1 <u>As long as</u> (on condition that) it makes her happy, I'll do it.
2 <u>As soon as</u> (immediately after) she goes out, I start missing her terribly.
3 He only washes twice a day <u>unless</u> (if … not) he's in love.
4 <u>Provided that</u> (on condition that) he feeds me, I'll let him stay here.
5 <u>When</u> (every time) I whine, she immediately jumps up.

Check it out

Conditionals
We use Zero Conditional to talk about facts or situations that are always true. If he is here, he spends eighty percent of his time asleep.
We use First Conditional to talk about situations that have a chance of happening in the future. If I keep training her, she will eventually give me all of it.
We use Second Conditional to talk about situations which are impossible now or in the future. What would our pets say about us if they knew how to talk?
Alternatives to *if* in conditional sentences: *when/ unless/ as soon as/ as long as/ provided that*

Mind the trap!

We often use *were* – not *was* – after *I*, *he*, *she* and *it*, especially in written English.

If I were you, I'd take your dog to the vet's.

6 Complete the sentences with the correct form of the verbs in brackets. What types of conditionals are they?

1 Fleas can jump up to thirty centimetres. If humans __would be__ (be) as good at jumping, as fleas they'd be able to jump 300 metres!
2 A cat can live for about fifteen years, provided that you __look__ (look) after it properly.
3 Reindeer get a special chemical from the food they eat – if they __didn't have__ (not/have) this chemical, their blood would freeze.
4 Some worms will eat themselves, if they __didn't find__ (not find) enough food.
5 When bats __leave__ (leave) caves they always turn left.
6 If you put a small amount of alcohol on a scorpion, it __will sting__ (sting) itself to death.

7 Complete the sentences. Then compare your answers with your partner.

1 As soon as I wake up in the morning, I … .
2 If there's nothing good on TV, I usually … .
3 I enjoy English lessons as long as we … .
4 I'll pass all my exams as long as … .
5 I never … unless … .
6 If I could change one thing in my life, I … .
7 If I had more …, I … .
8 If I were an animal, I … .
9 Provided that … this weekend, I … .

8 Work in pairs. Which animals make the best pets? Why?

As intelligent as ... ?

It looks like an alien, can copy other animals and can change colour, shape and size in a second. Alec Peters investigates a mysterious creature that might be too intelligent for humans to understand.

Ask a biologist what the most intelligent creatures are on Earth, and they'll probably come up with a fairly similar list: larger mammals such as horses, dogs, dolphins, pigs, the great apes as well as some birds like crows and ravens. But now some scientists believe that one of the most intelligent <u>beings</u> on Earth is in fact the octopus – which doesn't belong to any of these groups.

Every schoolchild knows that octopuses (or octopi) have eight legs and can shoot ink while trying to escape from enemies. But there are many other unusual things about octopuses. For example, the legs of some octopuses can grow to over nine metres in length and are extremely strong. If an octopus loses a leg, it can grow a new one. It also has three hearts and complex eyes, which seem to belong to a mammal rather than a sea creature. Octopuses also seem to be experts at escaping – they have extremely soft, flexible bodies and can escape through holes not much bigger than their eyes. There are many biologists who have stories about walking into the laboratory after lunch to find their octopus had escaped from its aquarium and was now hiding in a teapot or climbing a bookshelf!

However, even until quite recently, little was known about octopus intelligence. There are several reasons for this. Firstly, octopuses usually live at the bottom of river mouths and seas – areas which are not attractive to <u>researchers</u>. Secondly, they are not social animals so it can be difficult to <u>study</u> their interaction with others. Perhaps most importantly, octopus intelligence is not easy for humans to understand. When we observe mammals such as rats or dogs we can often instinctively understand their behaviour. Octopuses, however, can seem like aliens. Scientists need to have a lot of imagination to be able to understand what an octopus is thinking!

In the 1950s, the US Air Force sponsored scientists to study the way octopuses use their brains. They hoped that they could use this knowledge to help them build better computers. However, their brains were so <u>complex</u> that the scientists quickly gave up. And even today the octopus brain is a mystery. Octopuses have a very complex nervous system and recent research suggests that they have some of their intelligence inside each arm, which means that each arm can 'think' for itself. It also appears that they have good memories, perhaps similar to a cat's. Some octopuses in laboratories seem to play with objects as if they were toys – a sure sign of intelligence. Others could pick up complicated skills like opening jars.

Perhaps the most striking thing about octopuses is their ability to change their colour and body <u>pattern</u>. They do this to camouflage themselves and also to communicate with others. They can completely change their appearance in less than a second – a striped octopus can suddenly become spotted. It can change its skin to look like rocks, sand or plankton. A scientist once observed an octopus that changed its appearance nearly 1,000 times during seven hours of feeding! It can change its appearance to look like a dangerous predator – and can even copy its style of swimming.

Some scientists have even suggested that these different patterns and colours are in fact a very sophisticated language – and that each design is a different verb, adjective or noun. But nobody has been able to work out what they might be saying. It seems like the problem isn't the limitation of the animals ... but the limitations of humans!

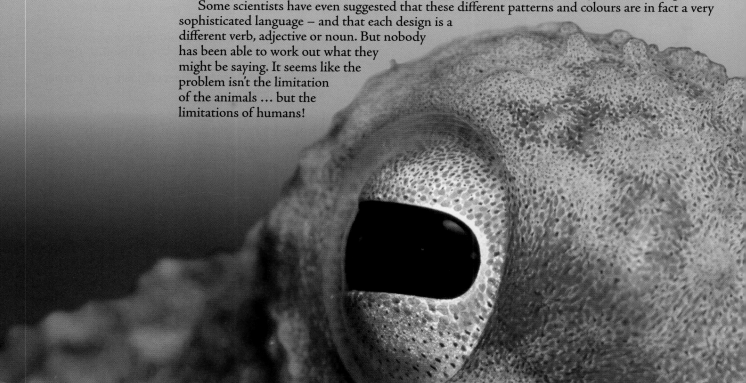

READING AND VOCABULARY

1 Work in pairs and complete the similes. Use a dictionary to help you. Then answer the questions below.

> brave   gentle   proud   quiet   blind   wise

as _____ as an owl   as _____ as a mouse
as _____ as a peacock   as _____ as a lamb
as _____ as a lion   as _____ as a bat

- Do you have similar similes in your language?
- Which animals are, in your opinion, the wisest/most intelligent?

2 Look at the photo and read the title and introduction of the article. What creature do you think the article is about?

3 [CD ROM] Quickly read the text and check your predictions from Exercise 2. What information did you find most interesting?

4 Read the text again and circle the correct answers.

1 Now some scientists believe that
a all octopuses are more intelligent than larger mammals.
b we can add the octopus to the list of most intelligent animals.
c the octopus isn't in fact a mammal.
d we should find a new group for octopuses.

2 An octopus's eye is
a something that even schoolchildren know about.
b rather unusual for a mammal.
c rather unusual for a creature that lives in the sea.
d not very complicated.

3 Octopuses are good at escaping because
a they can change the shape of their body.
b they choose surprising places to hide in.
c they have very small eyes.
d the scientists who study them often go out.

4 One of the reasons that we didn't know how intelligent octopuses are until recently was that
a they live in places where researchers don't like going.
b they don't like being observed.
c they don't like socialising with humans.
d they are so different from other animals we know.

5 One thing that suggests that octopuses are intelligent is that
a they were smarter than US Air Force computers.
b their brains are similar to cats'.
c they learn how to do complicated tasks.
d the octopus brain is a mystery.

6 One of the reasons octopuses often change their appearance is because
a they want to become less noticeable.
b they get bored when they are eating for a long time.
c they are very talkative.
d they enjoy copying other animals.

5 Find the <u>underlined</u> words in the text which have similar meanings to words a–e.

a design
b creatures
c sophisticated
d observe
e scientists

6 Think Back! Write as many words in each category as you can in three minutes.

Insects	Birds
beetle, bee, …	stork, eagle, …
Fish	**Mammals**
salmon, eel, …	zebra, rat, …

7 For each category below, give examples from Exercise 6.

Which animals/creatures are
- often hunted?
- in danger of extinction?
- often thought of as pests?
- often kept as pets?
- kept for milk, meat or fur?

8 Work in pairs. Tick the sentences you think are true. Then check your answers on page 140.

Animal Quiz

1 Elephants are the only animals that can't jump. ☐
2 A rat can survive for longer without water than a camel. ☐
3 Crocodiles can't stick out their tongues. ☐
4 A duck's quack has no echo – nobody knows why. ☐
5 Butterflies taste with their feet. ☐
6 An ostrich's eye is bigger than its brain. ☐

53

LISTENING

1 In pairs, read the notes. Which information do you find the most surprising?

AFRICAN ELEPHANTS

Numbers falling
1970s – 1.3 m
now – < 85 K

Statistics
• largest land animal
• height c. 4 m
• weight = 80 men
• runs at c. 40 km/hr = Olympic sprinter!
• excellent swimmer
• lifts > 250 kg with trunk
• skin 5 cm thick in places
• drinks 200 L water/day
• eats 100 kg leaves

2 CD1.34 What do you think these symbols and abbreviations in the notes about African elephants mean? Why do we use them? Then listen and check.

1 K   4 <
2 c.   5 >
3 =   6 m (two meanings)

3 In pairs, look at the notes in Exercise 1 again and answer the questions. Then study Train Your Brain and check your answers.

• Did the person who made the notes try to write down everything the speaker said? Did he/she write in full sentences?
• What sort of information did he/she make notes on: facts, memorable things, opinions?

TRAIN YOUR BRAIN | Listening skills

Taking notes – Symbols and abbreviations

a Don't try to write down everything you hear or write in full sentences!
b Concentrate on facts or the most interesting/memorable things you hear.
c Where possible, use symbols and abbreviations of common words/phrases to save yourself time.

---

4 Work in pairs and match the common abbreviations with their meaning.

1 i.e.   a very
2 e.g.   b in other words; which means
3 yr(s)   c usually
4 etc.   d etcetera/and so on
5 v.   e year(s)
6 usu.   f for example

5 CD1.35 Read the notes. Then listen and complete the information for gaps 1–5.

LIFESTYLE

• females and young live in herds – in other words [1] _family_ groups
• sometimes up to 20 elephants but usually [2] _6–10_ in herd
• sometimes elephants live together all lives – more than [3] _65_ years
• male elephants usually [4] _leave_ herd when teenagers
• form gangs and behave badly – for example they [5] _get_ very drunk on rotten fruit! (something)

6 Look at the notes in Exercise 5. Shorten any of the information you can. Use Exercises 2 and 4 to help you.

7 CD1.36 Read the notes. Listen to the last part of the lecture and fill in the missing information. Use abbreviations where possible.

RECENT RESEARCH

• communicate with subsonic noises – [1] _____ for human ear
• noises travel [2] _____
• different herds communicate with each other every evening, [3] _____
• few enemies
• stamp feet, [4] _____ to frighten predators
• generally [5] _____ animals – emotional maturity = [6] _____ old human

SPEAKING AND LISTENING

1 **CD1.37** Look at the photo. What do you think the situation is? Then listen and check.

2 **CD1.37** Study Speak Out. Then read and listen again. Put the underlined phrases in the correct places in the box.

SPEAK OUT I Expressing probability	
100% certain	will definitely/certainly ¹ _certain_
70%	will probably it is likely that he/she/it will ² _chances_
50%	may / ³ _might_ it is possible that he/she/it will perhaps
30%	probably won't ⁴ _unlikely_
0%	definitely/certainly won't

Presenter So, is Trixi going to win?
Deborah Oh yes, I think <u>it is certain that Trixi will</u> win this year. I mean look at her – beautiful fur, bright eyes, her gorgeous red ribbon.

Presenter And what are Rambo's chances of winning do you think?
Bill To be honest, <u>I think it is unlikely that he'll</u> win – there's too much competition. But I'm just here for fun really.

Presenter How are you feeling now, Bill?
Bill Well the judge seemed very, very impressed. I wasn't confident before but actually … now I think <u>the chances are that he'll win it!</u>
Presenter Well let's wait and see. And what about Trixi? Deborah, are you still confident?
Deborah Well everything started going well and then that nasty little dog next to us gave my poor Trixi a fright and she bit the judge. But she still <u>might</u> win, I mean she's won here twice already.

3 **Rewrite the sentences so that the meaning stays the same, using the words in brackets. Use Speak Out to help you.**

1 The chances are that the number of foxes in urban areas will increase.
The number of foxes _____ increase. (probably)

2 It is certain that the law will have a positive effect on the birds' situation.
The new law _____ a positive effect on the birds' situation. (definitely)

3 It is unlikely that penguins will become extinct.
Penguins _____ extinct. (probably)

4 It's possible that the new law will be a success.
The new law _____ a success. (might)

4 **Say how probable these things are. Use Speak Out to help you.**

1 There will be an English test next week.

The chances are that there will be an English test next week.

2 You will catch a bad cold next winter.
3 You will fall madly in love this year.
4 You will finish this book before the holidays.
5 You will go abroad next summer.
6 You will pass all your exams this year.
7 Your computer will catch a virus in the next six months.
8 Your favourite band/artist will give a concert in your town this year.
9 Your favourite sports club will win a major championship this season.

WRITING

1 Work in pairs. Look at the pictures and the newspaper headline and answer the questions.

- What problems connected with animals are presented here?
- What kind of animals are in danger of extinction?
- What is the best way to protect such animals?
- What are the advantages and disadvantages of keeping animals in zoos?
- Why are zoos popular places to visit?

2 Read the essay and answer the questions.

- Does the writer mention your arguments for/against zoos from Exercise 1?
- Is the writer generally for or against zoos?
- Do you find his/her essay convincing?

'Zoos Are Last Chance For Siberian Tiger'

English Essay

Zoos still have a useful function in the modern world. Do you agree?

1 Although the function of zoos has changed little during the last 250 years, zoos are very controversial today. Many people think they are cruel and have no place in the modern world. It is my own opinion that zoos, although not perfect, do have a useful function.

2 First of all, zoos are places of education. Zoos can help children to appreciate nature. Furthermore, research into animal behaviour is done in zoos and has increased our knowledge of zoology, genetics and even psychology. Above all, zoos can protect the future of many species of animal. Many species today are in danger of extinction and, thanks to breeding in zoos, many animals have a chance of survival. Indeed there are some animals which now only exist in zoos.

3 Opponents of zoos say that they are cruel. First of all, they argue, zoos cannot recreate the environment in which animals live and, because of this, animals are bored and depressed. Secondly, animals have frequent contact with human visitors which can be stressful. However, in my opinion, most zoos have improved recently. It is now quite rare to see animals in cages and most zoos try hard to recreate the environments in which different animals live.

4 In conclusion, although zoos are not a perfect environment for animals, I believe that they have more advantages than disadvantages. In an ideal world, zoos would not be necessary. But as long as man hunts animals for profit and destroys their environments, zoos are essential.

246 words

3 Think Back! Compare the Opinion essay opposite with the For/Against essay on page 38. Label the types of essay at the top of the table.

	a) _____ essay	b) _____ essay
Topic	Often includes 'Give arguments for and against …'	Often includes 'Do you agree?'
First Paragraph	Introduction	Introduction
Second Paragraph	Arguments for	Arguments that support your opinion
Third Paragraph	Arguments against	Arguments which are against your own opinion
Conclusion	A summary of the debate; your own opinion at the very end	A summary of the arguments, saying once again why you think you are right

4 Underline the sentences in the essay where the writer does these things.

- mentions his/her own opinion for the first time
- says why he/she disagrees with the arguments of his/her opponents

5 Look at these sentences from the essay. Which argument does the writer feel is most important? What words or phrases tell you this?

1 First of all, zoos are places of education.
2 Furthermore, research into animal behaviour is done in zoos.
3 Above all, zoos can protect the future of many species of animal.

6 Complete Train Your Brain with ideas a–d below, using your answers to Exercises 3–5 to help you.

a against   c most important argument
b debate   d opinion

TRAIN YOUR BRAIN | Writing skills

Opinion essay

Paragraph 1 – Introduction
- Make general points as in a For and against essay
- Mention your own [1]_____ at the end.

Paragraph 2
- Give your own opinion with two or three arguments/ examples.
- Give your [2]_____ last.

Paragraph 3
- Begin the paragraph with *Some people/Opponents say* … .
- Mention one or two arguments which are [3]_____ your own opinion.
- Then say why you disagree with them.

Paragraph 4 – Conclusion
Summarise the [4]_____ and say once again why you think you are right.

---

7 In pairs, look at the essay title and decide which arguments are against killing animals for fur. What is your own opinion?

It is wrong to kill animals for their fur. Do you agree?

1 It is cruel – animals which are kept for fur have short and unhappy lives.
2 Animal fur is warmer and more attractive than man-made materials.
3 It is unnecessary because we can now make man-made materials very cheaply.
4 Wearing fur is natural – Man has been wearing it for thousands of years.
5 It has no place in the civilised world in the twenty-first century.
6 Some animals that are hunted for fur are endangered species.

8 Now write your essay. Use Train Your Brain, your answers to Exercise 7 and the prompts below to help you.

Paragraph 2
My point of view
- *First of all*
- *Moreover/Furthermore …*
- *Above all …*

Paragraph 3
Arguments my opponents might use
- *Firstly*
- *Next/Secondly …*
Why I disagree with these arguments
- *However, in my opinion …*

'Frankly, I think killing animals for fur is barbaric.'

57

VOCABULARY AND GRAMMAR

1 Complete the sentences. Make new words from the words in capital letters.

1 I prefer cats to dogs because they
   are very _independent_   DEPEND ✓
2 I would like to become a scientific
   researcher and study the causes
   of floods.   RESEARCH ✓
3 Tom's dog isn't very _obedient_ –
   it never listens to him.   OBEY ✓
4 Some people keep rather _unusual_
   pets, like spiders or lizards. USUAL ✓
5 Some _endangered_ species are still
   hunted although it's illegal. DANGER ✓
6 Kittens are lovely and _playful_ –
   I can watch them for hours. PLAY ✓
7 Do you know which animals in your
   country are in danger of _extinction_? EXTINCT ✓
8 Keeping pets is _likely_ to help
   ill or depressed people get better. LIKE ✓

2 Complete the text with one word in each gap.

WHAT ARE WE DOING TO OUR PLANET?

You might not know this but, ¹_____ the
end of the century, scientists estimate that
over 10,000 species of animal, plant and
insect ²_____ be dead. You may think
that this is a long time in the future but, if I
³_____ you, I would start to worry now.
In the ⁴_____ five years, twenty animals
that are alive now will be extinct. You will
never see them, ⁵_____ something is
done quickly. This isn't a wild guess, this is
really ⁶_____ to happen.

**Don't wait until it's too late. We need
your help as ⁷_____ as possible.**

 **Telephone now to find out what
you can do: 0122 343 556**

3 Circle the odd word out in each group and explain why it doesn't fit.

1 zoology / psychology / biology / science-fiction
2 survive / kill off / become extinct / wipe out
3 scientist / optimist / zoologist / biologist
4 massive / epidemic / vast / limited
5 eel / bat / fly / owl
6 penguin / ostrich / skylark / bee
7 mosquito / cockroach / beetle / ape

4 Complete the sentences. Use *will*, *be going to*, the Present Simple or the Present Continuous.

1 When you _____ (arrive), we'll have
   dinner.
2 I promise I _____ (not tell) anyone about
   the surprise party.
3 A Would you like to go windsurfing with me?
     The weather is great.
   B Sorry. I _____ (meet) my sister at 12.
4 Who do you think _____ (win) the next
   World Cup: Germany or Brazil?
5 A I'm really hungry.
   B I _____ (make) some sandwiches.
6 A Congratulations on winning the lottery!
     What _____ (you do) with the money?
   B I want to see the world – my plane to Japan
     _____ (leave) at 8 tomorrow morning!

5 Use the words in brackets and rewrite the sentences so that they mean the same as the original sentences.

1 It is likely that the borders in Europe will
  disappear one day. (the chances)
  _____

2 We'll have a class test today if my History
  teacher doesn't forget. (unless)
  _____

3 I can only talk on the phone after I finish
  doing my homework. (as long as)
  _____

4 It is certain that Messi will be as famous as
  Pele one day. (certainly)
  _____

5 Letter writing might disappear because more
  and more people use email. (likely)
  _____

6 It is unlikely that hip hop will be more
  popular than rock music one day. (probably)
  _____

7 My mum won't let me go to the summer
  camp because my grades aren't good. (if)
  _____

PRONUNCIATION

1 **CD1.38** Listen to the words in the table. Now listen to
the words in the box and write them in the correct
columns. Then listen and check.

circle engine servant leisure petrol
worm urban observe pest penguin
fur essential

e	ɜː
pet	work

58

LISTENING SKILLS

1 **CD1.39** **Listen to a radio programme about exotic pets. Then circle the correct answer.**

1 More and more people want to keep exotic pets because …
   A there are so many of them.
   B they are becoming more and more popular.
   C it's getting easier to buy them.
   D they are so cute.

2 The British law is mentioned in the talk because …
   A all exotic animals are illegal in Britain.
   B all exotic animals are dangerous to people.
   C you are not allowed to keep any dangerous pets in Britain.
   D you are not allowed to keep some dangerous pets in Britain.

3 The best way to get the necessary information about the pet you want to keep, is to …
   A first of all, look for the information on the Internet.
   B most importantly, talk to vets about it.
   C use as many different sources of information as you can find.
   D just contact some people who have the same pets.

4 The advice concerning children and exotic pets is …
   A never buy a pet if you have children
   B all exotic pets are harmful to your skin and eyes
   C instead of buying an exotic pet, buy a less unusual pet, like a guinea pig
   D all pets are a good idea if you have children

5 It is important to remember that …
   A exotic pets cost a lot.
   B the cost of keeping the pet may be higher than the cost of the animal.
   C food for exotic pets is always very expensive.
   D pet sitters for exotic pets are more expensive than for ordinary pets.

6 In general, the speaker's attitude towards keeping exotic pets is …
   A encouraging and enthusiastic.
   B discouraging and pessimistic.
   C threatening and scary.
   D reasonable and balanced.

SPEAKING SKILLS

1 **Describe the photo and answer the questions below.**

   1 Why do you think the people in the photo have chosen to wear the same clothes?
   2 Do you think that unisex fashions and hairstyles (suitable for both men and women) will be more popular in the future?

2 **Choose one of the topics and prepare a 3-minute presentation.**

   A. Do you agree with the opinion that only the animals kept in zoos will survive if we do not change our attitude to the environment?
   B Justify the opinion that films and books about disasters will always be popular because people enjoy being scared.

Success!

Read, listen and talk about success and achievements, work and education.
Practise Third Conditional; *I wish*; *if only*.
Focus on giving advice; *had better*.
Write an application form.

GRAMMAR AND READING

1　Read the article and look at the life map. Which path did Hardeep take?

2　Read the article again and answer the questions.

• Why did Hardeep feel lonely as a teenager?
• Why did she become interested in art?
• Why didn't she go to her college interview?

[FIRST STEPS]

Happy Accidents

Hardeep Sidhu is one of Britain's top women comedians. She is appearing this week at the Buxton Comedy Festival.

When I was twelve, my parents moved out of London to a small village near Oxford. I was the only Asian girl in my school and I suddenly felt a bit lonely. I became a typical 'difficult' teenager – I hated school and I thought all the world was against me. But two important things happened. I realised that being funny was the best way to make friends. Perhaps if we'd stayed in London I would never have learned how to be funny! And then I had a brilliant Art teacher, Mrs York, who encouraged me to go to Art College. I would probably have left school as early as possible, if I hadn't met her. However, on the day of my college interview in Bath, I woke up late. I left the house wearing two odd shoes and didn't notice that my bottle of chocolate milk had spilled all over the paintings in my bag. Then when I finally got to the station I got on the wrong train! Who knows … if I had gone to Bath that day I might have become a professional artist. But I went to Swindon instead! I told the woman next to me on the train about what had happened and she sat and cried with laughter. It turned out she was the producer of a comedy programme on the radio. To cut a long story short, I got an invitation a week later to attend an audition for the show … and the rest, as they say, is history! I'm very lucky – my life has been full of happy accidents!

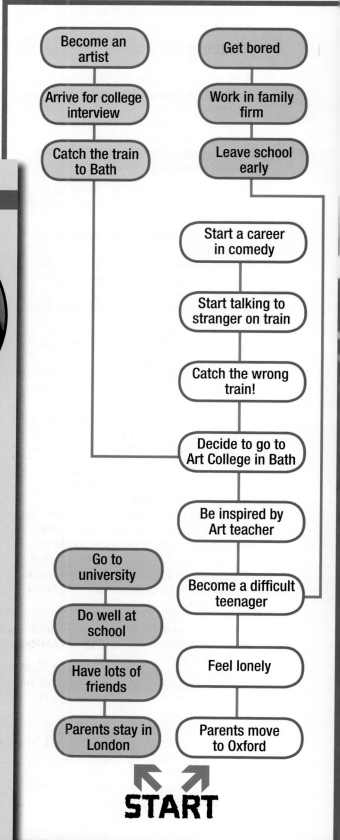

Become an artist

Arrive for college interview

Catch the train to Bath

Get bored

Work in family firm

Leave school early

Start a career in comedy

Start talking to stranger on train

Catch the wrong train!

Decide to go to Art College in Bath

Be inspired by Art teacher

Go to university

Become a difficult teenager

Do well at school

Feel lonely

Have lots of friends

Parents stay in London

Parents move to Oxford

START

Work it out

3 Look at the sentences and answer the questions.

> **a** I **would have left** school as early as possible if I **hadn't met** her.
> **b** If I **had gone** to Bath that day, I **might have become** an artist.

1 Do these sentences talk about the past, present or future?
2 Did these things happen in Hardeep's life?
3 What tense is used after *if*? What form is used in the other clause?

Check it out

Third Conditional

We use the Third Conditional to talk about a situation that had a chance of happening in the past but it didn't happen.

The condition	The result
if + Past Perfect,	*would/could/might/should/have* + Past Participle

If I had gone to Bath that day, I might have become a professional artist. (but I took the wrong train)
I would have left school early if I hadn't met her. (but she encouraged me to go to college)

4 Look at the life map in Exercise 1 again and complete the sentences. Use the Third Conditional.

1 If Hardeep's family had stayed in London, she ___ (had) lots of friends.
2 She probably ___ (go) to university if she had stayed in London.
3 She wouldn't have become a difficult teenager if she ___ (not feel) lonely.
4 If Hardeep hadn't had an amazing teacher, she ___ (become) interested in Art.
5 If she hadn't become interested in Art, she probably ___ (work) in the family business.
6 She probably would have got bored if she ___ (work) for the family business.
7 If she had caught the right train, she ___ (arrive) for her college interview.
8 She wouldn't have become a top comedian if she ___ (not start) talking to the woman on the train.

5 Think Back! Match sentences 1–3 with contexts a–c. Identify the First, Second and Third Conditional.

1 If I had time, I would learn more English.
2 If I work hard, I will pass all my exams.
3 If I had worked harder, I would have passed my exams.

a A situation in the past that didn't happen. ☐
b A situation that has a good chance of happening in the future. ☐
c A situation that is unlikely to change now or in the future. ☐

6 Complete the sentences with First, Second or Third Conditionals.

1 I learnt a lot at university. But I _____ (not graduate) if my parents _____ (not/help) me financially.
2 Don't panic! If we _____ (leave) now, we _____ (still get) there on time.
3 I doubt I'll get that job – and perhaps it's a good thing, too. If I _____ (get) the job, I _____ (have to) move to London.
4 Our day out has been a complete disaster. If I _____ (know) it was going to be so horrible, I _____ (stay) at home.
5 I don't know why you always listen to loud music when you're revising. If you _____ (concentrate), you _____ (remember) more.
6 It's your own fault that you failed. If you _____ (not play) computer games all night, you _____ (pass).

7 Complete the texts with the correct form of the verbs in brackets.

Picasso, Pablo
The great artist, Pablo Picasso, believed that his success was thanks to his parents. 'Would I have become an artist if my father [1]___ (not be) an art instructor? [2]___ (I have) the same determination to succeed if I hadn't had such a strong mother?' he wrote. Indeed, Picasso's mother always believed Pablo would be a success at anything. When he was young she once told him, 'If you become a soldier, you' [3]___ (be) a general; if you become a monk, you' [4]___ (end up) as the Pope.' Instead he became Pablo Picasso, perhaps *the* painter of the twentieth century!

Einstein, Albert
Albert Einstein was perhaps the best-known scientist of the twentieth century. As well as his scientific work he also took an active interest in political and social problems. For example, in 1939 he wrote a letter to President Roosevelt encouraging the US to start building an atomic bomb. Later, when he found out about Hiroshima and Nagasaki, he changed his mind. 'If I [5]___ (know), I [6]___ (become) a shoemaker.' he admitted.

8 Complete the sentences to make them true for you and write two sentences of your own. Then compare your sentences with your partner.

1 If I had got up an hour earlier today, I ___ .
2 If I had never met ___ , ___ .
3 I would never have read ___ if ___ .

READING AND LISTENING

1 Work in pairs and answer the questions.

- What period in history do you think the picture shows?
- What kind of lifestyle do you think the people have?

2 [CD ROM] Read the plot summary below and check your predictions to Exercise 1. Why do you think people are so intrigued by Gatsby's past?

3 [CD ROM] Now read the extract from the novel. What does Nick think of Gatsby after meeting him?

4 Read the story again and answer the questions. Tick true and cross false.

1 People didn't usually get invitations to Gatsby's parties. ☐
2 Nick arrived at the party just before the start. ☐
3 One of the guests believes that Gatsby hasn't always lived in the USA. ☐
4 The books in the library are not real. ☐
5 Nick starts enjoying the party more as it gets later. ☐
6 Gatsby's appearance was very different to what Nick had expected. ☐

5 Work in pairs. Do you think the guests' gossip about Gatsby is true? Why?/Why not?

THE GREAT GATSBY
BY F. SCOTT FITZGERALD

T he story takes place in the USA of the 1920s. Nick Carraway, the narrator, is a young graduate who has moved to New York to work on Wall Street. He had been in the army in World War One. He rents a small house in West Egg, an exclusive area of Long Island. He's single but has a busy social life and he spends a lot of time with Tom, an old college friend, and his beautiful wife Daisy, who live nearby. Everyone has a lot of money and spends most of their time going to parties.

Nick has never met his neighbour, Jay Gatsby, a lonely millionaire. Gatsby is famous for his extravagant and very popular parties at his luxury home but he is also the subject of much gossip about his past. One day, Nick receives an invitation to Gatsby's next party …

I believe that on the first night I went to Gatsby's house I was one of the few guests who had actually been invited. People were not invited – they just went there. Sometimes they came and went without meeting Gatsby at all.

When I arrived, the garden was already full of music and laughter. I tried to look for Gatsby but nobody knew where he was. Finally I found a familiar face – Jordan Baker, a friend of Daisy's. She was talking to a group of guests who I didn't know.

'Have you been to Gatsby's parties before?' Jordan asked the girl beside her.

'The last one was the one I met you at,' answered the girl, in a confident voice.

'When I was here last, I tore my dress on a chair,' said another girl, 'and he took my name and address – and I got a package from Croirier's with a new evening dress in it. It cost two hundred and sixty-five dollars!'

'There's something funny about a guy that'll do a thing like that,' said the other girl. 'He doesn't want any trouble with ANYbody.'

'Who doesn't?' I asked.

'Gatsby. Somebody told me …'

Everyone leaned forward to listen.

'Somebody told me they thought he killed a man once.'

'Well I heard he was a German spy during the war.' One of the men nodded.

'I heard that from a man who grew up with him in Germany,' he said.

We all turned and looked around for Gatsby. But he wasn't there.

After supper Jordan and I went to look for Gatsby inside the house. In the library a fat, middle-aged man, with enormous glasses, was sitting at a huge table, staring at the shelves of books. He was a little drunk.

'What do you think?' he asked us, excited.

'About what?'

He waved his hand at the book-shelves.

'About that. They're real.'

'The books?'

He nodded.

'I thought they were just for show. But they have pages and everything.'

We went back into the garden. The moon was high in the sky. A famous opera singer sang in Italian, some actors played a funny scene and then a jazz band

THE GREAT GATSBY

BY F. SCOTT FITZGERALD

started playing. People were dancing now. Champagne was being served in huge glasses and the air was full of conversation and laughter. We sat at a table with a man of about my age and a little girl who giggled every time someone spoke. The man looked at me and smiled.

'I know your face,' he said, politely. 'Weren't you in the Third Division during the war?'

'Why, yes. I was in the Ninth Battalion.'

'I was in the Seventh Infantry. I knew I'd seen you somewhere before.'

We talked for a moment about some wet, grey little villages in France.

'Having a nice time now?' Jordan asked me.

'Much better.' I turned again to my new acquaintance. 'This is an unusual party for me. I haven't even seen the host. He sent over his chauffeur with an invitation – and I only live next door!' For a moment he looked at me as if he didn't understand.

'I'm Gatsby,' he said suddenly. 'I thought you knew. I'm afraid I'm not a very good host.'

He smiled again. It was a smile that you might come across maybe four or five times in your life – a smile that understood you as you wanted to be understood. It made me trust him immediately.

Gatsby left us to answer a phone call from Chicago. I told Jordan that I had expected Gatsby to be different – older, fatter, red-faced.

'Who is he? Do you know?' I asked Jordan.

'He's just a man named Gatsby …,' she answered coolly.

'Where is he from, I mean? And what does he do?' I asked her again.

'Well, he told me once he was an Oxford man. I don't believe it, though.'

There was something very mysterious about Gatsby's story – how had someone so young appeared from nowhere and bought such a grand house in West Egg? I suddenly noticed Gatsby again – he was standing alone on the steps, smiling at the lively scene below him. Looking at his tidy hair and his smooth, tanned skin it was difficult to see anything suspicious about him. A band started playing and people started singing. Girls rested their heads on their partners' shoulders. But no one rested their head on Gatsby's shoulder.

6 Check that you know these words before you listen to the next part of the story. Use a dictionary if you need to.

aristocrat (n)   courage (n)   medal (n)
bravery (n)   inherit (vb)   wealthy (adj)

7 **CD2.1** Listen and answer the questions.

1 Which university does Gatsby say he went to?
2 What is Gatsby's explanation for his wealth?
3 Which two characters realise they had known Gatsby years before?

8 **CD2.2** Listen to the end of the story. Put the events in the correct order. Then listen again and check.

a works for a millionaire ___
b returns to the US ___
c works for criminal gangs ___
d Gatsby is born into a poor family _1_
e studies at Oxford ___
f works on a farm ___
g earns enough money to move to West Egg ___
h joins the army and meets Daisy ___

9 Work in groups and answer the questions.

• What did Gatsby do as a child to help himself become a success?
• What did he learn when he was a teenager?
• What made him turn to crime in order to be successful?
• Do you agree with the way Gatsby achieved his success?

10 Work in pairs. Match the beginnings and endings of these quotations. Which one do you agree with the most and why?

1 'A man is a success if he gets up in the morning and goes to bed at night, ☐
2 'I owe my success to having listened respectfully to the very best advice, ☐
3 'Success is the ability to go from one failure to another ☐
4 'Success is a journey ☐

a with no loss of enthusiasm.' (*Winston Churchill*)
b and in between does what he wants to.' (*Bob Dylan*)
c not a destination.' (*Ben Sweetland*)
d and then going away and doing the exact opposite.' (*G. K. Chesterton*)

11 Work in pairs. Say which of the ideas below are closest to your own definition of success and why.

• being famous
• being the best at something
• accepting failure
• doing better than anyone expected
• winning an award/title
• being a positive influence on others
• earning a lot of money
• being happy
• finding your perfect partner
• spending your life as you want to
• recovering from illness, difficulties or prejudice
• doing better than your parents

12 Work in pairs. Think of someone who you feel is a good example of a success. It can be either a celebrity, a famous character in history or someone you know personally. Tell the class about your choice.

GRAMMAR AND LISTENING

> I wish I didn't have to play tonight.

> If only I could have a quiet evening at home.

> If only I hadn't left the band!

> I wish I had never entered the music business.

1 In pairs, look at the photo and answer the questions.

- Who do you think the person is? What's the situation?
- Would you like to be famous? Why?/Why not?
- What are the disadvantages of being famous? Use these ideas to help you.

autographs   interviews   bodyguards
pressure   fans   privacy

2 [CD2.3] In pairs, listen and decide why Colin is unhappy. Does he mention any of the disadvantages of fame you mentioned in Exercise 1?

Work it out

3 Read the sentences and answer the questions.

1 I wish I didn't have to play tonight.
2 If only I could have a quiet evening at home.
3 If only I hadn't left the band!
4 I wish I had never entered the music business.

Which sentence(s) talk about a regret …
- about the present? What tense do we use?
- about the past? What tense do we use?

Check it out

> **_I wish_/_If only_ for regrets**
>
> We use _I wish_/_if only_ when we want something to be true but know it is impossible or unlikely.
>
> We use _if only_/_I wish_ + the Past Simple to talk about regrets about the present. It means, 'It would be nice if … .'
> _I wish_/_If only_ I **could** have a quiet evening at home. (It would be nice if I could have a quiet evening. = It's a pity I can't have … .)
>
> We use _if only_/_I wish_ + the Past Perfect to talk about regrets about the past. It means, 'It would have been nice if … .'
> _I wish_/_If only_ I **hadn't left** the band. (It would have been nice if I hadn't left the band. = It's a pity I left … .)

4 Rewrite the sentences using the prompts so that the meaning stays the same.

1 It would be nice if you didn't have to leave so early.
   I wish _____
2 It would be nice if I could speak Spanish.
   I wish _____
3 It would be nice if you lived closer to us.
   If only _____
4 It's a pity I gave up learning German.
   I wish _____
5 I'm sorry I was rude to you.
   I wish _____
6 It's a pity that I lost his phone number.
   If only _____

5 Make sentences with _wish_/_if only_ for these situations.

1 You aren't very good at singing.
2 You argued with your parents last night.
3 You don't have any friends abroad.
4 Your ears are too big.
5 You didn't pay attention in the Maths lesson.
6 You don't understand your Maths homework.

6 Work in pairs. Think of a famous person and write down three regrets about the present/past which you think they might have.

Be a social success!

Shy? Lacking self-confidence?
Let me help you!

I am a fully-qualified personal coach and I have helped dozens of people to believe in themselves and make a success of their lives.

Phone to make an appointment now – the first consultation is free!

Natalie Edwards
01459 2 444333

SPEAKING AND LISTENING

1 Read the advert above. What do you think it means to be a social success?

2 Work in pairs. Tick the advice which you think is useful for people who want to be a social success.

- Mention your successes and achievements very often ☐
- Be yourself ☐
- Always introduce yourself first ☐
- Pay compliments as often as you can ☐
- Smile a lot ☐
- Sound confident ☐
- Speak with an educated accent ☐
- Tell jokes very often ☐
- Keep up-to-date with the latest films and music ☐
- Try and remember people's names and other details ☐
- Wear fashionable clothes ☐
- Use long, complicated words ☐

3 **CD2.4** Listen and <u>underline</u> the advice in Exercise 2 that Natalie, a personal coach, gives Marcus. Did you choose the same advice?

4 **CD2.5** Listen and decide which of Natalie's pieces of advice Marcus tried to use at his next party. Which was the most useful?

5 **CD2.6** Study Speak Out. Then listen and complete Natalie's sentences with a phrase from the box.

SPEAK OUT | Giving advice

You'd better (+ infinitive)
You ought to …
If I were you, I'd …
You should …
It's worth + -ing
It's a good idea to …
You might find it useful to …
Why don't you (+ infinitive) … ?
Remember to …

1 When you meet somebody for the first time ___ introduce yourself first.
2 ___ trying to memorise at least one detail about them.
3 ___ make notes on little cards.
4 ___ make more of an effort to keep up-to-date with what's going on.
5 ___ start reading a few film reviews.
6 ___ smile a lot.
7 ___ just be yourself?

Mind the trap!

You'd better (= *you had better*) is very strong advice. It means we don't expect the listener to ignore it! Its meaning is close to 'you definitely have to'.

Somebody's stolen my wallet.
You**'d better** contact the police.

6 Work in groups. Imagine that you work as a personal coach. Use Speak Out and try to give at least two pieces of advice for each situation.

What advice would you give to someone who …
- wants to make a good impression on a first date?
- has problems remembering appointments and birthdays?
- wants to earn some extra money to be able to go on holiday?
- needs to find out some information on Einstein for a class presentation?
- is having problems keeping up with English lessons?
- wants to make a good impression for a college/job interview?
- has just had a serious argument with their boyfriend/girlfriend/sister?
- feels bored in the evenings?
- is addicted to computer games?
- can't wake up in the mornings?

VOCABULARY AND WRITING

1 Complete the sentences with the correct form of the words in capitals.

1 Nobody expected them to ___ but they did! SUCCESS
2 I haven't passed my driving test for the ninth time. I feel like a complete ___ . FAIL
3 Losing your privacy is a price you have to pay for ___ . FAMOUS
4 She ___ took her employers to court and won compensation. SUCCESS
5 Your projects were excellent – you can all be very proud of your ___ . ACHIEVE
6 You're very talented, you know – you have an amazing ___ to predict problems. ABLE

2 Put the verbs or phrases in the correct group.

not be up to the task
do well (in a test, at school …)
mess up (an exam, an interview …)
do badly (in a test …)   flunk (an exam)
pass (an exam)

Succeed	Fail

3 Write the verb(s) or phrases which collocate with these words.

achieve   fulfil   miss
make the most of   overcome

1 ___
2 ___
an ambition
a dream
an aim

4 ___
5 ___
a chance
an opportunity

3 ___
a difficulty
a problem
an obstacle
a disability
a fear/phobia

4 Work in pairs. Choose two topics and take turns to talk about them.

Talk about a time when you:
• fulfilled a dream.
• missed an opportunity to do something.
• messed up something badly.
• made the most of an opportunity.
• felt proud of your achievements.

5 Complete the application form with phrases from Exercises 1–3.

OUTREACH

Application for the post of

Team Leader
(Summer Holiday Camp)

1 Please give details of any personal qualities which you think you could bring to the job.

I believe my two biggest qualities are patience and the ¹___ to get on with people. I also consider myself very hard-working.

2 Please give details of any recent achievements (either academic or personal).

Last year I ²___ my ambition of being the first girl in my college to get a diploma in motor mechanics. During my last holiday I ³___ my fear of heights when I went bungee jumping with friends. I believe these examples show that I am not afraid of challenges and I always try to ⁴___ any obstacles I meet in life.

6 Complete the application form in Exercise 5 to make it true for you. Use the vocabulary on this page and on page 37.

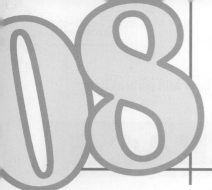

08 Taking a break

Read, listen and talk about holidays and travel.
Practise passive forms.
Focus on effective listening, interpreting statistics.
Write a description of a place.

GRAMMAR AND READING

1 Work in pairs. Look at the holiday brochure and answer the questions.

- What is unusual about the three hotels it describes?
- Which of the hotels would you prefer to spend a night in? Why?
- Have you ever stayed in an unusual place?

Work it out

2 Match sentences 1–6 with their passive versions a–f in the texts below.

1 They keep the temperature at about –5°C. ☐
2 They are already accepting reservations. ☐
3 Someone murdered two people while someone else was building the castle. ☐
4 The Clan McIntosh attacked the castle. ☐
5 Since then they have completely rebuilt the hotel many times. ☐
6 They won't complete the complex until next year. ☐

TOP 3 Extraordinary Hotels

**Want a holiday with a difference?
Have a look at these places …**

The Icehotel
Sweden **1**

200 kilometres north of the Arctic Circle, Swedish Lapland, The Icehotel is made of nothing but ice and snow! This amazing hotel was first built in 1990, and [a] since then it has been completely rebuilt many times. [b] The temperature is kept at about –5°C, but don't worry! Special hi-tech sleeping bags are included in the price!

Castle Stuart
Scotland **2**

Castle Stuart, which was built about 400 years ago, has a violent history. [c] Two people were murdered while the castle was being built. Not long after the building was finally completed in 1625, [d] the castle was attacked by the Clan McIntosh and was abandoned. Since then it has been fully restored and is now a luxury hotel. But it is said that the bedroom at the top of the East Tower is haunted.

The Bahamas **3**

The Poseidon is the world's first underwater luxury hotel. This five-star resort is being built eighteen metres below the sea in the Bahamas. It will be linked to land through two tunnels. The windows, which are made of transparent acrylic, offer fantastic views of the undersea life. [e] The complex won't be completed until next year, but [f] reservations are already being accepted.

3 Work in pairs. Look at sentences a–f in the texts. Answer the questions.

1 These sentences sound better in the passive than in the active because we are more interested in the …
   a actions. **b** people. **c** time.

2 Which auxiliary verb do we use in every sentence?
   a have **b** be **c** do

3 Every passive sentence has a(n) …
   a infinitive. **b** -*ing* form. **c** past participle.

4 To mention the person or thing that does the action we use the word …
   a because. **b** by. **c** for.

4 Work in pairs. Match tenses 1–6 with passive forms a–f. How many examples of each tense can you find in the texts on page 68?

1 Present Simple ☐ **a** has been rebuilt
2 Present Continuous ☐ **b** is kept
3 Past Simple ☐ **c** was being built
4 Past Continuous ☐ **d** was attacked
5 Present Perfect ☐ **e** won't be completed
6 Future ☐ **f** are being accepted

Check it out

The Passive

The Passive is used when the action is more important than the person who does it.
To mention the person or thing who does the action we use the word *by*.
To form the Passive we use the auxiliary verb *be* + the Past Participle.

The Icehotel **is made** of ice and snow.
This five-star resort **is being built** below the sea.
Two people **were murdered** while the castle **was being built**.
It **has been** fully restored.
It **will be linked** to land through two tunnels.

5 Complete with the passives of the verbs in brackets and then match questions 1–5 with answers a–e.

1 When ___ the Icehotel first ___ (build)? ☐
2 When ___ the building work ___ (usually/complete) each year? ☐
3 How many rooms ___ (build) next year? ☐
4 ___ everything ___ (make) of ice? ☐
5 ___ the Icehotel ever ___ (use) in any films? ☐

a It ___ (usually/finish) by mid-December.
b Next winter eighty-five rooms ___ (build).
c The first Icehotel ___ (build) in 1990. It ___ (build) every year since then.
d The ice hotel in the James Bond film, *Die Another Day*, ___ (base) on the Icehotel, but it ___ (make) of plastic.
e The restaurant ___ (not/make) of ice, but in the bar even the glasses ___ (make) of ice.

6 Complete the information about Castle Stuart. Choose a, b or c. Not all the sentences need the passive.

1 **a** are **b** have **c** –
2 **a** has **b** is **c** was
3 **a** has been **b** is **c** was
4 **a** are **b** have been **c** will be
5 **a** is **b** was **c** –
6 **a** being thrown **b** throwing **c** –
7 **a** is **b** was **c** will be
8 **a** is **b** was **c** –
9 **a** has he **b** was he **c** he was

Castle Stuart

Castle Stuart has eight bedrooms which [1]_____ all decorated in different tartans. Each one [2]_____ dedicated to a clan which fought for Charles Stuart 'Bonnie Prince Charlie' when he [3]_____ defeated at the Battle of Culloden in 1745. Over the years many stories [4]_____ told about the ghosts who haunt the castle. For example, one time a local man, Big Angus, [5]_____ spent a night at Castle Stuart to prove that it wasn't haunted. In the middle of the night he heard a loud noise. He looked out of the window and saw something strange. A man was [6]_____ out of a window. The next morning Angus [7]_____ found dead in the courtyard. He [8]_____ had a look of horror on his face. Did he jump or [9]_____ pushed?

7 **CD2.7** Change the active sentences below into the Passive. Listen and check.

1 Shop assistant: 'Is anyone serving you?'
   Are you being served?
2 Airport announcement: 'We are sorry to announce that bad weather has delayed Flight AJ439 to Athens.'
3 Hotel manager: 'I'm sorry. We don't allow pets here.'
4 Tour guide: 'A fire destroyed the church when they were restoring it.'
5 Travel agent: 'We highly recommend the trip to Paris.'
   Customer: 'Will you arrange transport from the airport to the hotel?'

Orraway *Adventure*

River bugs**Sphereing**Cliff jumping**Paintball**Quad biking**Snowboarding**White water raftin

Orraway is run by a group of professional outdoor instructors with one goal: to bring our love of adrenalin sports to you! We were recently voted one of the Top 50 Weekends in the UK by *The Independent* newspaper. Located in Abergavenny, South Wales, we are open 365 days a year.

River bugs

River bugging is the latest white-water activity sensation. This amazing action sport has never been offered to the public outside of New Zealand and Australia … until now! Only fifty River Bugs exist in the world, and we have ten of them! River Bugs look like a cross between a white water raft and an armchair. Designed for one person at a time, they give you all the thrill of white-water rafting, but on your own and in perfect safety. The user, who is known as a 'bugger', wears a helmet and is protected by inflatable chambers at the back and on the sides of the Bug. **1** ___d___ . Then, you will be taught how to control your Bug, told what to do and not to do, and then taken out to play on the river! River Bugging runs from April to October. It lasts half a day and costs only £45 per person. No previous experience is required, but you do need to be at least sixteen years old.

Sphereing

Rolling head-over-heels down a steep hill is guaranteed to give you a thrill. **2** ___f a___ . Sphereing! This involves climbing inside a four-metre plastic sphere that looks like a huge transparent golf ball, and then rolling down a hill at speeds of up to fifty-five kilometres per hour! **3** ___a___ . It only takes a few seconds but it's great fun! The sphere is big enough for two people so you can enjoy this fantastic experience with a friend. You are tied in the centre of the sphere to reduce the danger, but to make it more exciting, four litres of water may be thrown inside the sphere, too. Sphereing has to be experienced to be believed. One roll and you'll want to do it again. Two rolls and you'll be addicted! Sphereing runs from April to September and it costs £35 per person. No previous experience is required, but it is not recommended for anyone who suffers from epilepsy.

Cliff jumping

Cliff jumping starts at a huge smooth rock next to the river. The rock is wet so that you can slide down it easily! You can either just sit and slide into the water, or you can be brave and go head first. Next, you are taken to the first of our cliff jumping points where you will be taught the correct techniques for jumping and for entering the water correctly. **4** ___b___ . In fact, it has been adopted as part of the guidelines and regulations for cliff jumping around the UK. If your technique is good enough, you will be taken to the next level of jumping. Our first jumps are about one metre above the water. Our biggest jump is around twenty metres! **5** ___c___ ? It's up to you! Cliff jumping runs from May to October. It lasts half a day and costs only £40 per person. No previous experience is required.

Orraway – experience the art of adventure.

READING

1 Read the Orraway website and complete the text. Match sentences a–f with gaps 1–5. There is one sentence you don't need.

- **a** There is no steering, no brakes and absolutely no point
- **b** Our technique has been tried and tested many times
- **c** How extreme do you want to go
- **d** First, you will be provided with a wetsuit, a helmet and special gloves
- **e** Don't forget your camera
- **f** But now, a way has been found to make it even more exciting

2 **CD ROM** Work in pairs. Read the website again and find the most suitable activity for these people.

Talking Heads

Coby
'I want to do something really thrilling. I fancy bungee jumping, but I'm not ready for it yet. I used to be really good at diving when I was at school.'

Sonia
'Me and my boyfriend Steve want to do something really exciting for my birthday, but I can't swim. We're both speed freaks!'

Ray
'My job is really stressful and I want to do something that will let me forget all about it. I've got a week off in April, but my girlfriend doesn't want me to do anything too dangerous!'

3 Read the website again. Decide which activities match these statements – River bugging (R), Sphereing (S), Cliff jumping (C).

1 You do it alone.
2 It's the most expensive.
3 You can't do it in April.
4 You are sure to get wet.
5 If you do it once, you'll want to do it again.
6 Orraway are the only people in Europe to do it.
7 It doesn't take long to do.
8 You have to learn how to do it.

4 Work in pairs. Add these words to the table. Then use a dictionary and add more words.

boots   bungee jumping   elbow pads   hang gliding   jet skiing
kayaking   skiing   rock climbing   rope   scuba diving   skating

Water sports	Winter sports	Other extreme sports	Extreme sports equipment
Scuba diving white-water rafting	snowboarding Skiing	cliff jumping bungee jumping rock climbing	helmet boots elbow pad
hang gliding jet skiing kayaking	skating		rope

5 Work in pairs. Roleplay this situation.

Student A
You call Orraway to find out more information about the activities they offer. You begin the conversation.
- Tell them when you want to go there.
- Ask about prices and how dangerous the activities are.
- Book at least one activity.

Student B
You work for Orraway. Someone calls you to ask about the activities you offer.
- Say which activities are available at the time he/she wants to come.
- Give a brief description of two activities.
- Encourage him/her to book more than one activity.

6 Work in groups. Agree on one of the activities on the web page that you would all like to do.

A I'd love to try sphereing. It must be a lot of fun. Why don't we do that?
B Hmm, maybe. But I want to do a water sport. Let's try the River bugs.

The sphere isn't really designed for going up the hill, Mr Jones.

The adventure of Bob, Michelle and Maribel ...

LISTENING

1 CD2.8 In pairs, look at the photo and the notes in Part One and answer the questions. Listen and check.

1 Where are the people in the photo? How do you know?
2 What do you think they are going to do?
  - Go for a coffee
  - Fly to Madrid
  - Take a train to London

2 CD2.9 Use the photo to make predictions. Tick the sentences you think the girls will say. Listen and check.

1 A cup of coffee and an orange juice, please. ☐
2 Two for the Express to Victoria, please. ☐
3 How much is it? ☐
4 What time is the next train? ☐
5 Which platform does the train leave from? ☐

3 CD2.9 Listen again and answer the questions. Listen for the key words and don't worry if you don't understand every word.

1 Where are the girls going?
2 Do they buy single or return tickets?
3 How much are the tickets?
4 When does the train leave?
5 Which platform does it leave from?

4 Look at Exercises 1–3 and complete Train Your Brain with the words in the box.

context   Don't worry   key words   predictions

TRAIN YOUR BRAIN | Listening effectively

- Use the _____ (visual clues, audio clues and your knowledge of the world) to make _____ about what you're going to hear.
- Listen for the _____ .
- _____ if you don't understand everything.

5 CD2.10 In pairs, read Part Two and predict what kind of information is missing. Then listen and complete.

6 CD2.11 In pairs, read Part Three and predict what kind of information is missing. Then listen and complete.

Part One

Flight LJ 420, Madrid - Gatwick Airport, April 8 dep: 19.15, arr: 20.45.

Bob arrives at ~~9.30~~ 10.30 - Meet him at station (Victoria)
Simone's address - 23 Shannon Grove, ~~Brighton~~ Brixton

Part Two

Wed 11.45p.m. In a hotel in Brixton.

Bad news! Bob didn't get off the train from Brighton. The next train wasn't due for ¹_____ and when I tried to call him there was no ²_____ . So, we decided to go to ³_____ to see if he was waiting there for us. We asked for directions and a woman told us to take the ⁴_____ . But when we got to number 23 Shannon Grove, there was ⁵_____ there. We were really tired so we went to a ⁶_____ . The hotel room cost £85 for a night, but I would pay double just for the shower! The receptionist was from ⁷_____ - small world!

Part Three

Thu 10.30a.m. At Simone's flat.

Unbelievable! After we had a shower, we went to a late-night café to get something to eat. I had ¹_____ - it wasn't too bad. Suddenly I saw ²_____ . He was going into a ³_____ on the other side of the street. But by the time I got there Bob had already gone inside. They wouldn't let me in 'cause I had left my ⁴_____ at the hotel. But Maribel went inside and found Bob.

He had come from Brighton by ⁵_____ , not by train! When he saw we weren't at the ⁶_____ , he went to Simone's. The thing is she doesn't live at 23 Shannon Grove. It's 23 Shannon ⁷_____ ! Anyway, we went out dancing and we had a great time. The clubs in

VOCABULARY

1 Read 'at the airport' on the leaflet and check you know the <u>underlined</u> words. Then tick the things that are in the pictures.

2 Use the words in the illustration 'on the plane' to complete gaps 1–6 in the leaflet.

3 Match verbs 1–5 with their collocations a–e.

1 board ☐   a a flight on the Internet
2 book ☐   b the plane
3 check-in ☐   c passport control
4 fasten ☐   d your luggage
5 go through ☐   e your seat belt

4 **CD2.12** Work in pairs. Complete each gap with one word. Then match a–e below with sentences 1–7. Listen and check.

1 Would you like an _____ seat or one by the window?
2 Please have your passports and _____ cards ready.
3 Will passengers for _____ WA476 to London Gatwick please go to gate number twelve.
4 Please fasten your seat _____ and switch off all electronic equipment.
5 OK, go to _____ seventeen. Boarding starts at eleven fifteen.
6 I'm sorry for the delay, but we will be ready to _____ off in a few minutes.
7 In case of emergency there is a _____ under your seat and an oxygen mask above your head.

a a member of the cabin crew on a plane ☐ ☐
b a public announcement in the departure lounge ☐
c a security guard at passport control ☐
d someone at the check-in desk ☐ ☐
e the pilot ☐

5 Think Back! Check you know the meanings of the words and phrases in the box. Use them to complete the sentences below.

resort booked cancelled delayed
due in reservations return single

1 Her flight was _____ at 8p.m. but it was _____ for over an hour due to bad weather.
2 What kind of ticket would you like? A _____ or a _____ ?
3 I've _____ a holiday in a five-star _____ on the coast. I'm really looking forward to it.
4 I'm too busy at work now so I've _____ our _____ for the weekend in London.

6 Roleplay the situation. Work in pairs and follow the instructions. Student A, look at page 142. Student B, look at page 143.

TRAVELLING BY PLANE

AT THE AIRPORT

1 Look at the <u>departures board</u> ☐ to find out which <u>check-in desk</u> ☐ to go to.
2 Check in your <u>luggage</u> ☐, and get your <u>boarding card</u> ☐.
3 Go through passport control and the security check.
4 While you wait in the <u>departure lounge</u> ☐ you can do some shopping at the <u>duty-free shop</u> ☐.
5 When you hear the <u>announcement</u> ☐ of your flight, go to your <u>gate</u> ☐ and wait until it's time to board the plane.

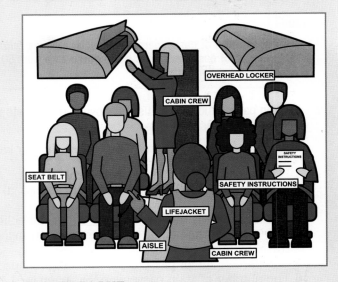

ON THE PLANE

1 Put your hand luggage in the ¹_____ or under the seat in front of you. Don't leave anything in the ²_____ .
2 Read the ³_____ carefully and listen when the ⁴_____ show you how to use a ⁵_____ .
3 Fasten your ⁶_____ and switch off all electronic equipment.

Holidays abroad by UK residents by destination

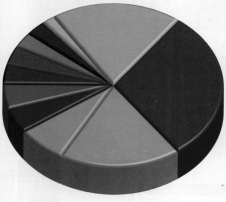

19% Other countries	5% Italy
2% Turkey	5% USA
3% Netherlands	7% Greece
3% Cyprus	18% France
4% Ireland	30% Spain
4% Portugal	

Journeys by public transport in the UK 1970–2010 (in millions)

	1980	1990	2000	2010 (projected)
Total journeys	8,000	8,000	6,800	7,000
Bus	6,200	5,300	4,620	4,450 (63.5%)
Train	1,750	1,700	2,000	2,250 (32%)
Plane	50	100	180	300 (4.5%)

SPEAKING

1 Work in pairs. Study the information in the pie chart and the chart and circle the correct words in the sentences in Speak Out.

SPEAK OUT | Interpreting statistics

Proportions

- **About a third** of British people who take holidays abroad go to *Spain / France*.
- *France / Greece* is visited by **7 percent (%)** of the holidaymakers.
- **Nearly one in five** go to *France / Italy*.
- **Most** travellers go to *Mediterranean / Northern European* countries.

Trends

- **The percentage of** passengers travelling by plane is *falling / rising*.
- **The number of** passengers has *gone down / up* from 50 million to almost 300 million in under thirty years.

2 Work in pairs. Study the statistics above and complete the sentences with the words/phrases in the box.

4%   down   falling   one in twenty   most   nearly half   rising   up

1 _one in twenty_ British holidaymakers went to Italy.
2 _Nearly half_ of the British who holiday abroad go to either Spain or France.
3 Portugal was visited by ___4%___ of the holidaymakers.
4 _Most_ of the people who take public transport in the UK travel by bus.
5 The percentage of passengers travelling by bus is _down (falling)_
6 The number of train passengers has been _falling_ slowly. (rising)
7 The number of total journeys by public transport went _rising_ [down] from 1980 to 2000 but it is expected to go _up_ again.

3 Work in pairs. Look at the graph on page 140. Use the language in Speak Out to talk about the statistics.

B I really love the old town which goes from the Castle to Holyrood Palace. There are lots of amazing old buildings there. But my favourite place is the Royal Park. It's a huge park with an ancient volcano called Arthur's Seat. From the top there is an incredible view of the river and the surrounding countryside.

WRITING

1 Work in pairs. Match the words/phrases below with definitions 1–8. Use a dictionary to help you. Which of these words describe the place where you live?

countryside ☐   village ☐
old town ☐   suburbs ☐
spa town ☐   city ☐
commercial zone ☐
industrial port ☐

1 a place to swim and improve your health
2 historic centre of the city
3 residential districts on the outskirts of a city
4 a land outside towns and cities with farms, villages, forests, etc
5 a part of town with lots of shops and businesses
6 a place with large ships and tankers
7 a large important town
8 a small town in the countryside

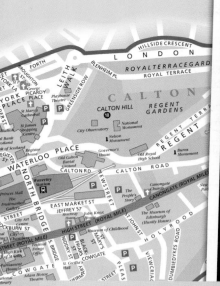

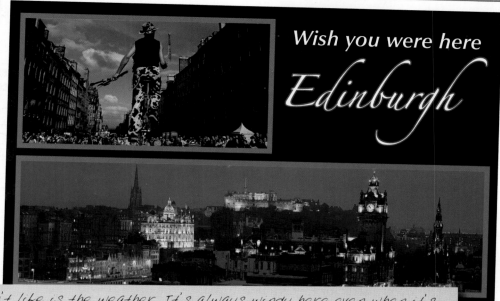

Wish you were here
Edinburgh

C The only thing I don't like is the weather. It's always windy here even when it's sunny. There are some really nice beaches nearby but it's too cold to go swimming.

D You can't get bored in Edinburgh. There are lots of things to do especially in August. That's when the international arts festival takes place. There are some very interesting museums and galleries, and you can also go on some great historical tours about ghosts and so on. Another thing I like about Edinburgh is it's great for shopping. It's got all the major chain stores and some interesting little shops.

E Edinburgh is my favourite city. There are lots of things to see and do and it's not too big, so you can get to most places on foot.

2 Read the statements about the city of Edinburgh. Tick true and cross false. Then look at the school project and check.

1 It's in the north of England. ☐
2 It's the capital of Scotland. ☐
3 It's a historic city. ☐
4 It's situated inland near some very high mountains. ☐
5 It's a centre for arts. ☐
6 It isn't a very commercial place. ☐

3 Read the description of Edinburgh again. Which of these things are mentioned?

Background information

• the population
• the geographical location
• how to get there
• local transport
• some historical details
• the major industries
• the weather

Things to see and do

• the surrounding area
• tourist sights
• shops
• nightlife
• sports and leisure activities
• museums and galleries

4 Read the description again. In which paragraphs A–E does the writer mention points 1–5? *HW*

1 Good points ☐
2 Bad points ☐
3 Background information ☐
4 Things you can see and do ☐
5 Conclusion ☐

5 Complete Train your Brain with points 1–5 in Exercise 4.

TRAIN YOUR BRAIN | Writing skills

Describing places

• Organise your description in paragraphs.
• Start with an introduction: mention [1]_____ – where it is, how old it is, what kind of place it is, how to get there.
• Give your opinion – use a variety of adjectives to describe the place. Mention [2]_____ and [3]_____.
• Mention the [4]_____ there.
• End with a [5]_____ in which you sum up what you think of the place.

6 Work in pairs and follow the instructions to plan a description of a place.

• Think of a place you both know well.
• Agree on which background information you want to include.
• Agree on the good and bad points.
• Make a list of things to see and do there.

7 Use Train your Brain and your ideas from Exercise 6 to write a description of the place you have chosen.

• Write a first draft.
• Give it to your partner to check it for errors.
• Write a final version.

VOCABULARY AND GRAMMAR

1 Circle the correct word.

1 Living in countryside / rural / village areas is safer than in big cities.
2 When you go diving in cold water, you need to have a rope / lifejacket / wetsuit.
3 I'm afraid of flying, especially when the plane takes in / up / off.
4 No previous / earlier / extraordinary experience is needed for this job.
5 Sophie lives on the suburbs / outskirts / residential area of London.
6 You need a fresh air / an open air / an outdoor instructor to learn how to ski. (not in room, outdoor)

2 Complete the sentences. Make new words from the words in capital letters.

1 As a pilot during World War II my grandfather showed a lot of __bravery__ . BRAVE
2 It's hard to believe but Amsterdam has only about 750,000 __inhabitants__. INHABIT
3 I'd like to make an __appointment__ with Dr Green, please. APPOINT
4 If you get to the airport too early, you'll have to wait in the __departure__ lounge. DEPART
5 Have you heard the __announcement__ about our train being delayed? ANNOUNCE
6 Could I make a __reservation__ for the morning flight to London? RESERVE
7 Some sports stars don't want their __privacy__ invaded by reporters. PRIVATE

3 Complete the text. For each gap circle the correct answer.

Tips for Surviving at University

■ Always ¹ _d_ all your classes – if you skip classes, you're sure to fall behind.
■ Always ² _c_ attention. Take an interest ³ _d_ what the tutors are saying – if it's difficult, take notes.
■ Study often and early – after all, you do want to keep ⁴ _d_ your fellow students.
■ ⁵ _c_ a good impression on your instructors – smile a lot and sound confident.
■ If you ⁶ _c_ an exam, don't feel like a failure. Accept it. Learn to ⁷ _a_ difficulties.
■ If you pass, celebrate! You've done ⁸ _b_ !

1 a come for	b go at	c visit	d attend
2 a give	b attract	c pay	d turn
3 a at	b to	c for	d in
4 a up to	b up with	c on with	d on to
5 a Make	b Do	c Give	d Leave
6 a pass	b take	c fail	d sit
7 a overcome		c keep up with	
b pass		d fulfill	
8 a good		c best	
b well		d the best	

4 Complete the sentences so that they mean the same as the original sentences.

1 I wore a helmet and that's why I didn't get hurt when the kayak hit the rock.
If I _____ .
2 They have just built a five-star resort on the coast.
A five-star resort _____ .
3 I'm sorry I can't go with you to the Open'er Festival in Gdynia.
I wish _____ .
4 You must revise a bit more before a unit test.
You'd _____ .
5 They are restoring a little church near where I live.
A little church _____ .
6 I'm so angry I forgot to take my camera.
If only _____ .
7 Matthew didn't revise for the exam. No wonder he flunked it.
If Matthew _____ .
8 I'm sure they will buy hi-tech equipment for the expedition.
I'm sure hi-tech equipment _____ .

5 Complete the text with the correct forms of the verbs in brackets.

The Taj Mahal is a monument located in Agra, India, which ¹_____ (construct) between 1631 and 1654. The Muslim Empero Jahan ²_____ (begin) its construction as a mausolem for his wi Mumtaz who ³_____ (die) in childbirth. The Taj Mahal ⁴_____ (construct) using materials from all over India and Asia. Over 1,000 elephants ⁵_____ (use) to transport building materials during th construction. Today the Taj Mahal ⁶_____ (consider) the finest example of a style that ⁷_____ (combine) elements of Islamic, Indian, Persian and Turkish Architecture. It ⁸_____ (describe) as one of the seven wonders of the modern world.

PRONUNCIATION

1 **CD2.13** Listen to the words in the table and look at the word stress patterns. Now listen to the words in the box and write them in the correct columns. Then listen and check.

abandon   achievement   adrenalin
advertisement   application   departure
concentration   development   disaster
industry   influence   inhabitant
inspiration   memorise   percentage
prejudice   reservation

●••	•●•	•●••	••●•
passenger	equipment	activity	destination

76

READING SKILLS

1   Read the article. Are the statements true (T) or false (F)?

1 It took Kukuczka less time than Messner to climb all the 14 highest summits. ☐ T
2 The Polish climber reached nine new peaks in winter. ☐ F
3 Kukuczka's equipment was of rather poor quality. ☐ F
4 Nobody climbed without oxygen before Messner. ☐ F
5 Messner stopped climbing mountains after his brother died. ☐ T
6 Messner showed photographs of the Yeti in his book. ☐ F

Rivalry at 8,000 metres

The Himalayas have been the scene of many rivalries over the years. Few, however, have been as long or heroic as the battle between Jerzy Kukuczka and Reinhold Messner during the early 1980s. Both men were trying to be the first to reach all 14 peaks in the world which are over 8,000 metres. Messner completed this remarkable achievement a year earlier than Kukuczka. However, it took Messner 16 years to do it whereas the Polish climber did it in only 8 years.

Kukuczka, who was born in Katowice, Poland in 1948, was a brilliant mountaineer. While trying to reach the 14 highest summits, he established nine new routes, reached one summit by himself, and did four of them in winter. In fact, many consider his achievement to be greater than Messner's, especially considering that his equipment was often hand-made and his clothes second-hand. Unfortunately, Kukuczka died attempting to reach the top of Lhotse in 1989. He was buried by his friends in a Himalayan glacier.

Messner, on the other hand, is a living legend among climbers. Born in South Tyrol (Italy) in 1944, he is one of the world's most successful and famous mountaineers. He was the first person to climb Mount Everest alone without oxygen and he has also crossed Antarctica on skis.

But Messner's career has had its tragic moments too. During his first major Himalaya climb in 1970, both he and his brother, Günther Messner, reached the summit. However, Günther died two days later on the way down the mountain.

Messner, who is now a wealthy man, has no intention of settling down in his castle in the Italian Alps. He keeps on exploring, climbing, writing and having new adventures; in 2004 he walked 2000 kilometres through the Gobi desert. Curiously, Messner is one of the few western people that claim to have seen the Yeti. He says he has met it twice, and has photographic evidence to prove it! However, in his book about the Yeti there is no real proof. Instead he just speculates that the Yeti is a large, long haired bear.

SPEAKING SKILLS

1   Roleplay this conversation.

Student A
You are on a language course in England. Unfortunately, although you have been on the course for some time, you are still having problems with understanding English. You have gone to your teacher for advice.
- Say that you have a problem. Explain that you don't understand the listening exercises in class or people on the street.
- Ask for advice.
- Thank him/her for the advice and ask when you will begin to make progress.

Student B
You are a teacher on an English language course. One of your students has come to ask you for advice. Comfort him/her, explaining that most foreign students have the same problem.
- Say that all contact with English is necessary and helpful (for example, listening to recordings in a language laboratory, listening to the radio and watching television).
- Advise him/her that the more conversations he/she has in English, the sooner he/she will start to speak and understand fluently.

2   Look at the table and talk about the statistics. Then answer the questions.

HARLEY HIGH SCHOOL PROJECT The sports we play	1996	2001	2006
football	51%	45%	33%
volleyball	42%	40%	38%
snowboarding	26%	30%	37%
swimming	40%	41%	40%
cycling	52%	52%	54%

In 1996 football was the most popular sport – more than half of the students said they played it.

1 Why do some sports become popular among teenagers? What is the role of sport stars and media coverage of sporting events?
2 Which sports are becoming less popular, and which more popular in your country? Why?

To err is human

Read, listen and talk about work and school.
Practise reported speech.
Focus on talking about visual materials.
Write a report of a conversation.

b

GRAMMAR AND LISTENING

1 Work in pairs. Use a dictionary to check the meaning of the words and phrases below. Then describe pictures a–c. What do they have in common?

a parachute / stuck / torch / Statue of Liberty
b drive through fence / sink / pool
c road sign / speed limit / make a mistake

2 **CD2.14** Listen and match dialogues 1–3 with pictures a–c.

Dialogue 1 ☐   Dialogue 3 ☐
Dialogue 2 ☐

3 **CD2.15** Work in pairs. Match speakers a–c with sentences 1–7. Then listen and check.

a Wendy   **b** Darren   **c** Christophe

1 I can't get up or down.
2 This number doesn't look right.
3 We're doing it wrong.
4 I had my first lesson yesterday.
5 I will call back later.
6 I've been here for ten minutes.
7 I had never driven a car before.

Public Works Dept. Incident report.
Worker involved: **Wendy Dickens**

We were painting the speed limit – forty miles per hour – on the road at Coombe Bissett and I told Ted we were doing it wrong. I said that ª <u>that</u> number didn't look right because the sign at the side of the road said thirty. Ted said that Bill had given him his instructions ᵇ <u>the week before</u> – and the speed limit was forty. So, I called up Bill and he told us it was thirty, so we had to change it.

Signed   *Wendy Dickens*

You won't believe what happened the other day. My sixteen-year-old neighbour, Darren, drove his mum's car through the fence and into our swimming pool! He explained that he had had his first driving lesson ᶜ <u>the day before</u>, and admitted that he had never driven a car before then. He said he had thought that ᵈ <u>that day</u> was his chance to get some practice because his mum wasn't there ᵉ <u>at that time</u>. And then he looked really worried and said that his mum would be home ᶠ <u>the next day</u> and that she was going to be furious.

New York Talk Radio

Carla
A Frenchman, Christophe Landry, said he was stuck on the top of the Statue of Liberty. He explained he was protesting against the use of land mines and told me his plan had been to land on the statue, but he had got caught on the torch. He claimed that he had been ᵍ <u>there</u> for ten minutes and added that he couldn't get up or down. He told me he had jumped from the Eiffel Tower ʰ <u>a few years earlier</u>. He promised that he would call back later, but could you call him to get an interview for the 6p.m. news bulletin?
See you   Judy

Work it out

4 Read the texts opposite and <u>underline</u> how sentences 1–7 from Exercise 3 were reported. Then complete gaps 1–6 in the table.

Direct speech	Reported speech
Present Continuous We're doing it wrong.	**Past Continuous** I told Ted we were doing it wrong.
Present Simple This number doesn't look right.	**Past Simple** I said that [1] _Christope s number didn't look right_
Past Simple I had my first lesson yesterday.	**Past Perfect** He explained that [2] _he has had first lesso years_
Present Perfect I have been here for ten minutes.	**Past Perfect** He claimed that [3] _He had been here for 10 minutes_
Past Perfect I had never driven a car before.	**Past Perfect** He admitted that [4] _he had never driven a car before_
can I can't get up or down.	**could** He added that [5] _He couldn't get up or down_
will I will call back later.	**would** He promised [6] _he would call back later_

Reporting verbs: *add, admit, agree, claim, complain, explain, point out, promise, protest, reply, say, tell, threaten*

5 [CD2.14] Match expressions 1–8 with their reported versions a–h in the texts. Then listen again and check.

1 now	☐	5 a few years ago	☐
2 this	☐	6 yesterday	☐
3 here	☐	7 last week	☐
4 today	☐	8 tomorrow	☐

6 Change these sentences to reported speech.

1 Ted I think it's wrong.
Ted said he thought it was wrong.
2 Wendy It definitely has a *c* and an *h* in it.
3 Kelly I've never seen anything like that.
4 Darren I don't know how it happened.
5 Darren I didn't mean to do it.
6 Darren My mum will be home tomorrow.
7 Christophe I can't talk now. A helicopter is coming.

7 Use the verbs in brackets to change this conversation to reported speech.

Tina You're not doing it right. (tell) You've made another mistake. (complain)
Tom I'm sorry. (reply) I don't usually make so many mistakes. (tell)
Tina This job is very important. (tell)
Tom Of course it's important. (agree) But you only told me about it yesterday. (protest) I can't perform miracles! (add)
Tina You're not trying! (claim)
Tom I am trying! (say) I didn't sleep well last night and I can't concentrate. (explain)
Tina When I got here, you hadn't even started it. (point out)
Tom I'll finish it tomorrow. (promise)
Tina That's too late. (say) I won't pay you if you don't finish it today. (threaten)

Tom was doing a job for Tina. She told him that he wasn't doing it right and complained that he …

8 Work in pairs. Correct the mistakes in the magazine article. Follow the example.

IS THIS THE WORST TV PRESENTER EVER?

TV presenter, Simon Forbes makes a lot of mistakes. Can you correct them?

1 'Manchester is the capital of England.'
2 'Pollution is making the planet colder.'
3 'The British don't drink much tea.'
4 'Scotland won the World Cup in 2006.'
5 'Rap music has been popular for fifty years.'
6 'Camels can live underwater for a week.'
7 'People will live on Mercury by 2015.'

Simon Forbes said that Manchester was the capital of England, but it isn't, it's London.

9 [CD2.16] Work in pairs. Read 1–4. What did the people actually say? Listen and check.

1 In 1888 the astronomer Simon Newcomb said that we were probably getting near the limit of all we could know about astronomy.

'We are probably getting …'

2 In 1901, two years before the Wright brothers' first successful flight, Wilbur Wright said that Man would not fly for fifty years.
3 In 1943 Thomas Watson, the chairman of IBM said that he thought there was a world market for maybe five computers.
4 After a meeting in Albuquerque, New Mexico in 1975 a banker said that Bill Gates had told him about his new company the day before. He said that he had never heard such a stupid idea and that that guy Gates couldn't be serious. He was sure that the business would never make any money.

It's not always easy to know what to do when you leave school. Alan Jeffries had an egg-citing experience!

A ☐ Alan had always been a good student. He had never <u>played</u> truant and had always <u>passed</u> all his exams easily. However, he wasn't ready for university. He enjoyed the freedom too much. He <u>skipped</u> a lot of classes and when he failed to <u>sit</u> his end of term exams, he was expelled. He said he didn't mind because he was going to <u>drop out</u> anyway. He had decided to take a year out in order to get some experience in the real world.

B ☐ Alan resigned before he was sacked. He started doing odd jobs for family friends again. And that autumn he was back at university studying Law. Maybe you're wondering what Alan does now. Well, believe it or not, he's a health and safety inspector in a large armaments factory. And he never eats eggs.

C ☐ Alan was a bit depressed about being out of work, but then, at last, he got a full-time job! It was in an egg factory. He was in charge of the machine that put the packs of eggs into large boxes ready to go to supermarkets around the country. The wages were low and he had to work long hours, but from the beginning, Alan's boss was impressed by his attitude. He clocked in on time, he was always happy to work overtime and he never took any time off. Before long, he had been promoted to a better job. Now he was responsible for driving a fork-lift truck and loading the boxes of eggs onto the supermarket lorries. He quickly became the fastest fork-lift driver in the factory. He was happy and proud to be earning his living.

D ☐ However, they say that pride comes before a fall. And so it was with Alan. One day, he decided to make his job more interesting by seeing how fast he could do it. He set his stopwatch and drove as fast as he could towards the boxes full of eggs. His foot was hard down on the accelerator, and the fork-lift was going at top speed, but Alan was sure he was in control. However, he was wrong. He waited one second too long. He hit the brakes but it was too late. The fork-lift crashed into a huge pile of boxes. There was a terrible crunching noise and then silence. When Alan's workmates went to see what had happened, they found Alan standing in the middle of the world's biggest omelette. Fortunately, he wasn't hurt, but he had broken more than twelve thousand eggs.

E ☐ Then he got a part-time job in a tea room. Unfortunately, it didn't last long. On his first day, he put salt in the sugar pot. On his second day he put tabasco sauce in some sandwiches and almost killed an old lady. And on the third day he dropped a tray and broke over two dozen cups and saucers. The manager of the tea room asked him to leave.

F ☐ 1 When Alan Jeffries left school, he wasn't sure what to do. His parents wanted him to go to university to <u>get</u> a degree in Law. They said that he would have great career opportunities when he graduated. So he took their advice and <u>enrolled</u> at Reading University.

G ☐ When he saw all the jobs on offer at the job centre, he was impressed. But it wasn't as easy as he had thought it was going to be to get a job, and he began to wonder if he had made a mistake. He applied for lots of jobs, both permanent and temporary – car mechanic, shop assistant, cook, hairdresser, security guard … But he was too young and inexperienced for some and overqualified for others. So he made some money doing odd jobs for family friends – painting a garage, babysitting, washing cars and so on.

You can't make an omelette without breaking eggs.

READING AND VOCABULARY

1 Work in pairs. Look at the photo and answer the questions.

- What kind of job do you think Alan had?
- Would you like a job like this? Why?/Why not?
- Have you ever had a job? If so, where and what was it like?

2 Read the article and order paragraphs A–G.

3 Find these words/phrases in the text and work out their meaning from the context. Then use the words to complete the summary below.

expelled (para A)	resigned (para B)
promoted (para C)	part-time (para E)
degree (para F)	career (para F)
graduated (para F)	applied (para G)
odd jobs (para G)	

After Alan left school, he began a ¹ _degree_ in Law. However, he was soon ² _graduated_ from _expelled_ university. Although he ³ _applied_ for lots of jobs, he didn't get any. For a while he did some ⁴ _odd jobs_ for family friends. And then he got a ⁵ _part-time_ job in a tea room. That didn't work out and he started working in an egg factory where he was soon ⁶ _promoted_ to the position of fork-lift driver. Unfortunately, he ⁷ _resign_ after an accident. He returned to university and ⁸ _graduated_ with an Honours degree. Then he began his ⁹ _career_ as a health and safety inspector.

4 Read the text again and answer the questions.

1 Why did Alan not complete his degree the first time he was at university?
2 Was it easy for him to find a job? Why?/ Why not?
3 How did he lose his job in the tea room?
4 How did he feel when he was unemployed?
5 What did Alan do in the egg factory?
6 How did he lose his job in the egg factory?
7 What did Alan do after that?
8 What is he doing now?

5 Work in pairs. Match people a–f with sentences 1–6.

a Alan
b the boss of the egg factory
c the manager of the tea room
d a university professor
e a worker in the egg factory
f Alan's parents

1 ___ wanted him to study Law.
2 ___ said Alan had missed too many classes.
3 ___ said she couldn't employ Alan any more.
4 ___ told Alan he was giving him a better job.
5 ___ said the boss wouldn't be happy with Alan.
6 ___ said he was going back to university.

6 Work in pairs. Complete questions 1–7 with verbs a–g. Read the article again and check your answers. Then ask each other the questions.

a drop out	c get	e play	g skip
b enrol	d pass	f sit	

1 Do you like to study the night before you ___ an exam? Why/Why not?
2 Which exams do you think you will ___ this term?
3 What do you think should happen to pupils who ___ truant?
4 Are you going to ___ at university when you leave school?
5 What kind of degree would you like to ___ ?
6 Do you think it's alright to ___ some classes at university? Why?/Why not?
7 Why do you think some people ___ of university?

7 Find the words and phrases underlined below in the article and check their meaning. Then match sentences 1–6 with their continuations a–f.

1 I want a permanent full-time position. ☐
2 Apply for a job in the building industry. ☐
3 The wages are too low, and I don't like the long hours. ☐
4 Last year I was out of work. ☐
5 My boss sacked me because I was always taking time off. ☐
6 You graduated with a Physics degree and now you're in charge of a burger bar! ☐

a And I usually clocked in late, too.
b Aren't you a little overqualified?
c Not a temporary part-time job.
d I resign!
e It offers good career opportunities.
f Now, I've got a job and I earn a lot of money, but I have to work a lot of overtime!

8 In pairs, prepare and give a short presentation on one of the topics below. Use the questions to help you.

1 Pride always comes before a fall. (What does this saying mean? Can you think of any other examples from life, films or books? Can pride be a positive attribute?)
2 Nowadays young people start their first job at a much later age than their parents did. (Why is this so? What are the advantages and disadvantages of this?)

Today your teacher is Katy

GRAMMAR AND WRITING

1 Work in pairs. Describe the photo and answer the questions.

- Do you think the girl in the photo is enjoying herself? Why?/Why not?
- Would you like to be a teacher? Why?/Why not?

2 **CD2.17** Listen to Katy's day as a teacher and put sentences a–g in the order you hear them.

a Have you done your homework? ☐
b Will you teach the class? ☐
c Can I teach what I want? ☐
d What are you doing? ☐1
e When did the French Revolution begin? ☐
f Please, don't make so much noise! ☐
g Go to the board! ☐

3 Work in pairs. Read what Katy told her friend and match phrases 1–7 with sentences a–g from Exercise 2.

'I arrived late for the history class and I was looking for my book when ¹ Mr Hill asked me what I was doing ☐. I explained and ² he asked me not to make so much noise ☐. Then ³ he asked me whether I had done my homework ☐. I said I had but then ⁴ he wanted to know when the French Revolution had begun ☐! I couldn't remember, and so ⁵ he told me to go to the board ☐ and then ⁶ he asked me if I would teach the class ☐! I was really surprised, but ⁷ I asked him if I could teach what I wanted ☐ and he said I could. Then, he sat down in the front row and I turned to the class and began to speak.'

Work it out

4 Study how Katy reported sentences a–g from Exercise 2. Then complete the table.

Reported questions and imperatives	
Yes/No questions	
Have you done your homework?	He asked me ¹ _____ my homework.
² _____ the class?	He asked me if I would teach the class.
Can I teach what I want?	I asked him ³ _____ what I wanted.
Other questions	
What are you doing?	He asked me ⁴ _____ .
⁵ _____ the French Revolution begin?	He wanted to know when the French Revolution had begun.
Imperatives	
Please ⁶ _____ so much noise!	He asked me not to make so much noise.
Go to the board!	He told me ⁷ _____ to the board.

5 Look at the sentences in the table and circle the correct words in rules 1–3.

1 When we report *yes/no* questions we use *if / that / whether*.
2 When we report imperatives we use *ask / say / tell + me, him, her … + to +* infinitive.
3 When we report negative imperatives we use *don't / not to +* infinitive.

Mind the trap!

When we report questions we cannot use interrogative word order.

I asked her where she lived.
NOT I asked her ~~where did she live~~.

6 CD2.18 Change sentences 1–10 to reported speech. Use the prompts in brackets to help you. Then listen to the second part of Katy's story and check.

1 'Do you know anything about computer games?' (I asked them …)
   I asked them if they knew anything about computer games.
2 'How many types of games consoles are there?' (I asked them …)
3 'Can we come in?' (The Maths teacher wanted to know …)
4 'Have you ever played any strategy games?' (I asked them …)
5 'Pay attention!' (I told them …)
6 'When did Lara Croft first appear in a game?' (I asked him …)
7 'Are you listening to me?' (I asked them …)
8 'Please don't throw things at me!' (I asked them …)
9 'What will you do about it?' (She asked me …)
10 'Don't shout!' (I told her …)

7 CD2.19 Work in pairs. Decide how you think Katy's story ends. Then listen and check.

8 CD2.20 Read Katy's report from her careers guidance meeting and write down what the interviewer said. Then listen and check.

[1] The advisor asked me how I was getting on, and I said I was fine, and then [2] he asked me what I wanted to do when I left school. I explained that I wanted to be an actress. He said that that was interesting, but [3] told me not to imagine that it was easy. Then [4] he wanted to know what my best subjects were. I told him I was good at Music and English, and [5] he asked me if I had ever acted in a play. I told him I hadn't and asked him what I could do to become an actress. [6] He told me to get some experience, to join a theatre group, and then to try to get into a good drama school. Then [7] he wanted to know if my parents knew about my ambition to be an actress, and I admitted that I hadn't told them, and [8] he asked me if they would be happy about it. I replied that I didn't know, and then he thought for a minute and [9] asked me if I had ever thought of becoming a teacher! That's when I told him about the dream I had had.

1 How are you getting on?

9 Work in pairs. Follow the instructions and roleplay a careers guidance interview.

• Take turns to be the careers guidance officer and interview your partner.
• Use the questions and imperatives in Exercise 8 and questions 1–4 below.
• Make notes of the questions and your answers.

1 What do you enjoy doing?
2 Would you like to go to university?
3 Have you spoken to your family about your plans for the future? What do they want you to do?
4 What is more important for you – money or job satisfaction?

10 Use your notes from Exercise 9 to write a report of your careers guidance interview. Use reported speech and a variety of reporting verbs.

"I REALLY ENJOY PARTYING ALL NIGHT AND SLEEPING ALL DAY– BUT I WOULDN'T LIST IT UNDER 'CAREER GOALS'!"

ROYAL NAVY RESCUE

07

707

HM Government

BFF1 5HX

Oops, sorry sir! More accidents at school than ever before

SPEAKING AND LISTENING

1 Work in pairs. Quickly look at the photos and circle the topic they suggest.

pollution / accidents / traffic problems

2 In pairs, quickly look at the other visual material. Tick the things you see and say what information they give you.

- a cartoon/illustration ☐
- a graph/chart/table ☐
- an extract from a newspaper/magazine ☐
- an extract from an informative leaflet ☐
- a newspaper headline ☐
- an advert ☐
- a quiz or survey ☐
- a note/message/email/online chat ☐

3 Read the material and look at the photos again. In pairs, write down three to five questions for discussion which the material suggests.

4 Read the questions. Are they similar to any of your questions in Exercise 3?

1 What issue does the material deal with?
2 What kinds of accidents are shown in the material?
3 What information can you get from the written material?
4 What can be done to reduce the risk of accidents?
5 How important is human error in most accidents?

5 **CD2.21** Listen and decide which two questions from Exercise 4 the student is answering. Then listen again and check.

public information leaflet

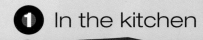

Most Accidents Take Place at Home

Find out how to avoid them

❶ In the kitchen

Britain's most dangerous jobs

1	Window Cleaner	4	Offshore fisherman
2	Soldier	5	Pilot
3	Fireman	6	Police officer

6 **CD2.21** Study Speak Out. Then listen again and circle the expressions you hear.

SPEAK OUT | Discussing visual materials

<u>As soon as you receive the materials</u>
- think of what topics the materials suggest.
- analyse the information the materials give you.
- think of questions the examiner may ask you.

<u>During the exam</u>
- Try to use the language from the examiner's questions in your answers.
- Use these phrases to talk about the materials in general.
  The material **seems to be about / deals with** …
  The table **is about / gives information about** …
  The photo **at the top / on the right / above the table** shows …
  It **looks like / looks as if / could be from** …
  The leaflet/advert/table/headline/article …
- Use these phrases to answer questions in which you have to give your opinion.
  It depends on … / **In my opinion** … /
  I believe … / **It could be** … / **What's more** … /
  Another reason is …
- Use the materials to give examples
  For example, … / **For instance,** …
  The headline **indicates / suggests** …
  It says in the leaflet that …
  We can see an example of this in the article/advert.
  We can see from the table that …
  The chart/graph **proves / shows** that …
  According to the newspaper headline …

---

7 **CD2.22** Listen and answer the questions.

1 What in her opinion is the key to reducing the risk of accidents?
2 How does the student use the language from the question in her answer?

8 **CD2.22** Listen again and complete the sentences with expressions from Speak Out.

1 I think _____ the place.
2 However, _____ that the risk of accidents can be reduced if people are trained well.
3 _____ in the leaflet that most accidents take place at home and _____ the newspaper headline the number of accidents at school is going up.
4 People who don't get good training are more likely to have accidents. _____ in the table of dangerous jobs.
5 _____ , in the picture on the right the man has had a car crash, but perhaps it wasn't his fault.
6 _____ , the key to reducing the risk of accidents is to train people.

9 Work in pairs and answer the questions in Exercise 4. Use the advice and the language in Speak Out.

10 Work in pairs. Look at the materials on page 140 and answer the questions 1–5 on page 141. Use the ideas in the Speak Out here and on page 74.

10 Mysteries

Read, listen and talk about mysteries.
Practise modals and modal perfects for speculation.
Focus on speculation, describing atmosphere.
Write a narrative.

GRAMMAR AND SPEAKING

1 `2.23` **Listen to the story. Are the statements true (T) or false (F)?**

1 Sheerness is a town which is near the sea. ☐
2 When police found the man, he was wearing formal clothes. ☐
3 The man was carrying a suitcase. ☐
4 The police arrested the man. ☐
5 The man pointed to Russia on the map. ☐
6 The man wrote his name on a piece of paper. ☐
7 The man refused to play the piano. ☐
8 His story became well-known across the world. ☐

2 `2.23` **Listen again and read the extracts. Match speakers' theories 1–6 with evidence a–e.**

1 He <u>could (*might/may*) be</u> an illegal immigrant.
2 He <u>must come</u> from Norway.
3 He <u>can't be</u> Norwegian.
4 He <u>might (*may/could*) have been</u> the victim of a crime.
5 He <u>must have been</u> in the sea.
6 He <u>can't (*couldn't*) have understood</u> you.

a He didn't write his name. ☐
b He seems very frightened. ☐ ☐
c He doesn't understand Norwegian. ☐
d He pointed at Oslo on the map. ☐
e His clothes are very wet. ☐

Officer 1 He seems very frightened. He <u>could be</u> an illegal immigrant.
Officer 2 Or he <u>might have been</u> the victim of a crime. Can you show us some identification, Sir? A passport, a driving licence?
Officer 1 He's obviously too shocked to speak.
Officer 2 No wonder – the poor guy's soaking wet. He <u>must have been</u> in the sea for a long time …

Officer 1 Where do you come from? France? Russia?
Doctor Let's give him a map. Perhaps that will help.
Officer 1 He's pointing at Oslo. He <u>must come</u> from Norway.

Officer 1 Well that was a waste of time – he <u>can't be</u> Norwegian, he didn't understand a word.
Doctor Perhaps if we give him a pen and paper, he'll write his name.
Officer 1 Good idea. Can you write your name for us, Sir?
Officer 1 He <u>can't have understood</u>. Wait a minute – he's drawing something …

Work it out

3 Look at the <u>underlined</u> phrases in theories 1–6 in Exercise 2 and decide in which situations a–c we use these modal verbs.

can't ☐   couldn't ☐   might ☐
could ☐   may ☐   must ☐

a The speaker is certain that it is/was true.
b The speaker thinks that it is/was possibly true.
c The speaker is certain that it isn't/wasn't true.

4 Look at the sentences below. Which one talks about a situation in the past?

1 He **must be** Norwegian.
2 He **must have been** in the sea.

Check it out

Modal verbs for speculation

We use *must/might/may/could/can't* + infinitive to speculate about whether something is true in the present.

He must come from Norway. (I'm certain it's true.)
He might/may/could be an illegal immigrant.
(I think it's possible.)
He can't be Norwegian. (I'm certain it isn't true.)

We use *must/might/could/can't/couldn't* + *have* + Past Participle to speculate about whether something was true in the past.

He must have been in the sea.
(I'm certain this really happened.)
He might/may/could have lost his passport.
(It possibly happened.)
He can't/couldn't have lost his memory.
(I'm certain it was impossible.)

Mind the trap!

The negative of *must* is *can't*, not *mustn't*.

He can't be French – I'm sure his parents are both from Wales. NOT ~~mustn't be~~
He started work five minutes ago. He can't have finished already! NOT ~~mustn't have finished~~

5 Complete the sentences. Use *might/could/may* and the correct form of the verbs.

1 Where's Jacob? He's not in his room.
A _____ (be upstairs)
B _____ (go to the gym)
2 I wonder why Monica speaks such good French?
A _____ (grow up in France)
B _____ (still have lessons)
3 Why is Paul in such a bad mood?
A _____ (receive some bad news)
B _____ (be tired)

6 Complete the sentences with *must, can't/couldn't* and the correct form of the verbs in brackets.

1 I phoned them last night but no one answered. They _____ (be) out.
2 You _____ (see) her at the station – she was at home with me!
4 What happened to sentence 3? They _____ (forget) about it! ☺
5 He lost his job and then his father died – it _____ (be) an easy time for him.
6 You're going out with Victor? You _____ (be) serious! In fact, you _____ (be) mad!
7 He _____ (be) hungry – he's just had lunch!

7 `2.24` Listen to the Mystery Guest. Make statements about him using *must/might/could/can't* and the ideas below.

live in France/the US   be married/divorced
have children   be a hooligan
be an actor   be famous
be French/American   be in his late teens

He might be a hooligan because he was in a dangerous fight …

8 `2.25` Listen to four situations. Decide what you think has happened. Make sentences with *might/may/could have*.

The machine might have taken his card.

9 `2.26` Read and listen to the story. In pairs, try to guess how the narrator knew that Paul was lying. Then complete the last sentence. Check your answers on page 141.

'Leo and I bumped into Paul in the café last week. We hadn't seen him for over a year. He walked up to us with a big smile on his face.

'Been somewhere hot, Paul?' I asked. We both looked at his badly sunburned face. He laughed.

'I just flew back from Botswana last night. I was working for a charity out there for a year. We were helping to build a primary school in a remote village. I've had the time of my life! Sitting on a warm beach every evening playing my electric guitar, an ostrich on the barbecue, amazing women … . But I tell you, you've no idea how good it was to have a really long hot bath and shave off my beard after eleven months.' Leo looked impressed but I knew that Paul was exaggerating as usual. He can't have _____ because _____ .'

READING AND VOCABULARY

1 Work in pairs. Look at the picture. What do you think might have happened?

2 Quickly read the story. Were your predictions in Exercise 1 correct? Then answer the questions.

1 Why is Framton Nuttel visiting the Sappletons?
2 Who is Mrs Sappleton waiting for during Framton's visit?
3 Why does Framton suddenly run out of the house?

3 Read the text and complete gaps 1–4 with the sentences below. There are two sentences you don't need.

A Framton was surprised to hear the word 'tragedy' in such a peaceful village.
B He looked around the living room and wondered if Mrs Sappleton was married or perhaps a widow.
C She didn't look very interested at all.
D She turned to look at him and laughed once more.
E The girl stopped speaking and just then her aunt came in and apologised for being late.
F The girl took Framton's coat and carefully placed it on the coat-stand.

4 🖥 **CD ROM** Read the text again. Are the statements true (T), false (F) or is there no information (NI)?

1 It is easy for Framton to talk to the girl. ☐
2 Framton comes from a large city. ☐
3 Framton's sister still lives in the village. ☐
4 The room suggests to Framton that there might be a man in Mrs Sappleton's life. ☐
5 Framton hadn't noticed the door was open until the girl mentioned it. ☐
6 Mrs Sappleton enjoys hunting. ☐
7 Framton feels sorry for the girl at one point. ☐
8 Mrs Sappleton had found Framton's topic of conversation strange. ☐

5 Work in pairs and answer the questions.

1 Do you think Mrs Sappleton is an unusual person?
2 What kind of person do you think the niece is? How do you know?

'Mrs Sappleton is upstairs – she'll be with us in a minute, Mr Nuttel.' said the girl. 'So you'll have to put up with me for a while.' She <u>giggled</u>.

Framton Nuttel tried hard to think of something polite to say to her. He had come to the village to relax after a long illness. His sister had lived there a few years before and she had given him a list of 'nice' people he should meet. But he was beginning to feel fed up with visiting strangers.

'Do you know many people in the village?' asked the girl, who was Mrs Sappleton's niece.
Framton <u>frowned</u>. 'Hardly anyone,' he answered <u>sighing</u>. 'But my sister used to live here and she gave me a list of people I should meet.'

'Oh, so you don't know anything about my aunt?' asked the girl.
'Just her name and address.' said Framton. ¹_____ . There was something very masculine about the room.

'You don't know about my aunt's tragedy?' asked the girl.
² _____

'You're probably asking yourself why we have the door open on an October afternoon, Mr Nuttel.'
For the first time Framton looked up at the open patio-door, which led to the garden.

'Well, let me tell you. Exactly three years ago today my aunt's husband, his dog and her two young brothers left the house to go hunting. They never came back. They were crossing some low ground near a river … it had been a very wet summer … well, their bodies were never found. And my poor aunt … she still thinks that they will come back someday and walk through that door. Which is why she keeps it open.' She stared at him for a moment and then <u>whispered</u>, 'Do you know, sometimes on quiet evenings like this, I almost get a strange feeling that they will all walk through that door!'

Framton <u>shuddered</u>. ³ _____
'I hope my Vera has been amusing you?' she said.
'She has been very interesting.' said Framton.

'I'm sorry to keep the door open but my husband and brothers will come back from their hunting trip soon.'

She talked for some time about hunting and birds. Framton felt terrible and tried to change the subject – but in vain. He could see that Mrs Sappleton wasn't really listening to him but was <u>gazing</u> at the door all the time.

'The doctors have told me to rest completely and not to do any exercise but they're not sure about the best diet for me,' said Framton, who thought the pair might be interested to hear about his illness. Mrs Sappleton <u>yawned</u>. ⁴_____

It was beginning to get dark and the room seemed a little gloomy.

'Here they are at last!' she said, suddenly. 'Just in time for tea!'

Framton turned to look sympathetically at the girl. She was also staring at the door with horror in her eyes. Surprised, Framton <u>glanced</u> at the door.

In the darkness, he could see three people <u>strolling</u> across the lawn, carrying guns. A dog was running behind them. One of the men was singing. Framton <u>gasped</u>. He suddenly got up out of his chair, took his hat and <u>dashed</u> out of the house and through the gate, away from the house as fast as he could.

'We're back, my dear,' said Mr Sappleton with a grin. 'Who was that who just left?'

'A very strange man called Mr Nuttel,' said Mrs Sappleton. 'All he could talk about was his illnesses and then he left without even saying goodbye … or sorry. It was as if he had seen a ghost!'

'It was probably the dog,' said her niece calmly. 'He told me he was terrified of dogs. He told me that once in India he had spent the night lying in an empty grave in a cemetery, trying to escape from a pack of mad dogs.'

6 Match these verbs with their definitions. Use a dictionary to help you.

giggle ☐ frown ☐ sigh ☐ whisper ☐
shudder ☐ gaze (at) ☐ yawn ☐
glance (at) ☐ stroll ☐ gasp ☐
dash ☐

a breathe in quickly because you feel very surprised/shocked
b breathe out with a long sound because you feel sad/disappointed
c open your mouth wide and breathe in deeply because you are tired or bored
d quickly look at someone/something
e stare without realising you are doing it
f laugh in a nervous or silly way
g to shake, usually because you are thinking of something unpleasant
h show you are worried, annoyed or confused by moving your eyebrows
i run very quickly
j speak extremely quietly
k walk in a slow, relaxed way

7 Work in pairs. Choose three verbs from Exercise 6 and act them out for your partner. Can you guess what your partner's verbs are?

8 Complete each sentence with a verb from Exercise 6. Sometimes more than one verb is possible.

1 Mark read the list and _____ . He hadn't been chosen for the school rugby team again!
2 Kirsty and Sam _____ the answers to each other during the German vocabulary test.
3 She quickly _____ at her watch and _____ out of the room. She was going to miss her flight!
4 The students _____ nervously after the teacher dropped a pile of atlases on his foot.
5 On Sunday afternoons they all enjoy _____ around the shopping centre.
6 During Chemistry lessons he _____ out of the window at the clouds and trees.
7 She _____ when she remembered her disgusting childhood school dinners.

G-AEPN

OAKLAND

HOWLAND ISLAND

LISTENING AND SPEAKING

1 **CD2.27** In pairs, look at the pictures. Have you heard of Amelia Earhart? Try and answer the questions. Then listen and check.

- In which period did she live?
- What was she famous for?

2 **CD2.27** Listen again and put the events in the correct order.

a born into a rich family   1
b trains to be a pilot   ___
c visits air show with her father   ___
d trains to be a nurse   ___
e flies solo across the Atlantic   ___
f drops out of university   ___
g finishes high school   ___
h works as a social worker   ___
i plans her round-the-world flight   ___

3 **CD2.28** Listen to Part 2. Did Amelia's plane ever reach Howland Island? Work in pairs. What do you think might have happened to her?

4 **CD2.29** Listen to Part 3. Were any of your ideas in Exercise 3 similar?

5 **CD2.29** Read the questions and possible answers. Then listen again and circle the correct answers.

1 The messages broadcast by Tokyo Rose
  A started in the 1930s.
  B were read by an American.
  C were very popular with Amelia's husband.
  D supported the USA.

2 Researchers couldn't find any information on Amelia in the FBI records because
  A she may have been killed by the Japanese.
  B researchers only started looking in the 1990s.
  C she probably wasn't a spy.
  D researchers didn't look for long enough.

3 When Amelia sent her last message
  A she still had gas for several hours' flying.
  B she was extremely worried about how much gas she had left.
  C she had already run out of gas.
  D she was about to crash.

4 The story about the metal plates on Nikumaroro suggests that
  A Amelia had met the islanders.
  B the plane might have landed or crashed nearby.
  C the US Navy hadn't searched the area near the island.
  D Fred Noonan wasn't good at navigating.

5 Bruce doesn't want to answer the question about *Star Trek* because
  A he hadn't seen it.
  B he didn't have any evidence for the theory.
  C he didn't think it was a serious question.
  D he didn't like the series.

6 Work in pairs. Which theory is most/least convincing? Take turns to give evidence for and against. Use Check It Out on page 87 to help you.

1 Amelia had worked for the Japanese against the USA.
2 She had been an American spy and was killed by the Japanese.
3 Her plane had run out of fuel.
4 She had tried to land on another island.

A She might have worked for the Japanese because the woman on the radio was American.
B She can't have worked for the Japanese because her husband didn't recognise her voice.

VOCABULARY

1 Match the words with definitions a–j. Then <u>underline</u> the adjectives that make a positive impression. Use a dictionary to help you.

deserted ☐   charming ☐   luxurious ☐
spacious ☐   shabby ☐   gorgeous ☐
cramped ☐   filthy ☐   cosy ☐   tacky ☐

a small, comfortable and warm
b small and uncomfortable
c extremely dirty
d cheap and tasteless
e in bad condition because it hasn't been looked after
f empty and quiet because there are no people
g pleasant or attractive
h extremely beautiful
i very comfortable and expensive
j large and pleasant with a lot of space

2 Circle the correct words.

1 There were no signs of life in the Market Square – it was *cramped / deserted*!
2 Their semi-detached house was too *cramped / tacky* for such a large family – so they moved into a more *spacious / gorgeous* detached house in the suburbs.
3 The kitchen was *cosy / filthy* – it looked as if it hadn't been cleaned in weeks!
4 She had a really *luxurious / shabby* apartment in the centre of town where she used to organise exclusive parties.
5 They loved staying in the *charming / filthy* hotel and went back every year.

3 Match the words that have a similar meaning.

1 depressing ☐   **a** tranquil
2 peaceful ☐   **b** superb
3 uninhabited ☐   **c** deserted
4 magnificent ☐   **d** gloomy

4 Work in pairs. Which adjectives from Exercises 1 or 3 could you use to describe these things?

1 A dark street in a poor district of a town.
2 The view from the window of a country cottage.
3 The ruins of an old castle.
4 A mansion in a large park.

5 Rewrite the sentences changing the <u>underlined</u> words/phrases to change the atmosphere.

1 The street was always <u>full of life</u> at any time of day. At the end of the street there was a <u>gorgeous</u> old church.
2 They lived in a <u>charming</u> old terraced house in the oldest part of the town.
3 The kitchen is <u>cosy</u> on dark, winter evenings.
4 They lived in a <u>shabby</u> block of flats.
5 They stayed in a <u>spacious</u> chalet by the beach.

I spend a lot of time in the Grassmarket, which is just a few minutes' walk from Edinburgh Castle. It's a spacious market square which is lined by magnificent stone townhouses, many of them dating from the sixteenth century. Some of the buildings are eight or nine storeys high – among the tallest in the city. Each house has a different style to its neighbour but together the buildings create a feeling of harmony. The Grassmarket doesn't get as crowded with tourists as other parts of the old town and there are a couple of charming cafés on the square where I sometimes go with friends between lectures. We just sit and enjoy the tranquil atmosphere – it's really magic!

6 Read the description above. Does the writer have a positive or negative opinion of the place? Which words suggest this?

7 Rewrite the text with adjectives to make the description more atmospheric.

Finally, Dan and Tonia found a bedsit in a district not far from the city centre – one room with a kitchen. It was on a street lined with detached houses. There was a view of the city centre from the window. The bedsit was unfurnished so they bought some furniture – a sofa bed, a coffee table and some armchairs.

8 Write a description of a striking, mysterious or magical place/building that you know. Mention its location and history. Write 200–250 words.

Rivals

Even at school there had been an unhealthy competition between George and Richard.

'I'll be the first millionaire in Coleford!' Richard used to boast.

'And you'll be sorry you knew me,' George would reply 'because I'll be the best lawyer in town!'

George never did become a lawyer and Richard never made any money. Instead both men opened bookshops on opposite sides of Coleford High Street. It was hard to make money from books, which made the competition between them worse.

Then Richard married a mysterious girl. The couple spent their honeymoon on the coast – but Richard never came back. The police found his wallet on a deserted beach but the body was never found. He must have drowned.

Now with only one bookshop in town, business was better for George. But sometimes he sat in his cramped, shabby kitchen and gazed out of the filthy window, thinking about his ex-rival. Perhaps he missed him?

George's passion was old dictionaries. He'd recently found a collector in Australia who was selling a rare first edition. When the parcel arrived, the book was in perfect condition and George was delighted. But while he was having lunch, George glanced at the photo in the newspaper that the book had been wrapped in. He gasped – the grinning face was older than he remembered but unmistakable! Trembling, George started reading.

'*Bookends* have bought ten bookstores from their rivals *Dylans*. The company, owned by multi-millionaire Richard Pike, is now the largest bookseller in Australia.'   (250 words)

WRITING

1 Read the story. Then, in pairs, answer the questions.

- What do you think might have happened to Richard after his honeymoon?
- How do you think George was feeling when he read the article? Why?

2 What kind of story is the text in Exercise 1? More than one answer is possible.

an action story
a fairy tale
a story with a moral
a mystery story
a romance
a comic story
a horror story
a personal story
(eg from a diary)

3 Think Back! **Read the text again and decide which tense(s) a–c or structures d–f we use in these situations.**

a Past Simple
b Past Continuous
c Past Perfect
d *used to*
e *would*
f a modal perfect

- to tell the main part of the story ☐
- to talk about something that happened even earlier in the past ☐
- to talk about past habits ☐ or ☐
- to show that a long activity was interrupted by a short one ☐ and ☐
- to speculate about what might have happened ☐

4 **In pairs, answer the questions.**

- Did George have a comfortable life or not? What adjectives in paragraph 4 help to create this impression? Look at the Vocabulary on page 91 to help you.
- Find verbs in paragraph 5 which make the story more dramatic. Look at Exercise 6 on page 89 to help you.

Mind the trap!

In stories we often put the reporting verbs (like *say*, *reply* and *ask*) before a noun or speaker's name. The meaning is the same but the style is more 'literary'. We can't do this with pronouns.

'How are you, John?' the girl asked.
OR 'How are you, John?' asked the girl.

'Where are you going?' she asked.
NOT ~~'Where are you going?' asked she.~~

5 **Change the punctuation in these sentences to make it correct. Use paragraph 1 of the story to help you.**

1 I'm really sorry he whispered it was an accident
2 didn't I tell you not to ever go in there she asked
3 be careful shouted Tom from the passenger's seat the road's really dangerous
4 I hope you've had enough sleep said Jacob because it's going to be a long journey

> As dawn broke the sky with flashes of pink, and the melancholy sound of a distant tram cut through the cold morning air, Sophie Hoffman strolled across the estate back to her flat. Her block of flats had been built in 1953 for the workers in the local car factory. The flats hadn't been renovated for years and the balconies were dangerous. She took off her ballet slippers and slowly climbed the stairs to the fourth floor. There were three other flats on this floor. Once inside her flat, she quietly put her filthy ballet slippers next to the lonely row of shoes by the front door. As she was passing the mirror in the hall she glanced at herself and gasped.

6 **Work in pairs. Read the beginning of the story above and answer the questions.**

1 Which information, in your opinion, does not add very much to the development or the atmosphere of the story? Try to cut the text by three sentences.
2 Compare your choices with another pair's. Were your choices similar?

7 Study Train Your Brain. **Look at Exercises 2–6 and decide which exercise practises each point.**

TRAIN YOUR BRAIN | Writing skills

Story

- Think about which format is best for a story eg a mystery/comic/horror story. ☐
- Use adjectives to create an atmosphere. ☐
- Use dramatic verbs to make your writing more exciting. ☐
- Do not go over the word limit. Edit your work and remove any information that does not add to your story. ☐
- Try to use a range of structures and tenses. ☐
- Using direct speech can make a story more interesting, but be careful with punctuation. ☐

8 **Work in pairs. Write a story of about 200–250 words which ends with the sentence** *'That was the last time he/she ever saw them.'* **Use these ideas and** Train Your Brain **to help you.**

- Think of a situation where someone might feel relieved, shocked or disappointed to stop seeing a group of people. Why did the characters not see each other again?
- Think of your characters' ages. Are they your age, younger or older?
- Think of the period in history and the place of your story.
- Think of the best style or format for your story and decide how you want to begin the story:
  a dialogue (direct speech)
  b a description of a person
  c the history of what had happened before the main part of the story
  d a background description of a place, the weather etc
  e a dramatic event which is key to the story

VOCABULARY AND GRAMMAR

1 Complete the text. For each gap circle the correct answer.

You don't have to be a psychologist to guess how students are feeling during a test or an exam. Just by observing their body language you can tell whether they will ¹_____ or fail. Just before the test starts, they will often say silly things and ²_____ nervously to hide their nervousness. When they get their papers, some of them will ³_____ to themselves – a sure sign they know the answers. However, if they feel the exam is hard, you may hear how disappointed they are when they sigh or see how annoyed they are when they ⁴_____ . Some will try to glance quickly at their neighbours' tests, and some will ⁵_____ to pretend that they are bored or tired while, in fact, they are just waiting for the teacher to turn away so that one of their mates can quietly ⁶_____ the answers to them. When they finish, some will immediately ⁷_____ out as if they were desperate to check their answers in their course book while others will ⁸_____ out slowly, relaxed and sure they have passed.

1 a take	**b** skip	**c** pass	**d** flunk
2 a gasp	**b** giggle	**c** glance	**d** sigh
3 a grin	**b** shudder	**c** glance	**d** frown
4 a giggle	**b** frown	**c** stroll	**d** grin
5 a shudder	**b** gasp	**c** yawn	**d** grin
6 a whisper	**b** giggle	**c** gasp	**d** shout
7 a stroll	**b** dash	**c** march	**d** jump
8 a run	**b** dash	**c** stroll	**d** shudder

2 Complete the sentences with adjectives. The first letter of each adjective is given.

1 That terrible motel had cheap, **t**_____ furniture in all rooms.
2 Olivia's room is plainly **f**_____ with a bed and a desk, but it's very cosy.
3 If you take away these armchairs, the room will look more **s**_____ .
4 Look at this dress! Isn't it a **g**_____ colour?
5 The castle was turned into a **l**_____ hotel with a swimming pool and big garden.

3 Complete the sentences so that they have the same meaning as the original sentences.

1 I'm sure he isn't English.
He _____ .
2 'Don't surf the net after midnight'.
My mother told me _____ .
3 I'm sure you're hungry.
You _____ .
4 'Will you come to the meeting?'
Ellie asked me _____ .
5 'Why didn't you tell the truth yesterday?'
The police officer asked the suspect _____
_____ .

4 Complete the text with the correct form of the words in brackets.

Dear Dave,

How are you? I'm having trouble finding a job at the moment. I've been ¹_____ (employ) for six months and there aren't many good career ²_____ (opportunity) available. I must have ³_____ (spend) too much time studying at school because I'm ⁴_____ (qualify) for most of the jobs advertised. I'm not asking for much, just a certain amount of job ⁵_____ (satisfy) - the kind you get from a large salary, a ⁶_____ (space) office and frequent business trips where the company pays for me to stay in a ⁷_____ (luxury) hotel! Oh well. I'll just have to keep looking!

Hope you're OK.
Phil

5 Complete the text with one word in each gap.

UNRESOLVED MYSTERIES
Famous ghost ship found

An expedition ¹____ discovered the final resting place of the ship Marie Celeste, one of the world's most puzzling mysteries. A group headed by the author Clive Cussler and film producer John Davis said they ²____ discovered the ghost ship's remains off the coast of Haiti. On 7 November 1872 the ship had sailed from New York for Genoa in Italy. Over a month after she left port, the ship ³____ found deserted and drifting off the Azores, and was then towed to Gibraltar. No crew member had ever ⁴____ seen again. According to a popular theory, the crew died after they ⁵____ to a lifeboat because they were afraid the ship's cargo ⁶____ explode. However, some suggested that the crew ⁷____ have been kidnapped by pirates or aliens. After that the ship sailed for 12 years before its last captain tried to sink it near Haiti. Dr Cussler said the fate of the crew ⁸____ probably remain a mystery. He also ⁹____ that he ¹⁰____ show objects found in the wreck to the public on Thursday.

PRONUNCIATION

1 **CD2.30** Listen to the words in the table. Now listen to the words in the box and write them in the correct columns. Then listen and check.

clothes   filthy   further   health
leather   smooth   strength   then
thrilling   wealthy   weather   worth

ð	θ
father	thanks

LISTENING SKILLS

1 **CD2.31** Listen to a lecture about the Nasca lines in Peru. Are the statements true (T) or false (F)?

1 It hasn't rained in the Nasca desert for 10,000 years. ☐
2 It's likely the drawings were made by taking rocks away by hand. ☐
3 You can only see the full shapes of the drawings from air. ☐
4 It is possible that the Nasca Indians knew how to fly. ☐
5 It hasn't been proved the lines are an astronomical map. ☐
6 Von Daniken's book changed most people's thinking about Nasca. ☐

SPEAKING SKILLS

1 Look at the visuals and get ready to present the material and discuss:
– why certain subjects are more popular than others,
– the advantages and disadvantages of studying in state and private universities.
Then answer the teacher's questions.

Teacher's questions:
1 What issues do the materials deal with?
2 According to the materials, what subjects do students more/less often choose to study at university? Why can this be problem?
3 Are exams a good way of testing how much knowledge a student has? Why/Why not?
4 Why do young people decide to study at private, not state, universities?
5 Which subject would you most like to study in the future? Why?

IT'S YOUR CHOICE

The number of people enrolling at colleges is soaring – every year sees a rise in the numbers of students-to-be. They most often choose political science, international affairs, psychology, sociology and computer studies. However, the problem is, will there be jobs for ALL of them in the future? Do we need that many sociologists or experts in politics?

Debate on the rising number of private colleges and universities – Ministry of Education asks: do we need so many?

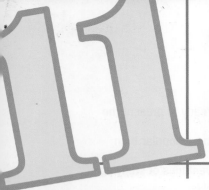

The body beautiful

Read, listen and talk about appearance and beauty.
Practise articles; *have something done.*
Focus on describing appearance; identifying text type.
Write a description of a person.

Beauty through the ages

A sign of <u>health</u> … or a sign of <u>wealth</u>?

Build: Nowadays, a woman who wants to make a career in the world of fashion has to watch her weight. However, during most of our history, being plump was considered more attractive for women: it showed that they didn't have to work and could afford good food. However, the story is a little different for men. In Greek or Roman society, people thought that a muscular physique was <u>the most attractive symbol</u> of <u>masculinity</u> and this idea has continued through the centuries with a few small changes. For example, in <u>the Middle Ages</u>, men wore tights or stockings so it was fashionable to have muscular legs and thighs. Today, in the age of the T-shirt, men worry more about arm and chest muscles. It is still fashionable for men to look fit as it suggests you take your health seriously.

Hair: Queen Elizabeth <u>The First</u> started going bald at an early age. She started a fashion for wigs in <u>England</u>. The fashion spread and eventually wigs were popular with both sexes for the next three hundred years. Wigs became a status symbol – the bigger the wig, the more important you were. However, there was another reason that wigs were an advantage. In those days, even rich people rarely washed and the unhygienic conditions attracted fleas and other pests. Shaving off your hair and wearing a wig was often the only answer. People used animal fat to keep the wigs in place – the smell must have been terrible!

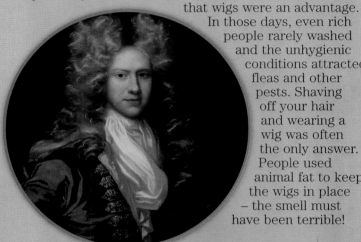

Skin: During <u>the Renaissance</u> in <u>Europe</u> it was unfashionable to have a dark complexion because it was a sign that you worked outside. Because of this, men and women did everything they could to keep their skin pale – often women used dangerous chemicals to paint their faces, which sometimes resulted in a painful death. This didn't change until <u>the 1920s</u> when Coco Chanel, a famous <u>fashion designer</u>, accidentally fell asleep in the sun. The suntan was born and remained popular for the rest of <u>the twentieth century</u> – an easy way to show that you were rich enough to spend your holidays in exotic, sunny places.

GRAMMAR AND READING

1 Read the texts and decide which of these did NOT use to be considered attractive in the past.

a suntan   **b** being slim   **c** a muscular body

2 **Think Back!** Complete rules 1–3 with *a*, *the* or Ø and match them with examples a–e.

1 We use ___ with plurals or
uncountable nouns.   [b] [d]

2 We use ___ when it is something unique
and when we mention the same noun
for the second time.   [c] [a]

3 We use ___ with singular countable
nouns when it is one of many.   [b]

a Coco Chanel fell asleep in <u>the sun</u>.
b Queen Elizabeth started <u>a fashion</u> …
c … <u>the fashion</u> spread …
d They wore <u>tights</u> or stockings.
e They could afford good <u>food</u>.

Work it out

3 For each example below choose the sentence with the same meaning. Use the texts to help you.

1 <u>Men in general</u> worry about their chest muscles.
  a The men worry about their chest muscles.
  b Men worry about their chest muscles.
2 <u>Any woman</u> who wants a career in fashion …
  c A woman who wants a career in fashion …
  d The woman who wants a career in fashion …
3 <u>The idea of a suntan</u> was born!
  e A suntan was born!
  f The suntan was born!

4 Now match your answers in Exercise 3 to the rules in the box below.

Articles – general statements

1 When we talk about things or people in general we use a plural or uncountable noun with no article (Ø).   ☐
2 We can also use a singular countable noun with *a/an*. It means *any/all*.   ☐
3 We can use a singular countable noun with *the* to refer to an invention/idea in general statements.   ☐

5 Look at the rules below. Then find <u>underlined</u> words in the texts that match each rule.

Articles – general uses

We generally use:
a/an with occupations
the with superlative adjectives; ordinal numbers; centuries; decades; historical periods
no article with continents; countries; abstract nouns

Mind the trap!

1 Generally all singular countable nouns need an article.

I bought **a hairdryer**. NOT I bought hairdryer.

2 It is unusual to use *the* in general statements with plural nouns.

Men are as vain as **women**!
NOT The men are as vain as the women!

6 Complete the sentences with *a*, *the* or Ø.

1 Actually, I think ___ shower was one of ___ greatest inventions ever!
2 Phil started ___ course to become ___ fitness instructor. But he found ___ course too boring and he dropped out.
3 Even ___ money can't buy you ___ health and ___ happiness.
4 In ___ 1970s ___ men and ___ women used to wear ___ flared trousers.
5 Everybody knows that ___ men in ___ Scotland sometimes wear ___ kilts. But ___ modern kilt was invented in ___ eighteenth century by Thomas Rawlinson, ___ Englishman!
6 ___ beautiful body doesn't always mean ___ beautiful mind.

7 Complete the texts with *a*, *the* or Ø.

Teeth: During [1] the sixteenth century, [2] ___ sugar started to become popular. But only [3] the richest people could afford it and it quickly became [4] a symbol of [5] ___ wealth. Of course [6] ___ toothpaste didn't exist in [7] ___ Europe then and [8] the people who ate a lot of [9] ___ sweet food usually had [10] ___ black teeth. In [11] ___ England [12] the women often used to paint their teeth black to make them look more rich and beautiful!

Tattoos: In [14] the 1990s [14] ___ archaeologists discovered [15] a man who had frozen to death on [16] ___ mountain between [17] ___ Austria and [18] ___ Italy. His body was covered in [19] ___ tattoos. [20] ___ archaeologists later calculated that [21] the man had lived 5,000 years ago and it was probably [22] the earliest known example of this kind of [23] ___ art.

8 In pairs, answer the questions.

1 In which situations do you spend a lot of time getting your appearance right before you go out?
2 Do you think that society takes beauty/appearance too seriously?

READING AND VOCABULARY

1 Work in pairs. Look at the list of different kinds of texts and put them into categories 1–5 below. Some items can go in more than one category.

advert	instructions
biography	invitation
catalogue	letter of application
dictionary	newspaper article
diary	note/message
email to a friend	novel
encyclopaedia	poem
essay	postcard
friendly letter	recipe
greetings card	rules
guidebook	

Purpose of text	Type of text
1 to give orders or instructions	signs and notices, …
2 to persuade the reader	newspaper editorial, …
3 to give (non-personal) information	website, …
4 personal, informal writing	blogs, …
5 literature	plays, …

2 Read text A and answer the questions. Don't worry if you don't understand all the words.

- What is the purpose of the text? Choose from categories 1–5 in Exercise 1.
- What type of text from the list above do you think it is?
- Do you think it is a modern text? Why?/ Why not?

3 Look at the information below. Then read text B and decide what type of style it has. Do you think the text is a piece of personal writing (eg a letter) or literature?

Informal style

- contractions (*I'd*) and ellipsis (missing words)
- quite simple language/slang
- usually quite short sentences
- exclamations and direct questions often used

Literary/formal style

- contractions and ellipsis not common
- sophisticated language
- long sentences and complex grammar
- exclamations and direct questions not used often

A

Sore throats
In the case of sore throats, the most effective remedy is bacon. Cut slices of fat, boneless bacon and season it well with black pepper. This should be tied around the patient's throat using a cotton bandage and worn for several hours until the pain decreases.

Poor appetite
There are several remedies which are suitable for patients with poor appetites. One can try rubbing the stomach with alcohol or taking a bath in beef soup. Now that electricity is becoming more popular in the home, one can also try electric shocks from a battery.

C

Face Mask

This face-mask will leave you feeling refreshed and your skin shiny and young.

You will need:
1 egg white
1 teaspoon sunflower oil
1 tablespoon lemon juice
1 teaspoon honey

1 In a bowl, beat the egg white until it thickens.
2 Add honey and continue to beat.
3 Lastly, add in the oil and the lemon juice. Mix well.
4 Apply to face and neck. Avoid the delicate areas around the eyes and lips.
5 Leave on face for ten minutes.
6 Wash off with warm water.
7 Enjoy!

B

The elderly passenger who was sitting on the north-window-side of that moving train was the one and only Professor Timofey Pnin. Ideally bald, sun-tanned and clean-shaven, he began rather impressively with that great brown dome of his, fashionable glasses (which hid his lack of eyebrows), ape-like upper lips, thick neck and muscular chest but ended, rather disappointingly, in a pair of skinny legs and almost feminine feet.

D

FOR YEARS experts have been predicting the growth of men's cosmetics. The market grew very slowly during the 1990s, but has grown rapidly since 2001. Manufacturers have spent a lot of time and money developing new products and packaging and finally it looks like their investments were worth it. Sales of men's deodorants and razors continue to grow but what is most exciting for the industry is that many products which used to be exclusively female are now being bought by men: skin cream, delicate shampoos, hair styling mousse and anti-ageing products. What isn't clear is whether men are becoming more vain or whether they simply have more money to spend on themselves.

E

From: Peterg@fmail.com
To: emmag@supamail.com
Subject: Hi again!

I promised to tell you about the Senior Prom (the formal ball we have to celebrate the end of High School). Our school had hired the ballroom at the Crown Plaza, a posh but pretty uncool hotel in town. Everyone had spent months getting ready for it – it's really important to have the most flattering hairstyle, the trendiest clothes and of course the right partner on the night! Luckily, I didn't have a problem – I'd always known my date was Toby ;). My parents bought me a really stunning lemon-coloured dress for the evening. Toby looked really smart in his tuxedo and bow-tie. And guess what? – Toby, Jon, Julie and I hired a limousine to drive us to the hotel! It was so romantic! Anyway, when we arrived at the hotel, all the girls suddenly looked ten years older than the boys. Isn't that weird? The Prom started with a big meal, which

---

4 Study Train Your Brain. Then read texts C–E and decide what type of text they are.

TRAIN YOUR BRAIN | Reading skills

Identifying text type

- As you read, think about what the purpose of the text is – it can help you decide what the type of text is.
- Look at the style – it can help you decide if the writing is personal or not.

5 Match these statements with texts A–E.

The text …
1 mentions a way to make you feel less tired. ☐
2 mentions dietary problems. ☐
3 describes somebody's appearance. ☐ ☐
4 talks about changes in people's behaviour. ☐
5 mentions ways to stay young-looking. ☐ ☐
6 mentions people who look older than they really are. ☐

6 Find adjectives a–i in texts B, D and E then match with definitions 1–9.

a skinny (text B)
b bald (text B)
c shiny (text C)
d vain (text D)
e trendy (text E)
f flattering (text E)
g stunning (text E)
h smart (text E)
i posh (text E)

1 making you look more attractive than usual ☐
2 looking clean and tidy ☐
3 too interested in your own appearance ☐
4 too thin ☐
5 expensive and used or owned by rich people ☐
6 fashionable ☐
7 bright because it reflects light ☐
8 with little or no hair ☐
9 very beautiful ☐

7 In pairs, prepare and give a short presentation on one of the topics below.

1 Are men more vain than women? Why?/ Why not?
2 Is it right that people have to dress formally in certain situations? (eg to a ball or an interview) Why?/Why not?
3 What 'folk remedies' for common illnesses or improving your appearance do you know?

TO DO LIST
have windows replaced ☐
have anniversary photo taken ☐
have hair done ☐
have eyes tested ☐
have washing machine repaired ☐
have grass cut ☐
have carpet cleaned ☐
have new roof put on garage ☐

Work it out

4 Look at the sentences and complete the rule below. Then find more examples of this construction in the text in Exercise 3 and <u>underline</u> them.

1 We <u>have had</u> all the windows <u>replaced</u>.
2 We <u>had</u> a new roof <u>put</u> on the garage last month.

have (in correct tense) + object + _____

Check it out

> **have something done**
>
> We use this passive construction when we arrange for somebody else (usually a professional) to do a job for us. To form it, we use the correct tense of the verb *have*, an object, and a Past Participle.
>
> Every week we **have** the grass **cut**.
> (A gardener does it for us.)
> I'm **having** the carpets **cleaned** this morning.
> (A specialist is doing it for me.)

GRAMMAR AND LISTENING

1 In pairs, describe the photo and answer the questions.

- Do you enjoy going to the hairdresser's/barber's? Why?/Why not?
- In what ways do people sacrifice time and comfort in order to look good? Is it worth it?

2 `CD2.32` Listen to the conversation. Tick the things that Sheila mentions to Jean in the To Do List above.

3 `CD2.32` Listen again and read. Did Duncan and Sheila do the jobs in Exercise 2 themselves?

'When Duncan retired we thought it's time to relax … and it's a chance to finally have all those little things done around the house. So we've already had all the windows replaced and we had a new roof put on the garage last month. And Duncan's back is bad and he can't work in the garden so we found a gardener and now every week we have the grass cut. And I'm having all the carpets cleaned this morning so I said to myself … "Sheila, why don't you go and have your hair done?" And I've made an appointment with the photographer … Duncan and I are going to have our portrait taken for our wedding anniversary. You know something, Jean? I don't know what to do with myself! It's so boring … when you have everything done by other people!'

5 Write sentences with *have something done* for these situations.

1 The optician tested Mark's eyes.
   Mark had his eyes tested.
2 The barber shaved Alex's head.
3 The manicurist is going to do Emily's nails.
4 The barber trims my dad's hair once every three months.
5 The hairdresser was dyeing Jade's hair when I saw her.
6 My friend has fixed my computer.

6 Work in pairs. Ask and answer the questions using the prompts.

1 Do you like/your photo/take?
2 How often/your hair /cut?
3 When was the last time/your eyes/test?
4 Would you like/your hair/dye?
   A Do you like having your photo taken?
   B I don't mind it actually!

1973
Ralph Coates

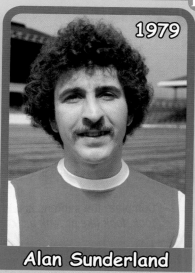

1979
Alan Sunderland

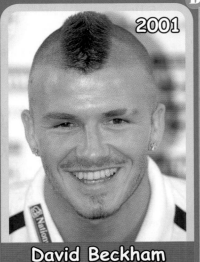

1987
Chris Waddle

2001
David Beckham

LISTENING AND VOCABULARY

1 Work in pairs. Look at the photos above and answer the questions.

- What sport do you think these people play?
- In your opinion, which hairstyle looks the worst?
- Have any of these styles been popular in your country?

2 Read descriptions 1–6 and match them with photos A–D.

1 a men's hairstyle in which the hair on top and at the sides of the head is short but the hair at the back is long ☐
2 a punk hairstyle in which the hair is shaved from the sides of the head but the part in the middle stands up ☐
3 some hair which has been dyed a paler colour than the rest ☐
4 hair that covers the forehead ☐
5 a line of hair that some men grow above their mouths ☐
6 a hairstyle where chemicals are used to make the hair curly ☐

3 **CD2.33** Listen and match the words below with descriptions 1–6 in Exercise 2.

a a fringe ☐   d highlights ☐
b a perm ☐   e a moustache ☐
c a mullet (slang) ☐   f a mohican ☐

4 **CD2.33** Listen again. Are the statements true (T) or false (F)?

1 In the 1960s, footballers didn't look much different from the rest of society. ☐
2 In the late 1970s, it became more common for players to earn a lot of money. ☐
3 Footballers in the 1970s looked like rock stars. ☐
4 Footballers probably choose their hairstyle to try and look more masculine. ☐
5 Players in the same club have always tried to have different hairstyles from each other. ☐

5 For each word or phrase, write the number of the hairstyle 1–4 which it is describing. Use a dictionary if you need to.

a bleached ☐   e dreadlocks ☐
b a pony tail ☐   f spiky ☐
c shoulder-length ☐ ☐   g wavy ☐
d straight ☐ ☐

6 Work in pairs and answer the questions. Use the vocabulary in Exercises 3 and 5 to help you.

- Which hairstyles are typical for footballers or other sports stars in your country?
- Which hairstyles are most popular for people of your age at the moment?

SPEAKING AND VOCABULARY

1 Think Back! **Put the words into the correct category.**

bald	dyed	trendy	muscular
pale	plump	shaved	shiny
skinny	smart	tanned	curly

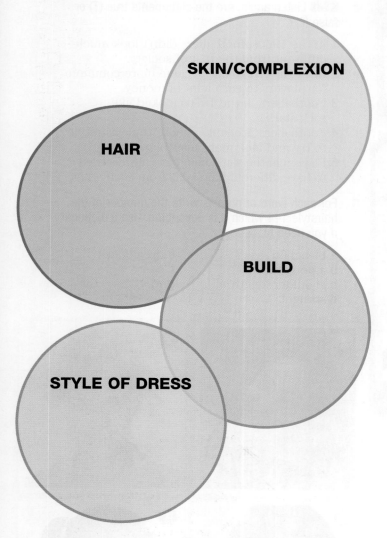

SKIN/COMPLEXION

HAIR

BUILD

STYLE OF DRESS

2 For each group, <u>underline</u> the words which have negative connotations and circle the words which are neutral/positive.

1 fat overweight plump skinny slim thin well-built

2 neat scruffy smart untidy well-dressed elegant

3 Circle the adjectives that can only be used to describe men. Then <u>underline</u> the ones for women only.

stunning
beautiful / attractive
handsome / pretty / good-looking
average-looking / ordinary-looking
ugly / unattractive

Mind the trap!

In British English we use:

look before an adjective   She **looks** very attractive.

look like before a noun   He **looks like** a student.

look as if before a noun/pronoun + verb
She **looks as if** she's in her teens.

4 Complete the sentences with the correct form of *look*, *look like* or *look as if*.

1 He _____ quite elderly.
2 It _____ they all really like each other.
3 He _____ he's in his late thirties.
4 They _____ typical businessmen.
5 He _____ he's looking for somebody.
6 Tom _____ very English, doesn't he?

5 Work in pairs and look at the pictures. How would you say these things in your language?

have a goatee beard   hair in plaits

have dimples

hair with a parting   have wrinkles

be unshaven/have stubble   have cropped hair

6 Work in pairs. Look at the photo and answer the questions.

- How old are the people? Where are they?
- What do you think they have in common? Do they have a good relationship with each other?
- What are the advantages and disadvantages of making friends with people from school/work?

7 CD2.34 Listen and read. Identify the person being described in the photo in Exercise 5.

❝She looks as if she's in her late teens or perhaps early twenties. She looks very slim and she's quite short. She's got straight black hair, which is quite long. She's got dark playful eyes and a cute little nose. She's wearing casual clothes – a blouse and baggy jeans – and she looks quite trendy. She looks like a student – perhaps in her last year of secondary school. I think she looks nice but also a bit moody, actually!❞

8 Study Speak Out! Read the text in Exercise 7 again and decide the order in which the things in bold below are mentioned.

SPEAK OUT | Describing appearance

When describing a person:

☐ Describe his/her **hair**. We usually mention adjectives in this order: general opinion/length/style/colour.
She's got **beautiful long dark hair**.
He's got **short spiky hair**.

1 Estimate the person's **age**.
He is **in his teens** but he **looks older**.
She **looks as if she is in her early/mid/late twenties**.
She **looks middle-aged/elderly**.

☐ Mention the person's **height/build/figure**. Try to use neutral, not negative, words.
She's **quite tall and slim**.   ~~skinny~~

☐ Mention any other **striking features**.
He's got **dimples** and **a goatee beard**.
She's got **dark, playful eyes** and **a small, cute nose**.

☐ Mention the **general impression** this person makes.
She **looks very well-dressed/scruffy**.
She **looks like a student**.

☐ Briefly describe **the clothes** he/she is wearing (or usually wears).
She usually wears **casual/smart clothes**.
He's wearing **a short-sleeved shirt and jeans**.

---

9 Choose another person from the photo. Describe him/her to your partner. Can your partner identify who it is?

10 Think of somebody you like very much. Write a description of him/her in about 200–250 words.

103

It's showtime!

Read, listen and talk about culture and entertainment.
Practise indirect questions.
Focus on participating in conversations.
Write a film review.

Woman	Excuse me, sorry to bother you, but _____ ? This place is so big and I can't find them.
Jens	Erm … yes, it's very big.
Woman	No, I mean, do you know where the toilets are?
Jens	Sorry?
Woman	Where are the toilets?
Jens	Oh, the toilets. No, I don't know.

GRAMMAR AND SPEAKING

1 You are visiting a capital city. In groups, decide what you would like to do from the list below.

- Museums (science, fashion, history)
- Art Galleries (traditional, modern)
- Live music (pop/rock, jazz, classical)
- Theatre (comedy, drama, opera)

2 Work in pairs. Look at the photos and read dialogues A–D. Which of the cultural activities in Exercise 1 is Jens enjoying?

Man	Excuse me, _____ ?
Jens	Good? Er … Oh, yes, … sure … . It is a good programme.
Man	Yes, but, could I have a look at your programme?
Jens	Oh, yes, of course. Here you are.

3 **CD3.1** Complete dialogues A–D with sentences 1–4. Then listen and check.

1 do you know how much it costs to get in
2 do you happen to know where the toilets are
3 do you think I could have a look at your programme
4 I wonder if you could give me change for a twenty-pound note

Work it out

4 Match direct questions a–d with indirect questions 1–4 in Exercise 3.

a Where are the toilets? ☐
b Could I have a look at your programme? ☐
c Could you give me change for a twenty-pound note? ☐
d How much does it cost to get in? ☐

Jens	Could you give me change for a £20 note?
Girl	No, sorry, I can't.
Jens	Thanks anyway. Eh, excuse me, _____ , please. I need it for the drinks machine.
Man	I think so … yes, here you are.

Check it out

Indirect questions

We use indirect questions to be more polite and hesitant when we:
- ask someone to do something for us;
- want to find out some information.

With indirect questions we use:
- affirmative word order;
- *if/whether* with *yes/no* questions;
- *when, where, what* with *wh-* questions;
- introductory phrases such as: *Do you think/I wonder/ Do you know/Do you happen to know/I don't know/ I'd like to know/Are you sure/Can anyone tell me/ Could you tell me/Would you mind telling me/ Have you any idea/Do you remember?*

5 Write indirect questions. Use the questions and the phrases in brackets to help you.

1 What are they talking about?
(Have you any idea …)
2 Was it really a good idea to give Shirley singing lessons? (I wonder …)
3 How does it finish? (Can anyone tell me …)
4 Have we come to the right place?
(Are you sure …)
5 Why did Juliet kill herself? (I'd like to know …)

6 Work in pairs. Match two of the indirect questions in Exercise 5 to the cartoons below.

Jens	Excuse me, _____ ?
Sharon	It's free.
Jens	Really? That's great.
Sharon	Where are you from? Your English is really good.
Jens	Thanks, I'm from Denmark. My name is Jens. Would you mind telling me what your name is?

7 **CD3.2** Write indirect questions. Use the questions and the phrases in brackets. Then listen and check.

1 Could you do me a favour? (Do you think …)
Do you think you could do me a favour?
2 Could you wake me up in an hour?
(I wonder …)
3 Why do we go out together? (I've no idea …)
4 What did we do in the last class?
(Do you remember …)
5 When do we use indirect questions?
(Could you tell me …)
6 What time is it? (Do you know …)

8 In pairs, complete the indirect questions with the words in brackets.

1 In a cinema. Ask the ticket seller about the finishing time of the film you want to see.
I wonder … (finish)
I wonder if you could tell me what time the film finishes.
2 In a restaurant. Ask the waiter for some salt.
Do you think … (bring)
3 In an art gallery. Ask an attendant for directions to the Renaissance section.
Could you tell me … (be)
4 At home. The film has already started. Ask about the action so far.
Would you mind telling me … (happen)
5 In an English class. Ask if anyone knows Shakespeare's birthplace.
Can anyone tell me … (be born)

9 In pairs, roleplay the conversation. Use indirect questions. Student A, look at page 142. Student B, look at page 143.

READING AND VOCABULARY

1 Work in pairs. Look at the photos, the fact box and the newspaper extract and answer the questions. Use Speak Out on page 85 to help you.

1 What issue does the material deal with?
2 How is the information in the fact box and in the newspaper article related to the photos?
3 What kind of damage can hurricanes cause?
4 How can we help people who have suffered natural disasters?
5 There appear to be more natural disasters than before. Why could that be?

2 [CD ROM] Read the article on page 107 quickly and choose the most appropriate title.

a Disaster in New Orleans
b We will survive
c The show must go on

3 Read the article again. Are the statements true (T) or false (F)?

1 One week after Hurricane Katrina everyone had left New Orleans. ☐
2 The writer compares Katrina to a bomb. ☐
3 By February 2006 most of the inhabitants of New Orleans had returned home. ☐
4 Not everyone agreed it was a good idea to celebrate Mardi Gras so soon after Katrina. ☐
5 There were no references to the Hurricane in the parades. ☐
6 The author is impressed by the reaction of the people of New Orleans to the disaster. ☐

| **FACT BOX** | **New Orleans,** Louisiana |

- 1718 – New Orleans is founded by the French.
- 1803 – Napoleon sells Louisiana to the USA for about $15 million.
- 1838 – The first Mardi Gras takes place.
- About 1900 – a new style of music is born – jazz!
- Many famous musicians such as Louis Armstrong and Lenny Kravitz were born in New Orleans.
- Population of New Orleans:
  - August 2005, before Hurricane Katrina – 484,000.
  - February 2006 – almost 200,000.

Monday 29 August 2005

Hurricane Katrina Hits New Orleans

Hurricane Katrina has hit New Orleans with winds of 200 kilometres per hour. The levees which protect the city have broken and the waters of Lake Pontchartrain are pouring through the streets. Large areas of the city have been flooded and emergency services are looking for survivors.

4 Put these words from the text in the correct categories.

artist   audience   band   concert   drawings
exhibition   festival   frames   galleries
group   guitarist   play (n)   performance
playwright   portraits   sculptor   sculptures
songwriter   stage   venue

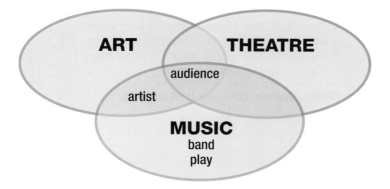

5 Work in pairs. What kinds of music are mentioned in the text? Can you think of any more? Make a list and compare it with another pair's.

6 Circle the correct words.

1 Although the main [1] *audience / venue* was destroyed in a fire, the music [2] *festival / frame* was a great success. The organisers built a temporary [3] *concert / stage* in the local park and the [4] *bands / plays* were able to perform there.

2 A small metal [5] *sculptor / sculpture* has been stolen from the modern art [6] *exhibition / portrait* in the Warehouse gallery.

3 After the first [7] *festival / performance* of her new play, the [8] *artist / playwright* spoke to the [9] *audience / venue* for more than an hour.

7 Work in groups and discuss one of the questions below. Use Speak Out on pages 9 and 31.

1 Do you think it was right to celebrate Mardi Gras so soon after Hurricane Katrina?

2 Can you think of any times when it is better to give in than to carry on? Choose from the ideas below:

a fight   a war   a sporting match   an exam
a job   a journey

New Orleans

Tuesday 28 February, 2006

I went to New Orleans only a week after Hurricane Katrina. Many streets were still under water and the city was a sad and lonely place. There was no music to be heard, only the sound of helicopters as rescuers searched for survivors. More than a thousand people had died. Tens of thousands had lost their homes. Perhaps four hundred thousand had fled.

The devastation was terrible: street after street of ruined houses and wrecked cars, dirty refrigerators under rotting trees. The city that many considered to be the most beautiful in North America looked as though it had been hit by a neutron bomb.

Six months later and it's Mardi Gras in New Orleans. Mardi Gras is French for Fat Tuesday and it's the culmination of twelve days of parties and parades. A celebration of life, food and fun. The city is full of people in masks and costumes, spectacular floats drive along the streets, jazz bands play outside grocery stores. Music has returned to New Orleans.

There are not as many people as usual but that's hardly surprising. Less than half the population has returned home since Katrina and much of the city is still a disaster zone. What might seem surprising is that there is anyone celebrating at all. Samuel Spears, a refugee in Houston, is angry, 'I can't go home, but they can have a parade? That's ridiculous!' However, Rob Clemenz, a lawyer

wearing a clown costume believes that the festivities will help the city to recover. 'We have to laugh. We need joy.' Katrina has not been forgotten in the parades. There are people with hats that look like storm-damaged roofs, and others with dirty lines on their trousers like the flood lines on the sides of their homes and a group dressed as blind men with walking sticks and dark glasses. On their T-shirts are the words 'levee inspector'.

But there is more to New Orleans than Mardi Gras. Songwriter Bob Dylan once said that New Orleans is a poem. It's a city of culture, a city of art and music is at its heart. This is the birthplace of jazz and home to a wonderful mix of funk, R'n'B, country, reggae and hip hop.

The French Quarter is alive with music again. On one side of the street a rock group plays a concert, on the other a blues singer gives a performance to make you cry and on stage in the Maple Leaf venue a jazz guitarist has his audience in the palm of his hand. Artists sell drawings and portraits without frames on the streets. A sculptor has collected bits of broken buildings and used them to make fantastic sculptures in a park. A dozen art galleries in the Warehouse District recently held a four-day exhibition to show they are back in business.

And it won't stop with Mardi Gras. At the end of March there is the annual festival in honour of playwright Tennessee Williams, who set his play *A Streetcar Named Desire* in the French Quarter. And at the end of April the Jazz and Heritage festival will take place as usual. It's all summed up by a slogan on a T-shirt. It reads, 'Katrina didn't wash away our spirit.' And it's true. The spirit of this amazing city, the joy of music and the strength of life have survived the hurricane.

The Modern World
Damian Parc

1

The Modern World
Damian Parc

2

LISTENING AND SPEAKING

1 **Work in pairs and answer the questions.**

1 Where are the women?
2 What do you think they are talking about?
3 Why do you think the works of art are called
   The Modern World?
4 Which work of art do you prefer? Why?

2 **CD3.3** **Listen to the conversation between Jun and Vanessa. Which photo corresponds to the exhibit they see?**

3 **CD3.3** **Listen again. Are the statements true (T), false (F) or is there no information (NI)?**

1 Both Jun and Vanessa love modern art. ☐
2 Jun's boyfriend is an artist. ☐
3 Jun has been to this gallery before. ☐
4 They find *The Modern World* very easily. ☐
5 Vanessa doesn't understand its meaning. ☐
6 Jun thinks the empty space represents
   the emptiness of modern life. ☐

4 **CD3.4** **Listen and circle the best answers.**

1 When Damian arrives, he …
   a is delighted to see Jun.
   b doesn't talk much.
   c is enthusiastic about the exhibition.
   d is interested in Vanessa.

2 Vanessa tells Damian she thinks *The Modern World* is …
   a alright.   c interesting.
   b terrible.   d amazing.

3 When Jun tells Damian how much she loves
   his work of art, he …
   a wonders where it is.
   b says it doesn't exist.
   c agrees with her.
   d says it isn't in the right place.

4 Damian is angry because …
   a *The Modern World* isn't there.
   b Jun hasn't understood it.
   c he thinks Vanessa doesn't like it.
   d he doesn't like the sign next to it.

5 When Damian goes away, Vanessa …
   a complains about the world today.
   b tells Jun she doesn't like *The Modern World*.
   c agrees with Jun.
   d laughs at what Jun says.

5 **CD3.5** **In pairs, decide what has happened to *The Modern World*. Listen and check.**

6 **CD3.6** **Listen and write E if the speaker is enthusiastic and I if the speaker is ironic.**

1 It's really great! ☐
2 It's absolutely wonderful! ☐
3 How fantastic! ☐
4 Amazing! ☐
5 I love it! ☐
6 It's very interesting! ☐

7 **Work in groups. Look at page 141. Use the expressions to discuss the works of art.**

SPEAKING AND LISTENING

1 Work in pairs. Describe the photo and answer the questions.

　1 What kind of performance is this?
　2 Do you enjoy going to performances like this?

2 `CD3.7` Listen to the conversation. Match the speakers (K) Kelly, (S) Sebastian and (B) Brendan with statements 1–8.

　1 ___ suggests going to an opera.
　2 ___ says young people don't go to operas.
　3 ___ points out that opera isn't as popular as other forms of entertainment.
　4 ___ claims young people aren't educated to enjoy opera.
　5 ___ thinks opera is too expensive for young people.
　6 ___ complains about the length of some operas.
　7 ___ says young people are too impatient to enjoy operas.
　8 ___ finds it strange that people sing to each other in operas and musicals.

3 `CD3.7` Complete Speak Out with headings a–f. Then listen again and check your answers.

　a Asking for explanation
　b Asking for repetition
　c Clarifying your message
　d Encouraging others to speak
　e Politely interrupting
　f Holding attention

SPEAK OUT | Participating in conversations

1 ☐
Excuse me, can I say something?
That's a good point, but …
Do you know what I think/(dis)like/find strange about …

2 ☐
Just a second, I haven't finished.
Hold on! Let me finish!

3 ☐
What I mean is …　The thing is …
Let me put it another way.

4 ☐
Do you see what I mean?　What do you think?
Why don't you tell us what you think/your opinion?

5 ☐
I'm sorry, I didn't get that. Could you say it again?
Sorry, I wasn't listening. Do you think you could repeat that?

6 ☐
Do you mean … ?　I'm not sure what you mean.
Are you saying … ?

4 Complete the conversation with one word in each space. Then look at Speak Out to check your answers.

Sebastian So, Brendan … Why don't you [1]_____ us what you think?
Brendan It was better than I expected.
Kelly Are you [2]_____ that you enjoyed the opera?
Brendan Well, I'm not going to buy a season ticket, but it was alright, I suppose.
Sebastian I'm sorry, I didn't [3]_____ that. Could you say it again?
Brendan Well, yeah, I kind of enjoyed it, but the second act was a bit hard to believe. Do you [4]_____ what I mean?
Kelly Not really.
Brendan Well, [5]_____ I mean is why didn't he tell her the truth?
Sebastian She won't let him. She keeps asking …
Brendan That's a good [6]_____ , but …
Sebastian Hold on! [7]_____ me finish! She keeps asking questions and he doesn't want to hurt her.
Brendan Yeah, I suppose it makes sense.
Kelly Do you [8]_____ what I think?
Sebastian What?
Kelly Madame Butterfly has got a new fan.

5 Work in small groups. Prepare your ideas on one of the topics below and then discuss it together. Use the expressions in Speak Out.

　1 The MTV generation have no patience. They want instant satisfaction.
　2 *Imagination without skill gives us modern art.* (Tom Stoppard)

VOCABULARY

1 **CD3.8** Check the meaning of the adjectives in the table. Then listen and add these modifying adverbs to the table. Which adverb goes with both kinds of adjectives?

a bit   extremely   really   totally   rather
quite   completely

Base adjectives

good   bad   silly   funny   attractive   exciting
surprising   interesting

Use: very, pretty, _____ , _____ ,
_____ , _____ , _____

Strong adjectives

brilliant   pathetic   ridiculous   hilarious
stunning   thrilling   amazing   fascinating
spectacular   dreadful

Use: absolutely, _____ , _____ ,
_____

Mind the trap!

We only use *a little/a bit/a little bit* before an adjective to give a negative opinion:

It's **a bit silly.** NOT It's a bit interesting.

We can't use it before an adjective + noun phrase:

The story is **a little bit boring.**
NOT It's a little bit boring story.

2 Cross out the adjectives which don't go with these adverbs.

1 a bit ~~brilliant~~ / *monotonous*
2 absolutely *brilliant* / *good*
3 totally *stunning* / *attractive*
4 quite *good* / *pathetic*
5 very *interesting* / *amazing*
6 absolutely *bad* / *dreadful*
7 totally *exciting* / *spectacular*

3 **CD3.9** Check film-making words a–g below. Use a dictionary to help you. Then listen and match them with expressions 1–7 from Exercise 2.

a acting ☐   e screenplay ☐
b directing ☐   f soundtrack ☐
c final scene ☐ g special effects ☐
d plot ☐

4 In groups, talk about films you have seen recently. Use the language from Exercises 1–3 to give your opinions.

A Have you seen … ? It's really good, isn't it?
B Good? It's absolutely brilliant! The special effects are totally amazing!

WRITING

1 **Think Back!** Work in pairs. Guess which kinds of films your partner likes.

action   cartoon   romance   documentary
comedy   fantasy   thriller   crime
horror   western

A You like thrillers, don't you?
B No, I don't.

2 **CD3.10** Work in pairs and circle the correct words in the quiz. Guess if you don't know. Then listen and check.

1 Nick Parks is *American / Australian / British*.
2 The characters are *computer images / drawings / made of plasticine*.
3 Wallace is a *dog / man / rabbit*.
4 Wallace loves eating *carrots / cheese / meat*.
5 Gromit is a very clever *dog / man / rabbit*.
6 The director, Nick Parks, has won *two / four / six* Oscars.

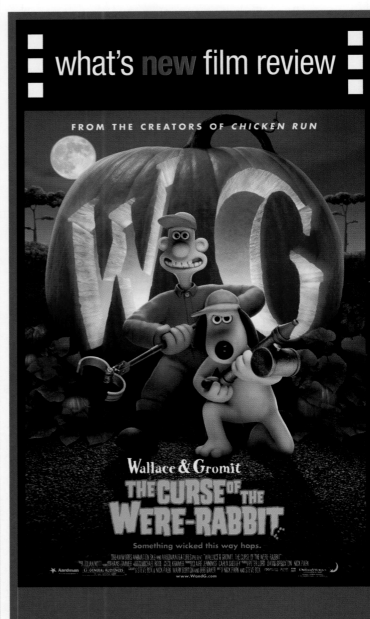

110

3 Read the film review and match points 1–4 with paragraphs a–d.

1 opinion of acting, screenplay ☐
2 summary and recommendation ☐
3 background information (name of film and directors, genre of film) ☐
4 plot and main characters ☐

4 Read the review again and tick the true sentences.

When writing a film review, you should:
• describe the plot with present tenses. ☐
• say what happens in the final scene. ☐
• use adjectives, adverbs and modifiers to give your opinions. ☐
• make a recommendation in your conclusion. ☐
• use either an informal or a formal style but not both at the same time. ☐

5 Read Train your Brain to check your answers to Exercises 3 and 4.

Scary Bunny

A *The Curse of the Were-Rabbit* (2005) is the first full length feature film made by directors Nick Park and Steve Box with their amazing plasticine characters Wallace and Gromit. It won an Oscar in 2006, and if you watch it, you'll understand why. It's an absolutely brilliant animated comedy.

B Cheese-loving inventor Wallace and his brainy dog Gromit have started a company to protect the town's vegetables from hungry rabbits. However, just before the annual Giant Vegetable Competition, an enormous rabbit begins terrorising the town. It is eating all the vegetables and destroying everything in its path. The competition organiser, Lady Tottington hires Wallace and Gromit to catch the monster alive. But they will have to find the were-rabbit before gun-crazy hunter Victor Quartermaine, who is desperate to kill it.

C The screenplay is witty and full of hilarious visual jokes. As usual, the voice of Peter Sallis is absolutely perfect for the role of Wallace, and Gromit is so beautifully animated he can express a huge range of emotions without saying a word. And both Helena Bonham-Carter, who plays the part of Lady Tottington, and Ralph Fiennes as Victor are really funny.

D To sum up, *The Curse of the Were-Rabbit* is an amazing film which is suitable for both children and adults. If you liked Wallace and Gromit's previous adventures and you appreciate the British sense of humour, you'll love this film. Don't miss it!

TRAIN YOUR BRAIN | Writing skills

A film review

Plan your review and use clear paragraphs:

Paragraph 1
• Give some background information: name of film and directors, genre of film, date, prizes won.
• If relevant, mention where and when the film is set.

Paragraph 2
• Describe the plot and the main characters.
• Use present tenses.
• Don't give too many details.
• Don't say what happens at the end.

Paragraph 3
• Give your opinion of some different aspects of the film: acting, screenplay, soundtrack, directing.

Paragraph 4
• Summarise your opinions.
• Make a recommendation.

Remember to:
• Use a variety of adjectives (strong adjectives and modifying adverbs).
• Avoid vague adjectives like *good, bad, nice.*
• Use either formal or informal style but don't mix them.

6 Work in pairs. Use the words in the box to complete these sentences from film reviews.

character   comedy   directed   fantasy
part   plot   set   soundtrack   stars

1 It's a _____ film in three parts.
2 It's _____ in Africa.
3 It's _____ by Tim Burton.
4 It _____ Orlando Bloom.
5 The main _____ is an archaeologist.
6 It's a really hilarious teen _____ .
7 Angelina Jolie plays the _____ of an evil gangster.
8 The acting is quite good, but the _____ is totally ridiculous.
9 I loved the _____ , which was composed by Danny Elfman. It's absolutely brilliant.

7 Write a review of a film you have seen recently.

• Choose a film you have seen recently or know very well.
• Make a plan with clear paragraphs. Use Train your Brain to help you.
• Use the language from Exercises 5–7 and from the vocabulary section on page 110.

VOCABULARY AND GRAMMAR

1 Circle the odd one out and explain why it does not fit.

1 a fringe   c pony-tail
  b plaits   d tonsils
2 a chest   c dimples
  b wrinkles d eyebrows
3 a razor   c skin cream
  b shampoo   d mousse
4 a scruffy   c smart
  b trendy   d fashionable
5 a hairdresser c body-builder
  b manicurist   d barber
6 a dyed   c cropped
  b bleached d pale
7 a plump   c slim
  b overweight d fat
8 a stubble   c suntan
  b moustache d goatee beard

2 Complete the sentences with the words in the box.

animated audience brilliant directors,
effects exhibitions festivals sense
soundtrack special stage stars witty

1 I have a season ticket so I pay less to go to
all the _____ in the local museum all
year round.
2 When the band appeared on _____ , the
_____ started clapping their hands.
3 A 'The _____ _____ in Lord of the
Rings were absolutely _____ , don't you
think?'
B 'Yes, and the music was really great. I think
I'll buy the _____ .'
4 I love going to film _____ where you can
not only see hundreds of feature films, but
also meet film _____ and _____ .
5 Although this _____ film was made for
children, adults can also appreciate the
_____ dialogue and the main characters'
_____ of humour.

3 Complete the text with the correct form of the words in brackets.

'The Body Beautiful' [1] _____ (exhibit) at the Town Hall
is a fascinating collection of photos taken over the last
sixty years by local photographers. It shows us that there
is more than one idea of beauty and that our ideas of a
perfect shape and look soon become outdated and
[2] _____ (fashion). Women considered beautiful in the
1950s would be thought [3] _____ (weigh) compared
to the skinny models of today. The [4] _____ (muscle)
male heroes of the 1950s are very different to those of
2006 and I'm sure they would think our casual look was
very [5] _____ (attract) compared to their elegant suits
and dresses. They certainly spent a lot of time in the
bathroom and the first [6] _____ (shave) face to be
seen was probably in 1995 when George Michael was
making facial hair popular.

You can see 'The Body Beautiful' all this week. Admission is
free and I very much recommend that you visit.

4 Complete each gap with *a*, *an*, *the* or no article (Ø).

Make-up

During [1]____ nineteenth century it was
unfashionable to wear [2]____ cosmetics. But
[3]____ rich women began using them again after
[4]____ First World War. In 1921 Coco Chanel
created Chanel Number 5, which became
[5]____ best-selling perfume in [6]____ world.
When [7]____ make-up became cheaper in [8]____
1940s it finally became popular with [9]____
ordinary women.

Wigs

[10]____ wigs have been worn for [11]____
thousands of years. In Ancient Egypt, for
instance, [12]____ people wore them to protect
their shaven heads from [13]____ sun. They
became popular in [14]____ sixteenth century:
[15]____ Queen Elizabeth of [16]____ England wore
[17]____ red wig, tightly curled, and King Louis
XII popularised wig-wearing among [18]____men
in [19]____ France. Today wigs are worn mainly
for [20]____ fun and to hide [21]____ hair loss. In
[22]____ Britain, [23]____ special wigs are worn by
[24]____ lawyers appearing in court.

5 Complete the sentences so that they mean the same as the original sentences.

1 We need someone to tidy up our garden.
  We need to _____
  _____ .
2 I must ask someone to check my printer.
  I must have _____
  _____ .
3 Kate is very similar to her aunt Alice.
  Kate looks _____
  _____ .
4 Where is the entrance to the gallery?
  Do you know _____
  _____ ?
5 Is this film a comedy?
  I wonder _____
  _____ ?
6 I must go to the hairdresser because my hair
  is too long.
  I must have _____
  _____ .

PRONUNCIATION

1 [CD3.11] Read the words. In each group circle the word that has a different vowel sound. Then listen and check.

1 free / cinema / ticket / instant
2 cleaner / feet / lips / teens
3 skin / fitness / artist / clean
4 slim / wig / build / keep
5 trim / middle / season / kilt
6 witty / feature / flee / goatee

FIT OR FAT?

The cheerful Mr Pickwick, the hero of the novel by Charles Dickens, is always shown in illustrations as someone who is plump – and happy. He is also one of Dickens' wittiest creations. But nowadays being overweight no longer has such positive connotations. [1]____

However, doctors are worried that despite these dangers, more and more British people are seriously overweight. What's worse, the number of children who are overweight before they reach their teens is growing rapidly. [2]____

Going on a diet seems the obvious answer, but is it? Not according to England's chief medical officer, Sir Liam Donaldson. [3]____ And the Health Secretary John Reid even said that not being active is as dangerous for your heart as smoking.

So, how much exercise should you do? According to Sir Liam Donaldson, at least 30 minutes of moderate activity five days a week. Is going to the gym the answer? According to a sports psychologist, Professor Biddle, gyms 'are not making the nation fit'. And experts at the Health Development Agency believe that physical activity that fits into people's lives may be more effective. [4]____

Indeed, there's new scientific evidence that too much exercise may actually be dangerous [5]____ The only people who should push their bodies to that level of exercise on a regular basis are trained athletes.

One final thought. How come people in the past didn't have gym facilities and yet were leaner and fitter than people today?

READING SKILLS

1   **Read the article. Fill gaps 1–5 with sentences a–f. There is one extra sentence.**

   a He says that physical activity is the key to reducing the risks of obesity, cancer and heart disease.
   b Scientists at the University of Ulster have found that if you are not used to aerobic exercise, it may actually be bad for your health.
   c The problem is so serious that even the government has decided it has to take responsibility for this expanding problem.
   d They suggest taking the stairs rather than the lift, playing active games with your children, dancing or gardening.
   e So, it's probably best to choose which diet is best for you.
   f Instead, being overweight might mean an increased risk of many diseases, like heart disease or strokes.

SPEAKING SKILLS

1   **Choose one of the topics and prepare a 3-minute presentation.**

   • Going to the cinema and theatre will disappear one day due to DVDs and the Internet.
   • Most popular music nowadays is not a product of imagination and passion, but only a commercial product to make money.

2   **Work in pairs. Take turns and describe a person from each category to each other. You have a minute to guess who your partner is describing.**

   1 one of your classmates
   2 one of your teachers
   3 a famous sports star
   4 a famous cartoon/TV series character
   5 a famous film star
   6 a famous television personality
   7 a famous pop star

13

Game over

Read, listen and talk about games and sports.
Practise quantifiers and possessives.
Focus on making and responding to offers.
Write a review, an opinion essay.

THIS WEEK'S REVIEWS

Some people say there aren't any original games nowadays, and it's true that there aren't many new ideas around. In fact, none of the games I've tested this week are original, but most of them are fun.

PC DVD ROM

Alien Control 3

16+   Legend Software

PC DVD ROM

Virtual History

3+   Retro Games

PC DVD ROM

DRIVE HARD

7+   21ST GAMES

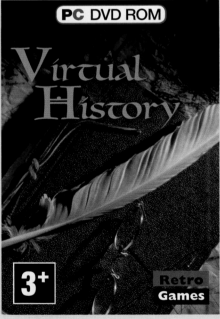

Most of my friends don't like historical games and think they're all boring. Personally, I thought both *Past Times* and *Heritage* were interesting, although it's true they weren't much fun. But *Virtual History* is different. It's just like travelling in time. It isn't easy. You need a little patience and some historical knowledge to help you reach the end, but it's a good game and it's got lots of fascinating puzzles.

Most gamers enjoy shoot 'em up games and all of my friends love *Alien Control*. Well *Alien Control 3* is even better! In both of the previous versions the aliens were in control. But now the humans are fighting back. The graphics are awesome. Is there a lot of violence? Well, yes, but none of the violence is unnecessary. The only downside is there are too many weapons and there isn't much time to choose which one to use.

Drive Hard is a car-racing game with too many accidents and too much blood. The controls are imprecise, there isn't any decent music and neither the sound nor the graphics are good. Are there any good points? Well, it has a few interesting ideas, but it hasn't got many options and it takes less time to play than it does to open the box. The makers of this game must think they can fool all of the people most of the time or most of the people all of the time. But they can't fool me. Boring!

	Alien Control 3	Drive Hard	Virtual History	The Shams at School
Multi-player	yes	yes	no	yes
Addiction Level	high	low	medium	medium
Our experts recommend	6/6	0/6	5/6	3/6
Value for money	90%	20%	90%	70%

BEST BUY

It depends what kind of games you like, but this week either *Alien Control 3* or *Virtual History* is the best buy.

More game reviews on next page.

GRAMMAR AND READING

1 Work in pairs. Look at the games and decide which one you prefer. Then read the reviews and say which game you would rather play and why.

2 Think Back! Which quantifiers below do we use with countable nouns (C), uncountable nouns (U) or both (B)?

1 (too) many	☐	**6** some	☐
2 (too) much	☐	**7** a few	☐
3 a lot/lots of	☐	**8** a little	☐
4 not many	☐	**9** not any	☐
5 not much	☐		

Work it out

3 Find sentences in the reviews including the words *all*, *most* or *none*. Then study the information in the table and use the words to complete the sentences.

1 ___ of the games are new.
2 ___ of them are fun.
3 ___ of them are original.

New	**8**
Fun	**7**
Original	**0**
Games reviewed	**8**

4 Find sentences in the reviews including the words *both*, *neither* or *either*. Study the rules in the table and then use the words to complete the example sentences.

---

both, neither and either

- We use *both*, *neither* and *either* to talk about only two people or things.
- *Both* is always followed by a plural verb.
- *Neither* and *either* can be followed by a singular or plural verb.
- We use *both + and*, *neither + nor*, *either + or*.

Game A is good and Game B is good.
1 _____ Game A and Game B are good.
2 _____ games are good.
Only one game is the best.
3 _____ Game A or Game B is the best.
Game A is bad and Game B is bad.
4 _____ Game A nor Game B is good.

Mind the trap!

When we talk about specific groups of people/things we can use quantifiers with or without *of*. But remember to use a determiner (*the/my* ...) after *of*.

Most people in **my** class like historical games.
Most **of the** people in my class like historical games.
NOT ~~Most of people in my class ...~~

We always use a quantifier with *of* before pronouns.

Most **of** them like these games.
NOT ~~Most them like ...~~

5 Work in pairs. Look at the table on page 114 and use the words below to complete the sentences.

a all	**c** both	**e** most	**g** none				
b any	**d** either	**f** neither	**h** some				

1 _____ *Alien Control 3* and *Drive Hard* can be played with another player.
2 _____ *Drive Hard* nor *Virtual History* is very addictive.
3 _____ of the experts recommend *Alien Control 3*.
4 *Drive Hard* didn't get _____ votes from the magazine's experts.
5 _____ of the experts recommend *Virtual History*.
6 _____ of the experts recommend *The Shams at School*.
7 The best game to buy is _____ *Alien Control 3* or *Virtual History*.
8 How many of the games offer 100 percent value for money? _____ of them.

6 Complete sentences 1–8 with phrases a–h.

a young people	**e** the cheats	
b strategy games	**f** them	
c games magazines	**g** time	
d my classmates	**h** these games	

1 I've read a few ___ .
2 Most ___ take days to play.
3 Which of these consoles do you like? – None of ___ .
4 None of ___ are too difficult.
5 Many ___ prefer playing to studying.
6 Some of ___ don't like computer games.
7 I already know most of ___ for this game.
8 You don't have much ___ to think in this game.

7 Use the words in brackets to rewrite the sentences so that they have the same meaning as the original sentences.

1 This is the best game. (any/as good as)
   There aren't any games as good as this one.
2 Look at these consoles. They are all expensive. (none/cheap)
3 Except for Tom, all of my friends play computer games. (most)
4 *Drive Hard* isn't very good and *Break Free* isn't very good. (neither)
5 *Virtual History* is an educational game. *Maths Fun* is educational, too. (both)
6 I'm going to buy a computer game. I like *Skypilot* and *Lost Treasure*. (either)
7 There are two games on my computer. (many)
8 I'm too busy to play games. (much/time)

8 Work in pairs. Use quantifiers from this lesson to write a review of three computer games. Then compare your reviews with your classmates'. (If you don't know any games, invent some!)

READING

1 Work in pairs. Describe the photo on page 117 and answer the questions.

1 Where do you think this place is?
2 Would you like to go to a place like this? Why?/Why not?

2 **CD ROM** Read the article and find out where the place in the photo is. Then choose the best summary of the article.

1 A guide to unusual sports facilities around the world.
2 A look at why we play games and how they may affect the future.
3 A historical guide to the development of sports and games.

3 Read the text again and circle the correct answers.

1 The writer finds it very surprising that Ski Dubai …
   a is so large.
   b is in the middle of a desert.
   c is not hotter.
   d has a ski-lift.

2 The writer thinks …
   a we should spend more on sports facilities.
   b our sports stars deserve the money they earn.
   c we don't spend enough time playing games.
   d we take games more seriously than real problems.

3 The writer …
   a is sure that all sports-lovers are obsessed.
   b crashed his car after a football match.
   c is addicted to football.
   d agrees that football is more important than life or death.

4 The article mentions the idea that …
   a sports fans take drugs.
   b humans play sports instead of fighting.
   c chess is the most peaceful game in the world.
   d armies should fight in stadiums.

5 A recent scientific study suggests that some computer games …
   a help people to relax.
   b may make people more violent.
   c may make people less aggressive.
   d encourage people to work together.

6 Which of these points does the writer mention?
   a It is a natural instinct to want to play.
   b Games can help people and animals adapt to life.
   c Games may become too realistic.
   d All of the above.

4 Match venues a–g with sports 1–7. Read the text again to check your answers.

a pitch   e course
b ring   f slope
c rink   g stadium
d court

1 athletics ☐   5 skating ☐
2 boxing   ☐   6 ski   ☐
3 football   ☐   7 tennis   ☐
4 golf   ☐

5 Find these linking words and phrases in the text and use them to complete these sentences.

however although despite what's more
instead of

1 I can't do anything about it _____ I know it's stupid.
2 Some computer games are very popular _____ being violent.
3 The ski-slopes were too crowded so _____ skiing we went for a camel ride.
4 It sounds crazy. _____ , it just shows how serious people are about having fun.
5 Games help us perfect our skills. _____ , they prepare us for survival.

6 Work in groups of three. Choose one role each and discuss the statement below. Use the language in Speak Out on pages 9 and 109.

'Too many people spend too much time playing games and sports.'

Student A You love sports. You run marathons, do aerobics and play in a volleyball team. You are very competitive and you always try to win. You believe that it is essential to have a healthy body and a healthy mind. You don't like watching sports or playing computer games.

Student B You love computer games. You believe they teach you a lot about the world and improve your hand-to-eye co-ordination and your computer skills. You don't like playing sports very much, but you enjoy watching football and tennis on the TV.

Student C You think young people should take part in sports, but should not be obsessed with winning. You also think most young people spend too much time watching sport on the TV. And you are worried that violent computer games make people aggressive.

7 Write an opinion essay on the statement in Exercise 6. Use the ideas from your discussion, the linking words in Exercise 5 and Train your Brain on page 57.

Sports Crazy

Look carefully at this photograph. What can you say about it? There are some people waiting to get on a ski-lift, others skiing down the hill, and the sky looks kind of funny.

In fact, it's one of the world's largest indoor ski-slopes. It covers an area of 22,500m² which is about the same size as three football pitches, and the temperature is a constant −1° to −2°C. However, the strangest thing about this place is that it's in the middle of the desert! It's called Ski Dubai and the outside temperatures can rise to more than 40°C!

It sounds crazy, but it just shows how serious people are about having fun. We spend huge sums on sports facilities. We pay our sports stars ridiculous amounts of money. And we spend hour after hour playing games although we know there are millions of people in the world with no water to drink and no food to eat!

It makes me wonder if all the sports-lovers and game-players in the world aren't a little bit obsessed. I know I am. I suffer from a very common obsession called football. It made me crash my car. I was driving past a football pitch where some kids were playing. I turned to watch and smashed right into the car in front of me. I can't help it. I see someone playing football and I've just got to stop and stare. I know it's stupid but I can't do anything about it. I'm addicted. As someone once said, 'Football isn't a matter of life and death. It's much more important than that!'

Of course, it isn't that important really. No game is. But the problem is that games are addictive. From the boxing ring to the skating rink, and from the tennis court to the golf course, you'll find participants and spectators who can't live without the drug of their choice. It could be a good thing. After all, despite being addictive, it's true that sports and games help us to relax. Maybe if it wasn't for sport, our societies would be more violent. Perhaps sport is a substitute for war? It's hard to think of a quieter, more peaceful game than chess, and yet what's the objective? Capturing your opponent's king. And surely, it's better to have wars in athletics stadiums rather than on battlefields? Even if we do have to put up with football hooligans.

What's more, playing is natural. Kittens chase balls of wool and puppies pretend to fight. Games help us perfect our skills and prepare us for the serious contest of survival. They are a rehearsal for real life.

But do all games help us relax and make us less violent? What about computer games? A recent article in *New Scientist* suggests that playing violent video games (and most of them are extremely violent) makes people more aggressive, more likely to commit violent crimes and less likely to help others.

Are these games a rehearsal for life or a substitute for life? Do we play instead of facing up to our real problems? Are games nothing more than an escape from boredom? And if that's so, then what will become of us in the future? Will games become so realistic that we won't be able to distinguish reality from virtual reality? Will they become so attractive that we will want to spend most of our time inside an artificial world? A Matrix?

I don't know. But what I do know is that I need a break. Something to help me relax. Skiing would be nice. I wonder how much it costs to get to Dubai?

GRAMMAR AND LISTENING

1 Work in pairs. Describe the photo below and answer the questions.

    1 What kind of sporting event do you think is going to take place?

    2 Have you ever been to a major sporting event? If so, what did you like/not like about it?

2 Check you know the meaning of this football vocabulary. Use a dictionary to help you.

    captain   corner kick   goalkeeper
    half-time   header   penalty   referee
    score (n)   score a goal   first/second half
    shot   team

3 **CD3.12** Work in pairs. Listen and complete the match statistics.

> **World Cup final – Brazil beat England**
>
> **Half-time score:** Brazil ___   England ___
>
> **Final Score:** Brazil ___   England ___
>
> **Goal scorer for Brazil:** Richardinho
>
> **Goal scorer for England:** ___

Work it out

4 Study the sentences in the table and complete gaps a–f with these words/phrases.

    1 people   **4** time expressions
    2 places   **5** groups of people
    3 things   **6** words like *end, top, front, middle*

Possessives
We use the possessive *'s* after: ᵃ _____ or animals, ᵇ _____ It's the **referee's** decision that counts. We were exhausted after last **Wednesday's** game.
We use *of* with: ᶜ _____ and for parts of things after ᵈ _____ Brazil are the winners of the **World Cup**. They lost a goal right at the **end** of the game.
We can use both forms after: ᵉ _____ , ᶠ The **team's** plan was to give the Brazilians no time. Des is talking to the captain of the English **team**. Ricardinho was playing football in the streets of **Rio** and now he's **Brazil's** most famous person.

> ### Mind the trap!
>
> When something belongs to two people we put the possessive *'s* after the second name.
>
> Bob and John**'s** team is the best.
> NOT ~~Bob's and John's team~~ …
>
> When it is clear which noun we are talking about, we can drop it.
>
> Whose team do you play for? – Tom**'s**.
> It is obvious we mean Tom's team.

5 **CD3.13** Circle the correct phrases. Then listen and check.

1 Brazil are the *World Cup's winners /*
winners of the World Cup.
2 Ricardinho scored at the *second-half's start /*
start of the second half.
3 It was *Sid's first goal / the first goal of Sid's.*
4 I'm not going to read *tomorrow's papers /*
the papers of tomorrow.
5 We only had *three days' rest / the rest of*
three days before the final.

6 Tick the correct sentences and correct the wrong ones.

1 The ball hit the net's back. ☐
2 England's fans behaved well. ☐
3 He's got a lucky rabbit's foot. ☐
4 They're the football boots of Tommy. ☐
5 The rules of our club are out of date. ☐
6 The game of last Saturday was cancelled. ☐
7 They lost a goal in the first half's middle. ☐

7 Read the prompts and write correct possessive phrases.

1 champions/last year
last year's champions
2 head/the cat
3 richest club/Europe
4 the end/the world
5 office/the manager
6 result/yesterday
7 star player/the team
8 the goal/the tournament

8 **CD3.14** Use phrases 1–8 from Exercise 7 to complete the story. Then listen and check. Who is speaking and what is the manager telling him?

I was in ¹*the manager's office* . There was a cat on
his desk and he was stroking ²_____ , but
he didn't look happy. He said, 'This is
³_____ . Right now we're the best, but
we've got to stay at the top. Our fans never
want to be ⁴_____ . They want to win every
game. Last year you were ⁵_____ . You
scored ⁶_____ in the World Cup last
summer. But in this sport you're only as good
as ⁷_____ and yesterday we lost and you
missed a penalty.' I defended myself. 'But we've
only lost one game. It's not ⁸_____ !' He
looked at me. His eyes were cold. 'Isn't it?'

9 Work in pairs. Tell each other about a sporting event. Use as many possessives as you can.

My sister's volleyball team was playing in a match to
celebrate the end of the school year and …

LISTENING

1 Work in pairs. Look at the list of games and pastimes and answer the questions. Use a dictionary to help you.

Cards ☐   Chess ☐   Cluedo ☐
Crosswords ☐   Draughts ☐   Jigsaws ☐
Monopoly ☐   Risk ☐   Scrabble ☐
Solitaire ☐   Sudoku ☐   Trivial Pursuit ☐

Which games and pastimes …
1 can you see in the photos?
2 have you played before?
3 are you good at?
4 are/aren't popular in your country?
5 do you prefer?

2 **CD3.15** Listen and tick the games and pastimes from Exercise 1 that you hear. Then answer the questions.

1 What is the name of the programme?
2 What kind of programme is it?
3 Who is the guest?
4 What has she done?

3 **CD3.15** Listen again and complete the table with information about the games and pastimes.

	Monopoly	*Chess*	*Sudoku*
When was it invented?	1935		
Who invented it?		Not sure – Indians/ Chinese?	
Why is it popular?			People like using their brains

4 Prepare a presentation about a game or pastime.

- Follow the advice in Speak Out on page 49.
- Find out when and where it originated, how popular it is, the rules.
- Say why you think people enjoy it.

119

badminton   golf   rugby   ice hockey

ice-skating   the long jump   cricket   gymnastics

boxing   windsurfing   squash   diving

water skiing   snowboarding   chess   handball

VOCABULARY

1 Work in pairs. How many of these types of sports can you find above?

indoor sports   outdoor sports   ball sports
team sports   individual sports
winter sports   water sports

2 Study the rules and match the sports from Exercise 1 to the verbs in the table. Then, in small groups, talk about the sports you do.

We use the verb *play* with games.
We use the verb *go* with outdoor activities ending in *-ing*.
We use the verb *do* with other activities and indoor activities ending in *-ing*.

play	*go*	*do*
ice hockey badminton	water skiing	gymnastics
————	————	————
————	————	————
————	————	
————		

A I go snowboarding every winter.
B Do you? I'd love to try that. I play badminton three times a week.

3 Work in pairs. Read clues 1–6 and work out which sports from the pictures opposite these people like.

1 All of them like outdoor sports.
2 None of them likes team sports.
3 Two of them like winter sports.
4 Gary hits a ball.
5 Ashley's sport is noisy.
6 Julie has to go up before she can come down.

Gary _____   Sol _____
Julie _____   Ashley _____

4 Read the text and match phrasal verbs 1–8 with their synonyms a–h. Use a dictionary to help you.

a exercise ☐   **e** recover from ☐
b continue ☐   **f** reduce ☐
c follow ☐   **g** start ☐
d gain ☐   **h** stop ☐

When I ¹gave up smoking I ²put on a lot of weight and my doctor told me to ³go on a diet and to ⁴take up a sport or a hobby. So, I ⁵cut down on sweets and joined a gym where I could ⁶work out every morning. Unfortunately, I hurt my back on the rowing machine so I stopped going.

When I ⁷got over my backache, I took up jogging. At first, it was great, but then I felt dizzy and I got a pain in my leg. Stupidly, I ⁸kept on running and I twisted my ankle.

The next thing I tried was hill walking but I got lost in a storm. The next day I had a terrible cold and a sore throat and I couldn't stop coughing and sneezing. I also had terrible blisters on my feet.

Then I went skiing. It was fun, but after the first day my knees were swollen, and on the second day I fell and broke my leg.

Finally, I went sailing. Never again! Before we had even left the port, I felt really ill and I couldn't stop vomiting.

Now I've taken up knitting. I haven't lost any weight, but at least I'm happy.

5 Read the text again and find the health problems that were caused by these sports. Use a dictionary to help you.

Rowing machine   backache
Jogging
Hill walking
Skiing
Sailing

6 Work in pairs. Use the ideas below to interview your partner.

- how/stay in shape
- how often/practise/favourite sports
- ever/take part/competitions
- win/medals/cups
- which sport/like/take up
- have/health problems/sport

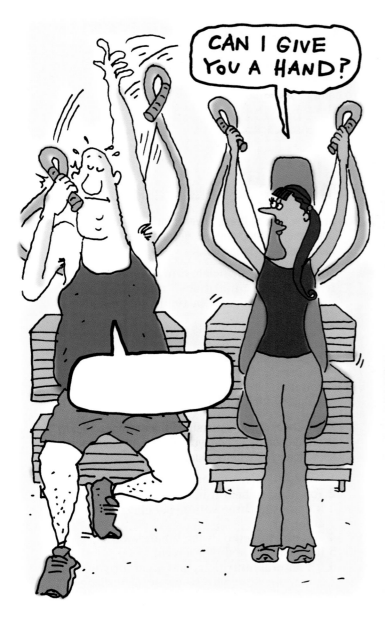

SPEAKING AND LISTENING

1 **CD3.16** Work in pairs. Look at the cartoon and choose the best response (a–c). Listen and check.

a That would be great, thanks.
b No, it's alright, thanks. I know what I'm doing.
c Yes, please. I've no idea what I'm doing.

2 **CD3.17** Listen and circle the correct answers (a–c). Then say what problems the people have.

1 Roger is …
 a watching a football match.
 b training for a football match.
 c about to start playing a football match.

2 Mary is …
 a playing a computer game.
 b buying a new computer game.
 c installing a game on her computer.

3 Jane is …
 a working out in a gym.
 b admiring a friend's exercise machine.
 c trying to make an exercise machine work.

3 **CD3.17** Listen again and complete the gaps in the Speak Out box with the words below.

alright   do   great   hand   like   look
please   Shall   want   Why   worry   Would

SPEAK OUT | Making offers

Offering help
I'll have a ¹_____ at it if you like.
Would you ²_____ me to do it for you?
³_____ I do it?
Can I give you a ⁴_____ ?
⁵_____ don't you let me try?
Do you ⁶_____ me to help?

Accepting
That would be ⁷_____ , thanks a lot.
Yes ⁸_____ , I haven't got a clue what I'm doing.
⁹_____ you? Thanks, I don't know how to do it.

Refusing
No, it's ¹⁰_____ thanks. I know what I'm doing.
I'd rather ¹¹_____ it myself. Thanks, anyway.
Don't ¹²_____ about it. I can do it on my own.

---

4 Match the words and phrases Then look at Speak Out to check your answers. What other combinations are possible?

1 I'll   ☐   a do it?
2 Would you like   ☐   b give you a hand?
3 Shall I   ☐   c have a look at it if
4 Can I   ☐   you like.
5 Why don't you   ☐   d let me try?
6 Do you want   ☐   e me to do it for you?
                              f me to help?

5 Work in pairs. Use expressions from Speak Out to roleplay these situations.

1 A Your bike has got a flat tyre. You don't know how to fix it.
  B Offer to help.
  A Refuse. You don't want your friend to get dirty hands.
  B Explain that you can wash your hands afterwards and offer again.
  A Accept.

2 B You can't finish a Sudoku puzzle.
  A Offer to help.
  B Refuse. Explain that you are almost finished.
  A Explain that you are very good at Sudoku and offer again.
  B Refuse again. You want to do it yourself.

3 B It's your best friend's birthday. You can't decide which computer game to buy her.
  A Offer to help.
  B Refuse, but say how difficult it is because there are so many games.
  A Explain that you know a lot about games. Offer again.
  B Accept.

The hard sell

Read, listen and talk about advertising; food; shopping and services.
Practise verb patterns; adjectives and prepositions.
Focus on making and responding to complaints, collocations.
Write a letter of complaint.

A

FRISCO'S
- Marvelbread -

Lets you see exactly the loaf you want

ENRICHED BREAD WRAPPED IN CELLOPHANE

A MODERN MARVEL!

B

Crosswell's *Garden-Pride* peas

Makes every meal special

Crosswell's Garden-Pride PEAS

GRAMMAR AND LISTENING

1 In pairs, look at these adverts for early American convenience food and answer the questions. Use the ideas below to help you.

(un)healthy   artificial/natural ingredients
fresh   frozen   nutritious   microwavable
pre-cooked   sliced   tasty/bland   tinned

- What sort of products are shown?
- Do they look tasty?
- How popular is convenience food in your country? What sort of products are most common?
- What's your opinion of this sort of food? Why?

2 **CD3.18** Check if you understand the sentences below. Use a dictionary to help you. Then listen and match sentences 1–7 with products A–C.

1 You need a saucepan to prepare it/them. ☐
2 You need to heat it in an oven. ☐
3 It comes in three varieties – chicken, beef and pork. ☐
4 You don't need to wash up afterwards. ☐
5 It doesn't go stale for a week. ☐
6 It's natural, nutritious and good for you. ☐
7 It can be eaten with stews or meat dishes. ☐

C

Agnew's TV Dinner

the convenient *choice*

for today's TV Family

3 **CD3.18** Listen again and match the adjectives with products A–C.

appetising ☐   convenient ☐   creamy ☐
delicious ☐   fresh ☐   juicy ☐   lean ☐
natural ☐   revolutionary ☐
sensational ☐

Work it out

4 Put the <u>underlined</u> phrases from the adverts into the table below.

1 Are you <u>tired of</u> eating the same meals?
2 You don't <u>need to</u> use plates!
3 Do you <u>keep</u> throwing out stale bread?
4 Every meal <u>can</u> be special.
5 They <u>make</u> soup taste more appetising.
6 Heat in a saucepan <u>before</u> serving!
7 We're <u>famous for</u> using only the best.
8 Do you just <u>hate</u> washing-up?
9 The next time you <u>feel like</u> cooking something truly sensational …
10 <u>It's worth</u> changing to Marvelbread.

Verb patterns

We use the *-ing* form after:
* some verbs (*admit, avoid, fancy, miss, stop, practise, enjoy, imagine, _____ , _____*)
* verb + preposition/phrasal verbs (*succeed at, apologise for, dream about, think about, look forward to, give up , _____*)
* adjective + preposition (*good at, interested in, proud of, sorry for, _____, _____*)
* some expressions (*after, by, instead of, when, I don't mind, I can't stand, without, _____ , _____*)

We use the infinitive with *to* after: (*agree, allow, decide, expect, hope, learn, manage, offer, promise, refuse, seem, want, would like, _____*)

We use the infinitive without *to* after:
modal verbs (*must, might, will, should, _____*)
other verbs with an object (*let, _____*)

Mind the trap!

There are some verbs that can go with more than one verb pattern but the meaning is basically the same.

She started/continued/began/prefers/loves **learning** English.
OR She started/continued/began/prefers/loves **to learn** English.

He helped me **install** the program onto my computer.
OR He helped me **to install** the program.

---

5 Complete the sentences with the correct form of the words in brackets.

1 Eating chilli peppers makes me _____ (sweat).
2 You should _____ (shake) the bottle before _____ (open) it.
3 I'm thinking about _____ (become) a vegetarian.
4 I'm tired of _____ (cook) – do you fancy _____ (eat) out?
5 Would you like _____ (help) me _____ (peel) these potatoes?
6 Why do you keep _____ (drink) coffee when you know you can't _____ (sleep) afterwards?
7 He decided _____ (go) on a diet – he's already managed _____ (lose) a few kilos.
8 The blackcurrant juice is on special offer this week. It's worth _____ (buy) a few extra cartons.
9 Do you feel like _____ (get) a takeaway pizza tonight?
10 Dad's a very nervous cook. He doesn't let anyone _____ (watch) him in the kitchen.
11 I was in a hurry so she offered _____ (make) me a packed lunch.
12 She seems _____ (relax) by _____ (eat) junk food in front of the TV.

6 Use the words/phrases in brackets to write a new sentence with a similar meaning.

1 Becky's parents only let her come home late at the weekends.   ALLOW
2 After several minutes, they succeeded in finding a table that was free.   MANAGE
3 I'd like to learn another foreign language.   INTERESTED IN
4 Do you feel like going for a cup of coffee?   FANCY
5 They didn't allow us to bring pets with us.   LET
6 We must book a table for this evening.   NEED
7 Do you want to order a takeaway pizza?   FEEL LIKE

7 In pairs, write the prepositions that go with these adjectives. Then use them to make sentences that are true for you. Use a dictionary to help you.

1 excited _____   5 keen _____
2 fed up _____   6 worried _____
3 fond _____   7 good _____
4 hopeless _____

I'm keen on swimming. I'm excited about finishing school in June.

READING AND VOCABULARY

1 Read the first paragraph of each letter A–C.

Which writer:
1 agrees with Judy Boyle's article. ____
2 partially agrees with Judy Boyle's article. ____
3 disagrees with Judy Boyle's article. ____

2 CD ROM Quickly read the letters and try to decide what Judy Boyle wrote about in her article.

3 Choose the best title for each letter to the editor A–C. There are two titles that you don't need.

1 More advertising clichés.
2 How advertising helps the economy.
3 Life before advertising.
4 Why advertising is a good thing.
5 How advertising makes us unhappy.

4 Find these words and phrases in the letters. How would you say them in your language?

Letter A: advertising   TV commercial
(advertising) slogan   ad-break
Letter B: ad/advert   advertising agency
Letter C: spam   billboard   junk mail
leaflet   poster

5 Read the letters again. Tick true and cross false.

1 Ashley Coates believes that, thanks to advertising, there is a bigger range of newspapers and magazines on the market. ☐
2 He suggests that the 1940s were an exciting decade to live in. ☐
3 He thinks that adverts take a lot of their ideas from pop videos. ☐
4 Duncan Grant uses the example of car adverts to show how exciting adverts can be. ☐
5 He suggests that stereotypes in adverts don't change very quickly. ☐
6 Jean Cox doesn't believe that people have contact with 3,000 advertising messages each day. ☐
7 She thinks that advertising makes us feel that what we own is never good enough. ☐

6 Work in groups and answer the questions.

1 Which of the opinions in the letters do you agree with most? Why?
2 What is your favourite billboard/TV advert? Why do you like it?
3 Can you think of any advertising slogans which have entered everyday language?
4 Can you think of any more clichés or stereotypes that are used in adverts?

Dear Sir/Madam,

I am writing in response to Judy Boyle's article, 'Time To Declare War on Advertising' which appeared in Saturday's paper. As someone who works in the advertising profession, I have to say that many of Ms Boyle's views are exaggerated or simply wrong.

Firstly, I'm surprised that Ms Boyle, a journalist on one of the biggest daily newspapers, doesn't realise that most of her newspaper's income comes from advertising. If advertising didn't exist, newspapers would be more expensive – and thinner! And there is no doubt that there would be fewer titles to choose from. This is also true of magazines and TV channels. Does Ms Boyle really want a return to the days without advertising – the Dark Ages of the 1940s – when there was one public TV
10   channel, two public radio stations and dull magazines and newspapers?

Ms Boyle complains about how irritating adverts are. I wonder if she has a sense of humour? Hasn't she noticed that adverts are entertaining and, above all, informative? It's a sad fact that there are often more ideas and creativity in a thirty-second TV commercial than there are in the programmes that come before or after it. Everyone has a favourite advert that we look forward to seeing. Adverts often capture the public's imagination and we talk about them and even start to use their slogans in everyday situations. Comedians make jokes about them. Pop video producers copy their ideas.

If adverts irritate Ms Boyle so much, there is a simple solution. The three-minute ad-break on TV is just enough time to make a nice cup of tea. And while you're in the kitchen, Ms Boyle, look at the box of teabags. Why did you decide to buy them? A long, serious discussion with friends about
20   different teabags? Or was it perhaps thanks to a memorable thirty-second advert?

Yours faithfully,

Ashley Coates
Coates Advertising Associates
LONDON N5

B

Dear Sir/Madam,

After reading Judy Boyle's article in Saturday's paper ('Time To Declare War on Advertising') I wanted to congratulate her on a brilliant piece.

Like Ms Boyle, I am also fed up with the ridiculous stereotypes you find in adverts. Look at car adverts, for example. In adverts, driving is never stressful or boring - it's one of the most exciting things a man can experience (for women it's eating chocolate). There are never traffic jams because when you buy a new car all the roads magically become empty of traffic.

10 There are other mysteries. Why does nobody wear glasses - unless it's an advert for an optician's? Why do women in adverts always slowly brush their hair in a kind of trance? How do they find the time? In my house, people would start banging on the bathroom door because they wanted to use the shower. And why do people who eat yoghurts always look as if they've just discovered the meaning of life? And are biscuits really that exciting?

I don't know anyone who behaves like the people who I have to watch on my TV every twenty minutes. And yet, I have been watching fools like these advertise products for the past twenty years! Do people who work for advertising agencies have any contact with real life? Or do they just sit in their offices and watch old adverts all day?

20 I wonder what other readers think.

Yours faithfully,

Duncan Grant

Falkirk STII

C

LETTERS TO THE EDITOR

Dear Sir/Madam,

I am writing in response to Judy Boyle's article, which appeared in your paper on March 22nd. Although I agree with many of the things Ms Boyle wrote, I feel she didn't mention some important points.

A recent report suggests that, on average, each person has to put up with about 3,000 advertising messages every day. At first sight, this number 10 seems impossible, but let's think about it. First of all, there are adverts in papers and magazines, on TV and on the radio. Then there's spam – emails with advertisements – and pop-up adverts on Internet pages. Then there are billboards in the street. Finally there is junk mail and leaflets, advertising slogans on T-shirts and shopping bags, posters in waiting rooms, on public transport, at sports matches and concerts. Advertising completely invades our lives.

20 Do you or I buy 3,000 products every day? No, of course not. So not only is advertising irritating and an invasion of our privacy, as Ms Boyle suggests – but it's a waste of money.

But there's another point that Ms Boyle didn't mention: advertising makes us dissatisfied. All of us are bombarded every day by adverts showing us people who are more attractive and successful than us and who have newer things than us. In reality, most of us have longer and much more 30 comfortable lives than our ancestors and yet people are more dissatisfied with their lives than ever before. A coincidence?

In short, advertising is one big lie. It tells us that luxuries are necessities and what you already have is not satisfactory. In fact, if you can relax in the evenings by watching adverts you already have all you need to live comfortably. The purpose of advertising is to make you forget this.

Yours faithfully,

Jean Cox
Brighton

"OF COURSE NOBODY NEEDS ONE, THAT'S WHY I CALLED YOU ADVERTISING PEOPLE IN."

We ❤ Shopping

WORK, EAT, BUY, CONSUME THEN DIE.

LISTENING AND VOCABULARY

1 Work in pairs. Do you enjoy shopping? Why?/Why not? Tell your partner.

2 **CD3.19** Listen to the conversation between Jason and his parents and answer the questions.

1 When is International Buy Nothing Day?
2 What do campaigners hope that people will do on this day?
3 Is Jason for or against supermarkets and chain stores? Why?
4 Would you find it easy to go for one day without buying anything? Why?/Why not?

3 **CD3.20** Match items 1–9 with places a–i. Then listen and check. Where can you buy them?

1 boot polish ☐   a baker's
2 pet food ☐   b butcher's
3 cosmetics ☐   c chemist's
4 bread ☐   d clothes store
5 vegetables ☐   e greengrocer's
6 stationery ☐   f grocer's
7 meat ☐   g newsagent's
8 salt ☐   h pet shop
9 underwear ☐   i shoe shop

4 **CD3.20** Listen again and answer the questions.

1 Why do Sue and Jeff think that life before supermarkets was worse?
2 What further arguments does Jason give against supermarkets?

5 Complete the compound nouns below with a word from the box.

cash (x 2)   chain   changing   department   ~~shop~~   shopping (x 2)

1 ___shop___ assistant – someone whose job is selling things in a shop
2 _____ trolley – a metal structure on wheels that is used for carrying things in shops
3 _____ store – one of a group of similar shops owned by the same company
4 _____ register – a machine that is used in shops for keeping money in
5 _____ centre/mall – a place where a lot of shops have been built close together
6 _____ rooms – a room in a shop where you can try clothes
7 _____ store – a large shop divided into several different parts, each of which sells different things
8 _____ dispenser – a machine, usually outside a bank, that you can get money from

6 In pairs, prepare and give a short presentation on one of the topics below.

• Small shops still have an important role to play in today's towns and cities. Do you agree?
• Shopping has become one of the most important leisure activities of our time. Is this a problem?

126

COMPLAINTS

Closed
Ran out
of excuses

SPEAKING AND LISTENING

1 Work in pairs. Look at the cartoon and answer the questions.

- Have you ever been dissatisfied with something you have bought?
- What did you do about it? Did you make a complaint?

2 Read the complaints below. When might someone say them? Use the ideas in the box. There is often more than one answer.

an Internet/online shop   a restaurant
a hotel   a clothes store   a bank
a store with electrical goods

1 It shrank the first time I washed it!
2 Your employee was extremely rude to me.
3 My order hasn't arrived yet.
4 It's faulty. I took it out of the box but I couldn't get it to work.
5 I'm not satisfied with the service.

3 **CD3.21** Match complaints 1–5 in Exercise 2 with responses a–e below. Then listen and check.

a <u>It's entirely our fault.</u> We'll send you a new one straightaway. ☐
b <u>I'm very sorry about that.</u> Would you like to exchange it for something else? Or would you like a refund? ☐
c <u>We're trying our best.</u> We've got a lot of customers in here this afternoon. ☐
d I'm so sorry. I'll talk to Mr Evans about his behaviour. <u>It won't happen again.</u> ☐
e Sorry – there must have been a mistake with your order. <u>We'll try to sort it out.</u> ☐

4 Study Speak Out. Complete the box with the <u>underlined</u> phrases in Exercise 3.

SPEAK OUT | Making complaints

Making complaints

It's broken/faulty.   It's not working.
There's a part missing.   It's shrunk/the dye has run.
My order hasn't arrived yet.   It's not what I ordered.
There's a mistake in the bill.   It's too tight/tough/noisy.

I'm not satisfied with the service.
One of your employees was extremely rude to me.
You've forgotten to … .

Responding to complaints

Apologising
I'm so sorry – there must have been a mistake.
1 _____
2 _____

Making offers and promises
We'll replace it straightaway.
Would you like a refund?
3 _____
4 _____

Defending yourself
Don't blame me! It wasn't my fault.
5 _____

Mind the trap!

In Britain, it's very typical to start making a complaint by apologising to avoid having a confrontation with somebody, even if you are angry.

I'm sorry to say there's a mistake in my bill.
I'm afraid my MP3 player isn't working properly.

5 In pairs, read the situations on page 141. Take turns to make complaints and respond to them. Use expressions from Speak Out to help you.

6 Work in pairs. Roleplay the conversation. Student A, look at page 142. Student B, look at page 143.

Yes it's faulty. I couldn't get it to work.

VOCABULARY

1 Look at the dictionary entry in Train Your Brain. Which words collocate with *complaint*?

1 verbs which collocate: __make__ , _____
2 prepositions which collocate: __about__ , _____ , _____
3 adjectives which collocate: __formal__ , _____

TRAIN YOUR BRAIN | Dictionary skills

Collocations

A dictionary can tell you not only the meaning of a word, but also collocations – the words it combines with.

complaint /kəmˈpleɪnt/ n a statement in which someone complains about something: *I would like to make a **complaint**.* | *The BBC received a lot of **complaints** after the programme.* | **formal/official complaint** | [+ **about**] *He was dismissed after **complaints** about the quality of his work.* | [+ **from/to**] **complaints** *from local residents.* |

---

2 Use the correct words from Exercise 1 to complete the collocations in the sentences below.

1 The school _____ many complaints _____ parents, who were unhappy with the cost of school trips.
2 She was unhappy with the service and _____ a complaint _____ the manager.
3 The hotel received a complaint _____ the quality of the food in the restaurant.
4 He was sacked after someone made a _____ complaint about his work.

3 Use a dictionary to find the meanings of the underlined words below. Then complete the sentences.

1 Phone Customer Services. I'm sure they'll _____ you a <u>refund</u>.
2 I'm afraid those trainers you wanted are now _____ _____ <u>stock</u>.
3 Would you like to <u>exchange</u> them _____ something else instead?
4 I wanted to use my credit card but they told me I could only _____ <u>cash</u>.
5 The new issue of *Hi!* magazine is _____ <u>sale</u> now!
6 This shirt was a real bargain! It was <u>reduced</u> _____ £25 _____ £8!
7 How much did you <u>pay</u> _____ that watch?

Dear Sir/Madam,

1 I am writing to express my dissatisfaction with the 2007 Punk In The Park festival which you organised.

2 I bought two tickets for me and my girlfriend for all three days, which cost me £90 in total. As I am a student, this was a lot of money to pay, but I believed it was worth it because of the quality of the bands which were being advertised.

3 On Friday afternoon the sound check lasted most of the afternoon. Although the first concert was going to start at 5p.m., the first band didn't appear on stage until 9p.m. Because of this, the last two bands (The Phoneys and Critical Age) didn't play at all. We were all very disappointed. On Saturday it started raining heavily. There were only two sets of toilets, both of them located in the lowest part of the field. There were very long queues for the toilets all day and when the toilets became flooded after just an hour of rain, the situation looked horrific. There clearly wasn't enough planning before the event.

4 I feel that in future you should plan such festivals more carefully.

5 I also think I should receive a refund for my tickets for one of the days (£30) because two of my favourite bands didn't play at all. I hope you will take my comments into consideration and I look forward to reading your reply.

Yours faithfully,

Mark D Smith

WRITING

1 In pairs, describe the photo and answer the questions.

- Why are such events attractive to many young people?
- What kinds of things can go wrong during such an event?

2 Read Mark's letter of complaint. What went wrong during the festival? Were any of your ideas from Exercise 1 correct?

3 What is the tone of Mark's letter? Tick the correct option. Do you think it makes the letter more effective? Why?/Why not?

1 aggressive and angry ☐
2 emotional ☐
3 polite but firm ☐

4 In pairs, look at Mark's letter again. Match the paragraphs with the content.

Paragraph 1 ☐   Paragraph 4 ☐
Paragraph 2 ☐   Paragraph 5 ☐
Paragraph 3 ☐

a Details about the service/product the customer bought and his/her expectations.
b Suggestions about how the company can improve its service.
c The reason for writing.
d What went wrong (in chronological order) and the problems it caused the customer.
e The compensation the customer expects.

5 Work in pairs. For each situation, choose the best form of compensation. Give reasons.

a financial compensation
b a replacement
c a refund
d an official apology

1 Some workmen have been fitting new windows. The work has lasted much longer than you expected and this has caused a lot of disruption to your family's life.
2 You bought a theatre ticket to see a play. One of the actors became ill so the play was cancelled just ten minutes before it was supposed to begin.
3 You bought a Discman. When you opened the box you found that the earphones were faulty.
4 You have just finished a project at college. A letter arrives from the college Principal which wrongly accuses you of cheating. You can prove this is untrue.

Mind the trap!

Compensation is uncountable.

I expect compensation. NOT ~~I expect a compensation.~~

6 Study Train Your Brain. Then, in pairs, read James's letter and decide what is wrong with it.

TRAIN YOUR BRAIN | Writing skills

Letter of complaint

- Start by giving your reason for writing. (*I am writing to complain about/express my dissatisfaction with …*)
- In the next paragraph(s), say what went wrong in chronological order and mention the problems it caused you. (*Because of this …*)
- If necessary, give suggestions about how the company can improve its service in a new paragraph. (*I feel that in future you should …*)
- At the end say clearly what kind of compensation you expect. (*I think I should receive …*)
- Remember to start/end your letter in a formal way. (*Dear Sir/Madam, Yours faithfully*)
- Make sure the tone is polite but firm and the style is quite formal.

Hi Guys,

I really hate your company now. I think I should get compensation or an apology or something.

I ordered an MP3 player (SoundBlast 3000) from you in February (the 3rd I think). This morning it finally arrived! I took it out of the box and it didn't work! And I'd paid lots of money for this! ☹

So what are you going to do about it?

But that's not all, actually. My MP3 player arrived after five weeks – it said on the website that delivery time was two or three days!!! At the beginning I waited and waited and nothing! Two weeks later I contacted your customer helpline. The guy told me that it was out of stock and that I had to wait another three weeks before it would be in stock again. Not very good service, is it?

Write back soon!

James Godfrey

7 In pairs, rewrite James's letter to make it more appropriate. Use your answers to Exercise 6 and Train Your Brain to help you.

8 Choose one of the situations from Exercise 5. Write a letter of complaint (200–250 words).

Say clearly:
- what has happened/gone wrong.
- the problems it caused you.
- how you feel about it.
- the type of compensation you would like.

VOCABULARY AND GRAMMAR

1 Complete the sentences. Make new words from the words in capital letters.

1 I've run out of cash – I need to
find a cash _____ . DISPENSE
2 Your staff were so rude to me that
I demand an official _____ ! APOLOGISE
3 Have you ever written a letter
of _____ ? COMPLAIN
4 I like _____ foods – they are
easy and fast to prepare but not
always cheap and healthy. CONVENIENT
5 Do you think _____ beer
on TV should be forbidden? ADVERTISEMENT
6 You can find a lot of recipes for
_____ meals in this book. NUTRITION
7 The cake didn't look very
_____ but it tasted delicious. APPETITE

2 Complete the second sentence so that it has a similar meaning to the first sentence using the word given. You must use between two and five words including the word given.

1 You can't have an apple. There are none here.
ANY
There _____ so you can't have one.
2 I don't want this book anymore. I think I'll
change it for that one.
OF
I'd like that book _____ one.
3 The result of the match last week was 2–0.
LAST
We won 2–0 _____ match.
4 It's a good idea to go shopping on Sundays.
WORTH
It's _____ shopping on Sundays.
5 I don't want to go out today.
FEEL
I _____ out today.
6 I don't like playing chess very much.
KEEN
I'm _____ chess.
7 I want to complain about the waiter.
A
I want to _____ about the waiter.

3 Fill in each gap with one word.

My friends call me crazy but I know I'm good.
I am good [1]_____ shopping. I'm famous
[2]_____ spotting a great top or jeans at a
discount prize and I don't [3]_____ spending
endless hours running around shops. I'm never
tired [4]_____ bargain-hunting. I wake up
in the morning and I immediately feel [5]_____
_____ going for a stroll to the nearest store.
Well, obviously I need to [6]_____ down on
shopping once in a while when I have no money
but I can't imagine [7]_____ it up completely.
Don't get me wrong, I don't just buy things for
myself – last week it took me hours before I
succeeded [8]_____ finding just the right gift
for my mum's birthday.

4 Read the text below and circle the correct answer for each gap.

Wimbledon is [1]_____ important sporting
event of the British summer. Since the first
tournament was played in 1877 in front of just
[2]_____ hundred spectators, the competition
has become a global sporting event attended
by over half a million people, and watched on
television by millions. [3]_____ the Wimbledon
tennis championship has been in existence for
just over a century, the sport of tennis has a
long history. [4]_____ experts agree that the
modern game has its origins in a courtyard
ball game played by French monks in the 11th
century.

It is definitely [5]_____ taking part in tennis
championships. The Wimbledon champion,
Roger [6]_____ total prize money has
amounted to nearly $17,000,000 since 1998.
[7]_____ the fact that Wimbledon has
traditionally been dominated by Americans and
Europeans, players from many other countries
are looking forward [8]_____ the tournament.

1 a most c most of
  b the most d the most of
2 a few b many c a little d a few
3 a However b Despite c Instead d Although
4 a Most b A lot c Much d Little
5 a famous for c without
  b worth d good at
6 a Federer c Federer's
  b Federers' d of Federer
7 a Although c What's more
  b Instead d Despite
8 a to win c of winning
  b to winning d as to win

5 Use the words in capitals and rewrite the sentences so they have the same meaning.

1 Tom isn't very tall. His twin brother Jack is
short too.
_____ NEITHER
2 I want to say I am really sorry for being late.
_____ APOLOGISE
3 There are five boys in my family and nobody
likes spinach.
_____ NONE
4 There are only seven girls in my class and
they are all very good at maths.
_____ ALL
5 I am really tired of my older sister talking
about her final exams.
_____ FED
6 Chess is a challenging game. Bridge is
challenging too.
_____ BOTH

PRONUNCIATION

1 **CD3.22** Listen and circle the word that has a different final consonant sound. Then listen and check.

1 tough / live / roof / self
2 tights / thighs / was / dimples
3 shop / club / top / jump
4 cons / pets / bags / games
5 leaves / takes / blames / plays
6 hers / days / shops / because

LISTENING SKILLS

1 **CD3.23** Listen to the radio programme. Put the events in the correct order.

a Mail order advertising catalogues appear in the USA. ☐
b The Volkswagen is advertised with 'Think Small' and 'Lemon' slogans. ☐
c Sales messages are used in Egypt. ☐
d Nokia is used by Tom Cruise in Minority Report. ☐
e Advertisements for books appear in British newspapers. ☐
f Cadillac advertises its cars in The Matrix Reloaded. ☐
g MTV appears with a lot of advertising. ☐

SPEAKING SKILLS

1 Roleplay the situations below. Pay attention to how formal or informal you need to be in each situation.

1 **A** Your parents are complaining about the loud music a neighbour of yours is playing. The neighbour is your age. You visit him/her to complain and suggest using headphones as it is quite late.
 B A neighbour of yours has come to complain about the loud music you are listening to. Apologise and accept his/her suggestion. Be friendly and polite.

2 **A** You've recently bought a personal stereo which will not play all your CDs. You go to the shop to complain about it. You are angry, but polite.
 B You are a shop assistant. A customer has come to complain about a faulty personal stereo he/she bought in your shop. Offer to replace it.

3 **A** You see a neighbour of yours, a young man/woman, who is shopping in your local supermarket. He/she is holding his/her baby and his/her trolley is full of shopping. You offer to help.
 B A neighbour of yours offers to help you in the shop where you are shopping with your small child. He/she offers to help you with your shopping. Accept politely and offer him/her a lift home.

2 Look at the visuals and get ready to present the material and discuss:
– the possible reasons why sport is becoming more and more commercialised.
– the advantages and disadvantages of being a sports star.
Then answer the teacher's questions.

Teacher's questions:
1 What issue does the material deal with?
2 What positive and negative sides of sport nowadays does the material present?
3 Can sport stars be positive role models to children and teenagers? Give examples.
4 Do you think there is too much violence in sport?
5 What sport/sports are a national obsession in your country? Why?

The end of football?

'We don't want spoilt football stars, who only care about their hairstyles and new clothes for their model wives', complain football fans. 'We want to watch real football'.

Sports stars raise money for earthquake victims in Asia

CULTURE SHOCK 1

THE BRITISH MUSIC SCENE

Glossary album reviews band/group/artist/singer/composer composition have (a hit) influence join (a band) lyrics music magazines music industry piece of music record company record shop rhythm solo styles

The Spice Girls

The Rolling Stones

SOME POPULAR MUSIC STYLES

Hard Rock/Heavy Metal
Macho rock played on loud guitars. Became popular at the end of the 1960s. Bands: Deep Purple, Led Zeppelin, Iron Maiden.

Progressive Rock
Experimental rock music with long, complex compositions, many long solos; often with keyboards. Popular in the early 1970s. Bands: Yes, Genesis, Pink Floyd.

Punk
Energetic, spontaneous and sometimes aggressive music – a reaction against commercialism and progressive rock. Popular at the end of the 1970s. Bands: The Sex Pistols, The Exploited.

Ska
A mix of Jamaican reggae and punk. Popular in the late 1970s. Bands: The Specials, Madness.

Goth
Cold, gloomy underground guitar rock, often with lyrics about death/suicide/alienation. Bands: Joy Division, Bauhaus, The Mission.

Acid House
A mix of disco rhythms and digital sound samples. Became popular at the end of the 1980s.

Jungle (Drum'n'bass)
Techno with very fast, complex rhythms and a very deep bass sound. First became popular in the 1990s.

Hip hop
A form of rap (words chanted to music) often with samples of other music and a reggae influence.

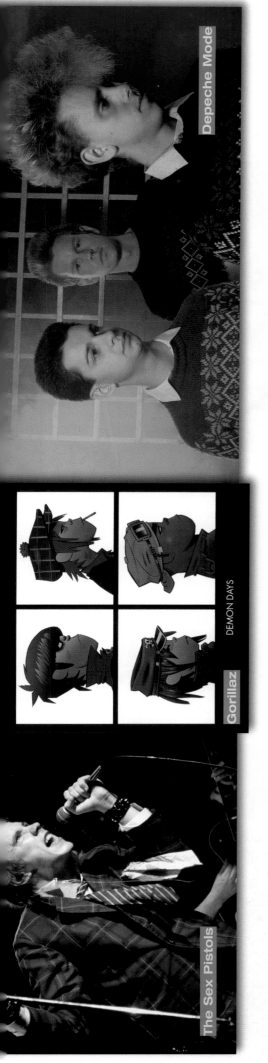

The Sex Pistols

Gorillaz

DEMON DAYS

Depeche Mode

1 **Work in pairs and answer the questions.**
- Are any of the artists/groups in the photographs (still) popular in your country?
- Can you remember any of their hits?
- Where do your favourite bands come from? Do you know anything about their biography?

Radiohead come from Oxford, I think. They started in the early 1990s. Their best album/best-known hit is …

2 **In pairs, look at the descriptions of popular music styles in the table above.**
- Do you like any of these styles?
- What's your favourite style of music?

3 [CD3.24] **Listen to the pieces of music and say how you feel about them. Use the adjectives and one of the expressions from the table below.**

(un)original atmospheric boring catchy dramatic energetic
fun melodic powerful

(very) positive	quite positive	rather negative/indifferent	(very) negative
I love it!	It's quite enjoyable!	It's nothing special.	What a load of rubbish!/crap!
It's cool/great!	I don't mind it!	I'm not mad about it.	It gets on my nerves.
It's terrific/fantastic.	It's not bad.	I'm not keen on it.	I can't stand it!
		It's not my cup of tea.	

A *It's really fun – I love it!*
B *It's not very original – it's not my cup of tea.*

4 [CD3.24] **Listen again. Try and guess the style of each piece of music you hear. Write the numbers of each piece in the Music Styles table. Then check your answers on page 141.**

☐ ☐

5 [CD3.25] **Read the questions then listen. Tick true and cross false.**

1 Pierre is a music critic in France. ☐
2 He thinks that Britain has produced many famous classical composers. ☐
3 He believes that the British are so successful because they speak English. ☐
4 Jeff grew up in London. ☐
5 Pierre was surprised to find that British cities were not as exciting as he had thought. ☐
6 Jeff thinks that British people stop being interested in music even after their twenties. ☐
7 He thinks it's easier for young British bands to get attention. ☐
8 Pierre believes that British people prefer to write songs about politics than take part in demonstrations. ☐

6 **Crossing Cultures Work in groups and answer the questions.**
- What are the most popular/successful groups or artists in your country? Have they had any success abroad? What kind of music do they play?
- Are there any cities or regions in your country that produce a lot of bands/artists?
- Where's the best place for seeing live music in your town/area?
- What's the best radio station for hearing new music in your country?
- Do artists in your country sing in English? What do you think about it?

CULTURE SHOCK 2

ACCENTS IN THE BRITISH ISLES

Glossary accents dialect drop a letter misunderstanding
national standard pronounce pronunciation

No place in the English-speaking world has more dialects than Britain and Ireland. According to some linguists, there are 'no less than thirteen' quite distinct dialects in Britain. Others put the number of dialects at forty-two – nine in Scotland, three in Ireland and thirty in England and Wales, but there could be even more. In only six counties in the north of England, seventeen separate pronunciations of the word *house* have been recorded. It would be no exaggeration to say that there are greater differences in pronunciation in the north of England between the Rivers Trent and Tweed (200 miles) than in the whole of North America.

Bill Bryson

North of England (Manchester)

In the North of England most people pronounce the 'uh' sound in *some* or *bus* like the 'oo' in *book*. Like people in the London area, they also tend to drop the 'h' at the beginning of words. So "ee 'ad soom foon,' means 'he had some fun.'

Scotland

In Scotland most people pronounce the 'r' strongly, even in words where the English do not pronounce it. 'I drrove my carr to the parrk' means 'I drove my car to the park.' The Scots also have their own words for many things, so 'Och aye, it's a bonny wee loch' means, 'Oh yes, it's a pretty little lake.'

Ireland

Many Irish people pronounce 'th' as 't' or 'd'. So 'I tink dere are tirty tree of dem' means 'I think there are thirty three of them.'

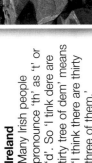

London

Many speakers in the London area do not pronounce the 't' clearly. They say 'a bo'le of wa'er' instead of 'a bottle of water'. They may also pronounce 'th' as 'f' or 'v'. So 'I fink it's your muver,' means, 'I think it's your mother.' They often drop the 'h' at the beginning of words. So "'ee 'as long 'air' means, 'He has long hair.'

3 **Read the fact boxes. Which two accents have something in common?**

4 **[CD3.26] Read the fact boxes again and identify what these people are saying. Listen and check.**

London: 'er li'le bruvver 'as go' somefing to say.
North of England: 'ee looves 'is moom.
Ireland: Deir tings are on de tird shelf.
Scotland: Therre's a wee birrd sitting in that trree.

5 **[CD3.27] Listen to speakers 1–4 and identify their accents.**

1 _____
2 _____
3 _____
4 _____

6 **Crossing Cultures Work in groups and answer the questions.**

1 How many different accents or dialects can you think of in your country? In which regions or cities are the accents very different from the national standard?
2 Do people in your country have misunderstandings because of different accents or dialects?
3 Do you think strong local accents are a problem or an advantage for languages? Why? Use the ideas below to help you.

- you know where people are from
- it would be sad if everyone was the same
- you can't understand some people
- science and business need a standard language
- variety is a good thing
- it creates a sense of identity
- it can confuse foreign visitors
- it can cause discrimination

1 **Read the extract from the book and choose the best summary.**

1 There are many accents in the English-speaking world.
2 It is amazing how many different accents there are in the British Isles. ☐ ☐ ☐
3 People in Britain are not sure how to pronounce the word *house*.

2 **Look at cartoons a–c. Work in pairs and answer the questions.**

1 What numbers are the customers saying?
2 What does the shop assistant understand?

BUDGET LONDON

Glossary abbey arts centre art gallery bus route bus pass/travelcard cathedral dungeon listings magazine (*What's on* guide) means of transport parliament sandwich bar takeaway food tourist attraction tours tower the tube

Key bus routes and tourist attractions in central London

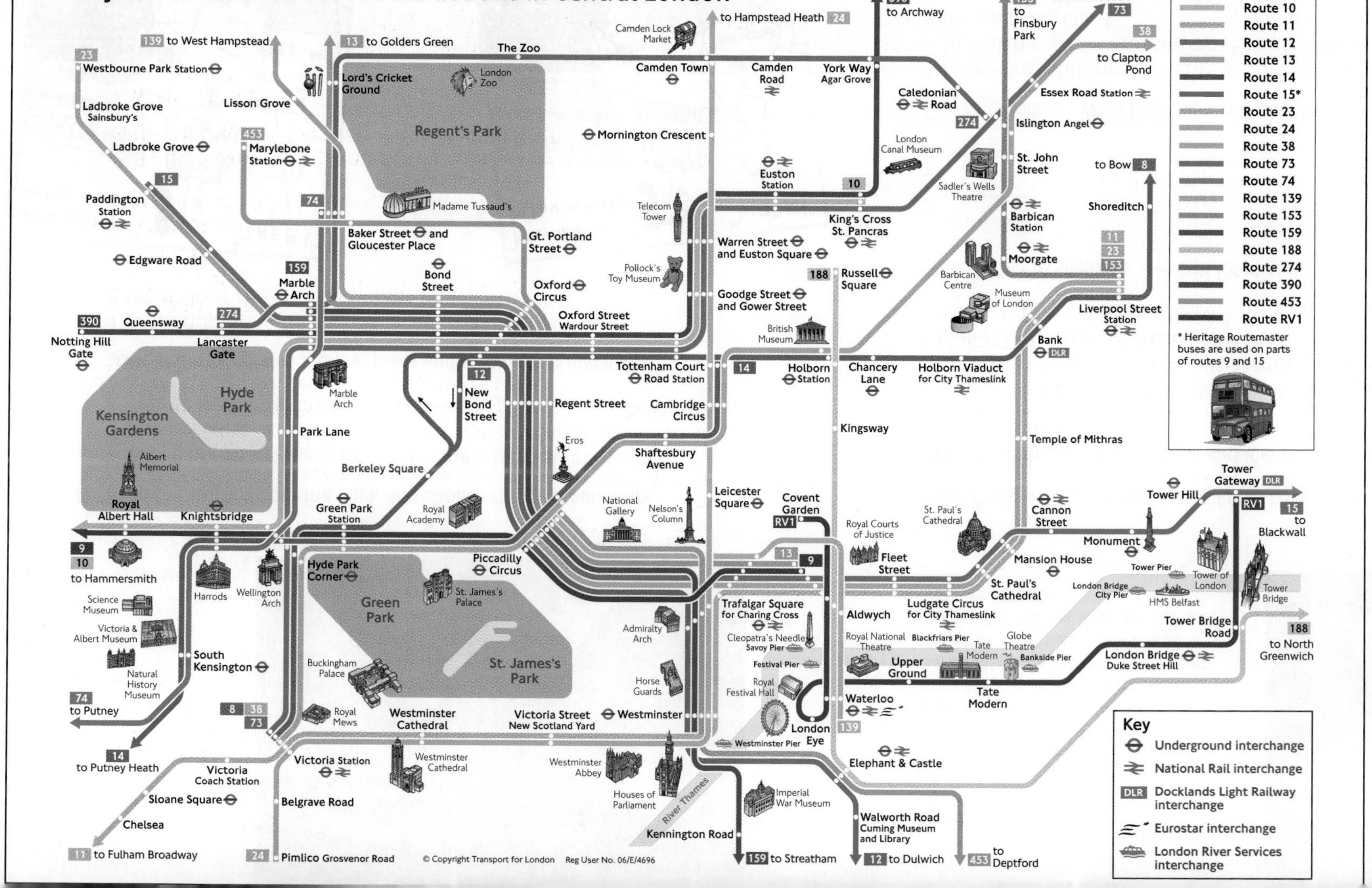

Routes:
- Route 8
- Route 9*
- Route 10
- Route 11
- Route 12
- Route 13
- Route 14
- Route 15*
- Route 23
- Route 24
- Route 38
- Route 73
- Route 74
- Route 139
- Route 153
- Route 159
- Route 188
- Route 274
- Route 390
- Route 453
- Route RV1

* Heritage Routemaster buses are used on parts of routes 9 and 15

Key
- ⊖ Underground interchange
- ⋙ National Rail interchange
- **DLR** Docklands Light Railway interchange
- ⊸ Eurostar interchange
- 🚢 London River Services interchange

© Copyright Transport for London   Reg User No. 06/E/4696

Key:

	Free
	Inexpensive (less than £5)
	Quite expensive (£5–£7.50)
	Expensive (£7.50–£12)
	Very expensive (more than £12)

Art Galleries
- National Gallery
- Tate Modern (contemporary art)
- Tate Britain
- ICA (Institute of Contemporary Arts)
- Courtauld Institute Art Gallery
- Royal Academy

Museums
- Science Museum
- Natural History Museum
- Imperial War Museum
- British Museum
- Museum of London
- National Maritime Museum
- Design Museum
- Fashion and Textile Museum
- Sherlock Holmes Museum

Other Tourist Attractions
- Royal Observatory – Greenwich
- Tower Bridge Exhibition
- HMS Belfast
- Westminster Abbey
- Globe Theatre – (reconstruction of a 16th century theatre)
- St Paul's Cathedral
- London Aquarium
- London Zoo (Regent's Park)
- Tower of London
- State Rooms, Buckingham Palace
- London Eye
- London Dungeon
- Madame Tussaud's

Hyde Park

The London Eye

Tate Modern

The Tower of London

Buckingham Palace

1 Work in pairs. Look at the map and the tourist information. How quickly can you find the answers to these questions?

1 Which art gallery is near Piccadilly Circus? Is it cheap to visit?
2 Which station is near Buckingham Palace?
3 Can you visit St Paul's Cathedral for free?
4 What bus(es) could you take from St Paul's Cathedral to get to Oxford Circus (the main shopping area)?
5 Which popular art gallery can you find on the south bank of the River Thames?
6 Which museums can you visit after shopping at Harrods?
7 Are museums in London generally expensive?

2 CD3.28 Read the questions and try to predict the answers. Sometimes more than one answer is possible. Then listen and circle the correct answer(s).

1 What is the cheapest way to travel around London?
a by tube   b by bus   c on a coach tour
2 Which museum is a good starting-point for visitors to London?
a The Science Musuem   b The Museum of London   c Madame Tussaud's
3 What's a good place to eat cheaply in London?
a a sandwich bar   b a Steak House restaurant   c a market
4 When is a good time to listen to classical music for free?
a at the weekends   b on Thursdays   c at lunchtimes

3 CD3.28 Listen again and complete what the speakers say about these things.

a Downing Street is the place where …
b 1666 was when …
c Borough Market is a place to …
d The Barbican is a place where …
e *Time Out* is a …

4 Work in pairs. Read the instructions and decide how you are going to spend the day. Then compare your plans with another pair.

You are visiting the UK and you have just arrived in London. You are leaving the next morning. You want to see as much as possible while spending as little money as possible! Make plans about:
• how you are going to travel around
• which museums, galleries and tourist attractions you plan to see
• where you are going to eat
• seeing some live music

Use the map above and your answers to Exercise 2 to help you.

5 Crossing Cultures Work in groups. Imagine a group of foreign visitors your age are visiting a town or city in your area. Use the ideas below to help you to give them advice about:

• the best means of transport for getting around cheaply and seeing as much of the place as possible
• the cheapest ticket or travelcard to buy
• eating out cheaply
• tourist attractions/museums which aren't too expensive
• cheap places to see concerts, plays or films and the best source of information about these

arts centre   bus/tram/metro   cathedral/abbey/church
exhibition/concert/recital   free/inexpensive   leaflet/guide
listings magazine   local newspaper   palace/tower   students union
takeaway food   Tourist Information Centre

A It's a good idea to …
B They should …
C It's worth …ing …

BRITISH SPORTS AROUND THE WORLD

Glossary associations to play by rules to draw up rules cheat fair play nil (scoreless) draw banned archery croquet committee tournament championship minority sport national sport

1 Match sports 1–6 with photos a–f.

1 Cricket ☐ 3 Golf ☐ 5 Rugby ☐
2 Football ☐ 4 Hockey ☐ 6 Tennis ☐

2 Read the introduction and tick the correct sentences.

1 We know where most sports originated. ☐
2 The British were responsible for organising many popular sports. ☐
3 Many sports became popular around the world thanks to the British Empire. ☐

INTRODUCTION: BRITISH GAMES?

People have played games throughout the ages from the ancient Egyptians to the Eskimos and the origins of most sports are lost in time. However, we do know when and where sports were first organised. And in many cases the first associations were formed and the first rules were written down in Britain. Then in the 19th century the British sent their soldiers, engineers and businessmen across their Empire and the rest of the world learnt to play by British rules.

Football may have been brought to Britain by the Romans, but the rules of modern football were drawn up in a tavern in London in 1863. The first game under the new rules ended nil nil (0–0). Nine years later the first international was played between Scotland and England. The result was another disappointing scoreless draw. It makes you wonder how football ever became the most popular sport in the world!

FOOTBALL

RUGBY

In 1823 a boy called William Webb Ellis was playing a game of football at his school, Rugby. Suddenly, he picked up the ball and began to run with it in his hands. This was against the rules. The boy had created a new sport – rugby football.

Great story. Unfortunately, it's not quite true. In fact, the rules of rugby weren't standardised until 1871 when the Rugby Football Union was founded in London. It has been said that rugby is a game for hooligans played by gentlemen, whereas football is a game for gentlemen played by hooligans.

CRICKET

Although the origins of cricket may be in Asia, the game has been played in England for over 700 years. It was probably first played by shepherds and it was so popular in the 15th century that it was banned by the king who was worried about the defence of his kingdom and who wanted his subjects to practise archery instead. The rules, which date from 1744, are so complicated that many people have no idea how it is played.

TENNIS

An early version of tennis was popular in monasteries in Europe more than a thousand years ago, but modern tennis didn't really become popular until 1875 when the All England *Croquet Club* tried to attract new members by offering Lawn Tennis as an alternative attraction. The new game was an instant success and in 1877 a committee was established to draw up the rules and to organise the first ever tournament. The Wimbledon Championship was born!

GOLF

There have been many sports in history in which you hit a ball with a stick, but it was 15th century Scots who first thought of hitting the ball into a hole. Scotland is home to the world's oldest golf courses and the famous course at St Andrews dates from the 16th century. The oldest surviving rules were drawn up by the Gentlemen Golfers of Leith, Edinburgh in 1744, and even today golfers must behave like gentlemen and must not try to cheat.

HOCKEY

In England in the 17th century, hockey was played by teams of up to one hundred players and games could last several days. The modern game was developed at Eton College in the 1860s, and in 1890 the English, Irish and Welsh hockey associations joined to form the International Rules Board. Hockey was introduced to India by the British Army in 1900 and today although it is a minority sport in England, it is India's national sport. In many parts of the world ice hockey is more popular than field hockey, but in India and in Britain hockey is usually played on grass.

---

3 Read about the sports described above and find out when the modern rules were agreed on.

Sport	Modern rules
1 Cricket	1744
2 Golf	_____
3 Football	_____
4 Rugby	_____
5 Tennis	_____
6 Hockey	_____

4 Read the texts again and match the sports with sentences 1–7.

1 It owes its popularity to another game. tennis
2 Fair play is even more important in this sport than in others. _____
3 It used to be popular in religious communities. _____
4 A monarch thought it was a danger to national security. _____
5 There is a popular myth about the origin of the game. _____
6 The first official matches didn't have very exciting results. _____
7 Now it is more popular in another country than it is in England. _____

5 `CD3.29` Listen and match sports 1–3 with the places a–c where they are played.

1 rugby ☐
2 cricket ☐
3 both ☐

a countries that used to be British colonies
b countries that didn't use to be British colonies
c hot countries

6 Crossing Cultures Work in groups and answer the questions.
- Which of the sports in the texts above are not popular in your country?
- Which of these sports is the most popular in your country?
- Which of these sports do you enjoy playing or watching?

Student Activities

Unit 2, Writing, Exercise 6, page 21.

Hi Daria,

Sorry I haven't written sooner, but I've been really busy. I'm exhausted! I've been studying really hard. I've got a big Maths test tomorrow. What else? Well, I've been taking driving lessons, too! My grandma is paying for them. I can drive quite well already. I want to pass my test so that I can get a part-time job.

The big news is that I've got you a present! The new Critical Age CD signed by Colin! We've been seeing each other quite a lot recently. He's really nice. You'd love him.

Anyway, that's enough about me. What about you? Have you decided to get that piercing yet?

Oh, before I forget, Chris called me up. Apparently, there's a really good theatre course on at the youth centre next week. Do you want to go? Come on! It'll be fun. I've got to go. My trigonometry book is calling me!

Write back soon.
Love, Neil.

Unit 3, Reading and Vocabulary, Exercise 5, page 26.

- Kathleen Robertson won $780,000.
- Wanita Young won $900, but got no money for pain and suffering. After winning the case, she said, 'I just hope the girls learned a lesson.'
- The jury agreed with Terrence Dickson and paid him half a million dollars.
- Kara Walton won $12,000 and dental expenses.

Unit 4, Reading and Vocabulary, Exercise 5, page 35.

- You probably have a type S (systemising/male) brain if your 6 sentences were mostly in this group of answers: 1, 2, 4, 5, 6, 10, 12, 16.
- You probably have a type E (empathising/female) brain if your 6 sentences were mostly in this group of answers: 3, 7, 8, 9, 11, 13, 14, 15.
- You probably have a type B (balanced) brain if your answers were a mixture of the two groups of answers (about 50% for each).

Unit 5, Vocabulary, Exercise 3, page 49.

Ideas
- Organise a concert
- A photo exhibition
- Sell lottery tickets or scratch cards
- A jumble sale (collect and sell second-hand things)
- A sports event, eg a football marathon
- Go out on the street with collecting tins

Unit 6, Reading and Vocabulary, Exercise 8, page 53.

All the answers are true.

Unit 8, Speaking, Exercise 3, Page 74.

Work in pairs. Use the language in Speak Out to talk about these statisitics.

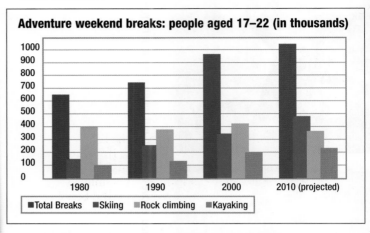

Adventure weekend breaks: people aged 17–22 (in thousands)

Legend: ■ Total Breaks ■ Skiing ■ Rock climbing ■ Kayaking

Unit 9, Speaking and Listening, Exercise 10, Page 85.

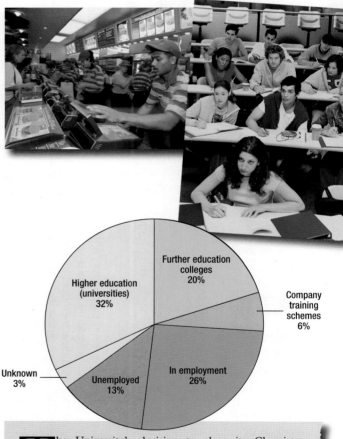

Pie chart:
- Higher education (universities) 32%
- Further education colleges 20%
- Company training schemes 6%
- In employment 26%
- Unemployed 13%
- Unknown 3%

The University's decision to close its Chemistry department from next year was criticised by the Education Minister yesterday. She said it was a pity for the economy of the future that more school leavers are choosing media studies or social sciences instead of hard science. She promised that the government would make a bigger effort to inform school leavers of the benefits of doing a science degree.

SKILLED BUILDING WORKERS REQUIRED

Reputable company
Good wages and conditions
For further information call 02387564

Questions

1 What issues does the material deal with?
2 What kinds of career choices for school leavers are suggested by the material?
3 What information can you get from the written material?
4 Why do you think most school leavers go on to higher and further education?
5 What are the advantages of getting a job instead of going to university?

Unit 10, Grammar and Speaking, Exercise 9, page 87.

Several possibilities – He can't have had a beard because his face was badly sunburnt. He can't have sat on the beach every evening because Botswana is hundreds of miles from any coast. It is unlikely that he had electricity to play his guitar on the beach.

Unit 12, Listening and Speaking, Exercise 7, page 108.

Bisbee

Simon Starling

Henry Moore

Work in groups. Use the expressions below to discuss the works of art.

What do you think it means?
I'm not sure …
I really like the …
I think the artist is saying that
It reminds me of …
I don't get it …

A *What do you think of the sculpture by Henry Moore?*
B *I think it's fantastic!*
C *What do you think it means?*

Unit 14 Speaking and Listening, Exercise 5, page 127.

Take turns to make complaints and respond to them.

1 **Customer in a restaurant** You ordered a steak and it's very tough – it's almost impossible to eat. Complain.
Waiter You are very apologetic and make an offer to satisfy the customer.

2 **Customer** You ordered some CDs from an Internet shop. When the parcel arrives you find that you have been overcharged – you have to pay more than you expected for the things you ordered. Complain.
Customer service employee You are very apologetic and make an offer to satisfy the customer.

3 **Customer in a shop** You bought a red and white striped T-shirt from a department store. After washing it for the first time, the red dye ran – now the T-shirt is completely pink! Complain.
Shop assistant You are very apologetic and make an offer to satisfy the customer.

4 **Manager of a supermarket** You're angry because you've just noticed that the shelves in the bakery department are empty. You're sure that your employees didn't remember to fill the shelves this morning. Complain.
Supermarket employee You defend yourself. You've already filled the shelves twice this morning but the customers are buying more bread than usual before the May Day holiday.

Culture Shock 1, Exercise 4, page 133.

1 Punk
2 Hip hop
3 Jungle
4 Acid house
5 Ska
6 Heavy metal

Student A Activities

Unit 2, Grammar and Reading, Exercise 9, page 15.

Student A
1 **Use questions 1–5 to interview your partner (Tracy from Critical Age).**

1 How long / know / Colin?
2 Where / meet?
3 How long / play /guitar?
4 Ever / meet / anyone famous?
5 What / listen / recently?

2 **You are Stephen from Critical Age. Use this information to answer your partner's questions. Use complete sentences.**

1 a couple of years
2 at a concert
3 not very long / about a year ago
4 no
5 techno

3 **Ask and answer similar questions about your own life.**

Unit 2, Speaking and Listening, Exercise 8, page 17.

Student A
Explain to your partner how to:

1 make a phone call.
2 store someone's number in the phonebook.

When your partner explains things to you, you must pretend that you know nothing about mobile phones.

Unit 3, Grammar and Reading, Exercise 6, page 25.

Student A

1 Use questions 1–4 in exercise 5, page 25 to interview your partner about a crime he/she saw. Take notes, and write about the crime your partner saw.

2 Imagine you saw someone committing a crime. Use prompts a–d below to answer your partner's questions. Use complete sentences and appropriate tenses.

a local shopping centre
b eat / ice-cream / friends
c man / steal / woman's handbag / run away
d run after him

3 Ask your partner if he/she has ever seen someone committing a crime. If so, ask him/her about it.

Unit 3, Vocabulary, Exercise 2, page 29.

Student A
Read these sentences to your partner. See if he/she can guess which acts of anti-social behaviour the people committed.

1 Sandy loved drawing, but her parents weren't happy when the police caught her. She was painting a picture on the wall of the bus station. (graffiti)
2 The maths teacher came into the toilets and saw Nelson. He was hitting Ralph and asking him for money. Ralph said it wasn't the first time that this had happened. (bullying)
3 After Donald had eaten his hamburger and drunk his beer, he left the empty containers on the park bench. (dropping litter)
4 The boys called Donna rude names just because of the colour of her skin. (racial abuse)

Unit 4, Speaking and Listening, Exercise 9, page 37.

Student A
Follow the instructions.

There is an important Maths test in two days. You have been absent from school recently and need to borrow your friend's classnotes. Talk to your friend and:
• explain your problem and politely make a request to borrow them.
• politely ask if it's OK to give back the notes the day after tomorrow.
• ask if it's OK to give them back tomorrow morning.
You start the conversation.

Unit 8, Vocabulary, Exercise 6, page 73.

Student A
Follow the instructions.

You work at the check-in desk at Gatwick airport. A passenger wants to check-in for flight PK387 to Rome.
• Ask him/her for his/her ticket and passport and if he/she has any luggage to check in. Ask if he/she packed the bag him/herself.
• The passenger's luggage weighs 17 kilos and the maximum allowed is 15 kilos. Tell him/her that there is a penalty of £25.

• Tell the passenger that there is a delay of one hour with this flight, give him/her a boarding card and indicate that boarding will be at 12.35 from gate 4.
You start the conversation.

Unit 12, Grammar and Speaking, Exercise 9, page 105.

Student A
Follow the instructions.

You are a foreign student in London. You're waiting in a queue to buy theatre tickets. You have a newspaper. The person in front of you has a theatre guide to *What's on in London*.
• Ask him/her if you can borrow his/her theatre guide.
• Accept his/her request and find out if there is a student discount on theatre tickets.
• Find out his/her name and where he/she is from and ask him/her what play he/she is going to buy tickets for.
You start the conversation.

Unit 14, Speaking and Listening, Exercise 6, page 127.

Student A
Follow the instructions.

You ordered a green medium T-shirt from Tee-Riffik, an Internet clothing company. However, the one you received was a pink extra large size. Your order also arrived very late – you had to wait ten days (the website promised a delivery time of two days).
• Call the Tee-Riffik helpline and make a complaint.
• Complain that you have received the wrong T-shirt.
• Politely mention any other problem you have with the order.
• Ask them to send you the correct item as soon as possible.
You start the conversation.

Student B Activities

Unit 2, Grammar and Reading, Exercise 9, page 15.

Student B
1 You are Tracy from Critical Age. Use this information to answer your partner's questions. Use complete sentences.

1 about six years
2 at a party
3 started guitar / primary school.
4 the singer Dido / going out with your cousin
5 blues

2 Use questions 1–5 to interview your partner (Stephen from Critical Age).

Interviewer
1 How long / know / Colin?
2 Where / meet?
3 How long / play / drums?
4 Ever / meet / anyone famous?
5 What / listen / recently?

3 Ask and answer similar questions about your own life.

Unit 2, Speaking and Listening, Exercise 8, page 17.

Student B
Explain to your partner how to:

1 send a text message.
2 change the ring tone.

When your partner explains things to you, you must pretend that you know nothing about mobile phones.

Unit 3, Grammar and Reading, Exercise 6, page 25.

Student B

1 Imagine you saw someone committing a crime. Use prompts 1–4 below to answer your partner's questions. Use complete sentences and appropriate tenses.

a disco
b dance / talk / friends
c group of boys / attack / another boy
d call / police

2 Use questions 1–4 in exercise 5, page 25 to interview your partner about a crime he/she saw. Take notes, and write about the crime your partner saw.

3 Ask your partner if he/she has ever seen someone committing a crime. If so, ask him/her about it.

Unit 3, Vocabulary, Exercise 2, page 29.

Student B
Read these sentences to your partner. See if he/she can guess which acts of anti-social behaviour the people committed.

1 Darren had just bought a new sound system for his car, so he drove round the streets with the windows down and played loud techno music. (noise nuisance)
2 Helen was in a hurry so she drove at more than 60 miles per hour in an urban area. (speeding)
3 Clive was really angry when he realised that he had lost his money. He stood in the street and shouted and used very bad language. (swearing in public)
4 Asif was very angry because his girlfriend had left him, so he took a knife and cut the seat on the bus. (vandalism)

Unit 4, Speaking and Listening, Exercise 8, page 37.

Student B

1 Your friend wants to visit you. You're not very happy about this but you agree.
2 You are a young woman with a heavy suitcase on a train. You are a feminist and you are the regional champion female weight-lifter. A student talks to you.
3 You ask a stranger at a party about his/her weight.

Unit 4, Speaking and Listening, Exercise 9, page 37.

Student B
Follow the instructions.

There is an important Maths test in two days. You plan to start revising tomorrow evening. Listen to your friend's request and:
• give permission.
• refuse permission and explain that you need the notes tomorrow evening.
• unwillingly agree.
Student A starts the conversation.

Unit 8, Vocabulary, Exercise 6, page 73.

Student B
Follow the instructions.

You are a passenger who wants to check in for flight PK387 from London Gatwick to Rome.
• Say that you have one piece of luggage to check in and one piece of hand-luggage.
• Explain that you have no British money left and offer to pay in euros.
• Complain about the delay of your flight.
Student A starts the conversation.

Unit 12, Grammar and Speaking, Exercise 9, page 105.

Student B
Follow the instructions.

You are a foreign student in London. You are waiting in a queue to buy theatre tickets. You have a theatre guide to *What's on in London*. The person behind you in the queue starts talking to you.
• Accept his/her request and ask him/her to lend you his/her newspaper.
• Tell him/her there is a discount for students. Then find out his/her name and where he/she is from.
• Explain that you want to see the musical *I love life!* and invite him/her to go to the theatre with you.
Student A starts the conversation.

Unit 14, Speaking and Listening, Exercise 6, page 127.

Student B
Follow the instructions.

You work in the complaints department of Tee-Riffik, an Internet clothing company. An unhappy customer calls you with a problem.
• Listen to the customer and deal with his/her complaint.
• Apologise.
• Defend your company. Invent an excuse for the poor service.
• Make an offer or promise to satisfy the customer.
Student A starts the conversation.

Irregular verbs

Verb	Past simple	Past Participle
be	was/were	been
bear	bore	borne
beat	beat	beaten
become	became	become
begin	began	begun
bend	bent	bent
bet	bet	bet
bind	bound	bound
bite	bit	bitten
blow	blew	blown
break	broke	broken
bring	brought	brought
build	built	built
burn	burnt/burned	burnt/burned
burst	burst	burst
buy	bought	bought
can	could	been able to
cast	cast	cast
catch	caught	caught
choose	chose	chosen
come	came	come
cost	cost	cost
cut	cut	cut
deal	dealt	dealt
do	did	done
draw	drew	drawn
drink	drank	drunk
drive	drove	driven
eat	ate	eaten
fall	fell	fallen
feed	fed	fed
feel	felt	felt
fight	fought	fought
find	found	found
fling	flung	flung
fly	flew	flown
forbid	forbade	forbidden
forget	forgot	forgotten
forgive	forgave	forgiven
freeze	froze	frozen
get	got	got
give	gave	given
go	went	gone
grow	grew	grown
have	had	had
hang	hung	hung
hear	heard	heard
hide	hid	hidden
hit	hit	hit
hold	held	held
hurt	hurt	hurt
keep	kept	kept
know	knew	known
lay	laid	laid
lead	led	led

Verb	Past simple	Past Participle
lean	leaned/leant	leaned/leant
learn	learned/learnt	learned/learnt
leave	left	left
lend	lent	lent
let	let	let
lie	lay	lain
lose	lost	lost
make	made	made
mean	meant	meant
meet	met	met
pay	paid	paid
put	put	put
read	read	read
ride	rode	ridden
ring	rang	rung
rise	rose	risen
run	ran	run
say	said	said
see	saw	seen
seek	sought	sought
sell	sold	sold
send	sent	sent
set	set	set
shake	shook	shaken
shine	shone	shone
shoot	shot	shot
show	showed	shown
shut	shut	shut
sing	sang	sung
sit	sat	sat
sleep	slept	slept
slide	slid	slid
smell	smelled/smelt	smelled/smelt
speak	spoke	spoken
speed	sped	sped
spell	spelt/spelled	spelt/spelled
spend	spent	spent
spill	spilt	spilt
split	split	split
spoil	spoilt	spoilt
stand	stood	stood
steal	stole	stolen
stick	stuck	stuck
strike	struck	struck
swim	swam	swum
take	took	taken
teach	taught	taught
tear	tore	torn
tell	told	told
think	thought	thought
throw	threw	thrown
understand	understood	understood
wake	woke	woken
wear	wore	worn
win	won	won
write	wrote	written